Family Support as Reflective Practice

by the same editors

Family Support
Direction from Diversity
Edited by John Canavan, Pat Dolan and John Pinkerton
ISBN 1 85302 850 9

of related interest

Enhancing the Well-Being of Children and Families through Effective Interventions
International Evidence for Practice
Edited by Colette McAuley, Peter Pecora and Wendy Rose
Foreword by Maria Eagle, MP
ISBN 1 84310 116 5

Safeguarding and Promoting the Well-being of Children, Families and Communities
Edited by Jane Scott and Harriet Ward
Foreword by Maria Eagle MP
ISBN 1 84310 141 6

Social Work with Children and Families
Getting into Practice, Second Edition
Ian Butler and Gwenda Roberts
ISBN 1 84310 108 4

Family Day Care
International Perspectives on Policy, Practice and Quality
Edited by Ann Mooney and June Statham
ISBN 1 84310 062 2

Helping Families in Family Centres
Working at Therapeutic Practice
Edited by Linnet McMahon and Adrian Ward
ISBN 1 85302 835 5

Domestic Violence and Child Protection
Directions for Good Practice
Edited by Catherine Humphreys and Nicky Stanley
ISBN 1 84310 276 5

Culture and Child Protection: Reflexive Responses
Marie Connolly, Yvonne Crichton-Hill and Tony Ward
ISBN 1 84310 270 6

Developing Good Practice in Children's Services
Edited by Vicky White and John Harris
ISBN 1 84310 150 5

Child Welfare Services for Minority Ethnic Families
The Research Reviewed
June Thoburn, Ashok Chand and Joanne Procter
Introduction by Beverley Prevatt Goldstein
ISBN 1 84310 269 2

Family Support
as Reflective Practice

*Edited by Pat Dolan, John Canavan
and John Pinkerton*

Foreword by Neil Thompson

Jessica Kingsley Publishers
London and Philadelphia

First published in 2006
by Jessica Kingsley Publishers
116 Pentonville Road
London N1 9JB, UK
and
400 Market Street, Suite 400
Philadelphia, PA 19106, USA

www.jkp.com

Library of Congress Cataloging in Publication Data
Family support as reflective practice / edited by Pat Dolan, John Canavan, and John
Pinkerton.
p. cm.
Includes bibliographical references and indexes.
ISBN-13: 978-1-84310-320-2 (pbk. : alk. paper)
ISBN-10: 1-84310-320-6 (pbk. : alk. paper) 1. Family services. 2. Child welfare. I.
Dolan, Pat, 1958- II. Canavan, John, 1967- III. Pinkerton, John, 1953-
HV697.F3673 2006
362.82'532--dc22

2005032271

British Library Cataloguing in Publication Data
A CIP catalogue record for this book is available from the British Library

ISBN-13: 978 1 84310 320 2
ISBN-10: 1 84310 320 6

Printed and bound in Great Britain by
Athenaeum Press, Gateshead, Tyne and Wear

Contents

Foreword   9
Neil Thompson

1. Family Support: From Description to Reflection   11
    Pat Dolan, National University of Ireland, Galway, Professor John Pinkerton,
    Queen's University Belfast, and John Canavan, National University of Ireland,
    Galway

Part 1   Engaging with Policy and Organisation

2. School as a Base for Family Support Services   27
    Ilan Katz, University of New South Wales, Australia

3. Family Support as Community-based Practice:
    Considering a Community Capacity Framework
    for Family Support Provision   42
    Robert J. Chaskin, University of Chicago, US

4. Supporting Families through Local Government:
    A Danish Case Study   61
    Peter Steen Jensen and René Junker, Municipality of Odense, Denmark

5. Implementing Family Support Policy: Empowering
    Practitioners   75
    Alex Wright, Glasgow University, UK

6. A Comparative Perspective: Exploring the Space
    for Family Support   88
    Michelle Millar, National University of Ireland, Galway

Part 2 Using Concepts, Frameworks and Tools

7. Safeguarding Children Through Supporting Families 103
   Ruth Gardner, University of East Anglia, UK

8. Youth Advocacy: Programming Justice-focused Family
   Support Intervention 118
   *Jeff Fleischer, Judy Warner, Carla J. McCulty and Michael B. Marks, Youth
   Advocate Program, Inc.*

9. Supporting Families with Disabled Children:
   A Case Study 134
   Rosemary Kilpatrick, Queen's University, Belfast

10. Enhancing Support for Young People in Need: Reflections
    on Informal and Formal Sources of Help 149
    Pat Dolan and Brian McGrath, National University of Ireland, Belfast

11. Cultural Competence, Cultural Sensitivity and Family
    Support 165
    Fatima Husain, National Family and Parenting Institute, UK

12. Reframing Practice as a Family Support: Leaving Care 181
    John Pinkerton

13. Assessment, Intervention and Self-appraisal Tools
    for Family Support 196
    Pat Dolan

14. Culturally Appropriate Family Support Practice:
    Working with Asian Populations 214
    *Monit Cheung, Children and Families Concentration and Child Welfare
    Education Project, and Patrick Leung, Graduate School of Social Work,
    University of Houston, TX, and US Council on Social Work Education*

Part 3 Advancing Evaluation

15. Developing an Outcome Evaluation Framework
    for Use by Family Support Programs   237
    Charles Bruner, Child and Family Policy Center, US

16. School- and Family-level Income Effects in a Randomized
    Controlled Prevention Trial: A Multilevel Analysis   250
    W. Todd Abraham, Daniel W. Russell, Max Guyll, Linda Trudeau,
    Catherine Goldberg-Lillehoj and Richard Spoth, Iowa State University, US

17. Towards an Inclusive Approach to Family Support
    Evaluation   266
    Jackie Sanders and Robyn Munford, Massey University,
    New Zealand

18. Reflecting for Action: The Future of Family Support   280
    John Canavan

    List of Contributors   290

    Subject Index   294

    Author Index   300

Foreword

This collection, edited by three highly respected figures in the field of child welfare, offers important food for thought in relation to a very important, but often neglected field of study and practice. Family support, often overshadowed by child protection on one side and the post-Waterhouse emphasis on good practice in residential child care on the other, is a subject worthy of detailed and extensive consideration in its own right. This important book makes a significant contribution to that end.

With chapters on a variety of themes, the book offers readers no shortage of insights and stimulating reflections on difference aspects of family support. As such, this book makes an important contribution to taking forward our thinking and thus having a platform from which to develop policy and practice.

The earlier work of this editorial team (Canavan *et al.*, 2000) argued that family support needed to find direction. Both books, this one and its predecessor, help take matters forward in this regard. The emphasis on establishing clarity and focus is one I especially welcome, as I have been concerned for some time that the pressures involved in child welfare work, combined with the complexities arising from various policy initiatives in a fast-changing political context, can lead to immense uncertainty, confusion and disorientation. Too often, in my view, the result is practices that lack direction, clarity and focus.

This is not necessarily a criticism of individual practitioners, but rather a recognition that unclear and unrealistic expectations of staff can be very counterproductive and undermining of good practice. This book, I am delighted to say, will be very helpful in establishing some of the clarity needed.

I particularly welcome the book's emphasis on reflective practice. In recent years there have been various steps that can be seen to increase the procedural elements of child and family welfare and thus undermine professional autonomy. However, given the complexities of the work, there will always be a role for professional assessment and decision making – and reflective practice is an essential part of developing good practice in that area. Non-reflective, uncritical approaches to such a complex and constantly changing set of circumstances are dangerous in the extreme. The editors and authors are therefore to be congratulated on an excellent contribution to promoting a critically reflective approach to family support.

Dr Neil Thompson
Avenue Consulting Ltd

Chapter 1

Family Support: From Description to Reflection

Pat Dolan, John Pinkerton and John Canavan

Introduction

This is the second set of descriptions of family support in its varied forms that
we have assembled as editors (see also Canavan, Dolan and Pinkerton 2000). The
message of the earlier book was that family support needed to find direction
within its diversity. It was unsustainable as a challenging policy and practice
direction if it could not move on from 'being one of those warm and fuzzy
terms which by being all inclusive ends up meaning nothing' (Pinkerton
2000). There was a need for description, clarification and definition. That was
the emerging agenda which needed to be addressed through policy, operational
management, practice and research. Five years on, family support has become a
major strategic orientation in services for children and families. It now occupies
a significant place within the array of care and welfare interventions. It has
global currency. Not only does it shape policy and practice in different countries but it accords strongly with the unifying global agenda for children and
their families: the United Nations Convention on the Rights of the Child. Yet
despite that continued development family support remains elusive. It's there,
governments are promoting it, agencies are organised for it, workers are delivering it and families receiving it – but what is it?

The clarification agenda still needs to be addressed. Family support continues to be remarkable for being so under-conceptualised. Its policy roots and
practice implications have yet to receive definitive programmatic attention.
Family support practitioners – and by that term is meant anyone involved in
making it a reality, whether through front line service delivery, management,
policy or evaluation – continue to work without a common view as to its
meaning. That lack of clarity is a shared challenge to all of us involved with
family support. It is that challenge of how to take a firm position on the content

and meaning of family support in policy and practice that represents the context in which this book was born for us as editors.

The challenge took two forms. The first was the involvement of two of the editors in launching a post-graduate programme of training in family support (www.nuigalway.ie/soc) and having to find the secure conceptual grounding that such an enterprise required. The second resulted from a concern we all three shared about a policy vacuum around family support. That led us to facilitate a national policy symposium on family support in Ireland in 2002. In turn this prompted a request from the Irish Department of Health and Children to formulate a definition of family support as part of the consultative process leading to the development of a national Family Support Strategy. Responding to the challenge of those two 'critical incidents' in the development of our thinking about family support forced us to take a position on what we regard it to be. We are now working to an explicit, albeit provisional, definition of family support.

Our definition, like all the others which are being applied, implicitly or explicitly, within the field of family support, must be compared and contrasted and tested in practice. A sound, shared understanding of family support can only emerge through such a process of reflection. The varied accounts we have assembled here on practising family support, and the lessons there are to learn from that practice, provide an opportunity to reflect on our definition and to develop future directions in our thinking and activity. We also hope the chapters will add to the readers' existing stock of concepts and frameworks of understanding, while developing their appreciation of how that knowledge can become a part of their practice.

This first chapter represents our guide to reading the chapters that follow. We begin by proposing social support as the theoretical linchpin to an understanding of family support. That is followed up with a model of family support linked to a definition and set of practice principles. With our position made explicit as a reference point we set out an approach to reflective practice and offer some guidance as to how to operate in this mode. It is our intention to encourage readers to respond from their own experience and understanding to our definition and in doing so move into reflective mode. Reflective reading, like reflective practice, must begin with clarifying what the starting point is for the individual reader. What any reader makes of this book will depend on his or her own experience of family support and sets of ideas about that experience. This means that certain chapters will have more immediate appeal for some readers than for others. The final part of this chapter provides summary information on each of the book's chapters which may help readers select which are closest to their interests. However, whether engaging with the book on a selective or a comprehensive basis, we urge readers to stick with the tasks set in this first chapter of connecting thinking to practice in order to address the clarification agenda necessary if family support is to maintain and develop its position within child welfare.

Understanding family support

Despite the recognition of family support as a major strategic orientation, it is still at a relatively early stage in its development (Pinkerton, Dolan and Percy 2003). The dominant focus in child care services since the early 1990s has been on the protection and care of children who are at risk. There has been interest in preventive approaches to child welfare, involving support to families and children, aimed at avoiding the need for further more serious interventions later on (Gardner 2003; Jack and Jordan 1999). However the level of that interest has been dependent on the contingencies of an ever changing national policy climate (Tunstill 2003). Lurking in the shadows of the debate over family support, there is a much sharper political, social and economic challenge (Hardiker, Exton and Barker 1991; Pinkerton *et al.* 2003). Accordingly secure ground needs to be sought in understanding what exactly family support means in terms of services, policy and organisational contexts. It is timely to focus on developing a definition. That in turn requires a more explicit position on the theoretical underpinnings of family support.

Underpinning family support with social support theory

There is no dominant theoretical underpinning apparent in the literature that attempts to address the thorny question of what is family support. However, social support theory is a strong candidate for filling that space as the link between it and the practicalities of supporting families is so clear. There is strong research evidence gathered over the last 30 years that social support plays a crucial part in successful coping (Eckenrode and Hamilton 2000). It is known that its presence assists resiliency, has a buffering effect in dealing with stress and aids positive mental health (Rutter, Giller and Hegel 1998). Informal social support between family members and amongst friends can be seen as forming a 'central helping system' (Canavan and Dolan 2000). Whittaker and Garbarino in the 1980s neatly described social support within families as being the 'bread and butter' source of help (1983, p.4).

In the main, people access support from the informal sources of the nuclear and extended family and to a lesser extent friendships (Canavan and Dolan 2003; Cutrona 2000). When such natural support is deemed to be weak, non-existent or incapable of offering the help required, a person is more inclined to turn to formal sources of support. This is not to counterpoise the informal and the formal as an 'either/or' choice, for both have advantages and disadvantages. Whereas informal support is non-stigmatising, cheap and avail-able outside of 'nine to five', there are forms and degrees of need where professional help is clearly required (Gardner 2003). Additionally, as Gardner (2003) and Belsky (1997) have cautioned, families can also be the main source of strife, including abuse. In such cases direct intervention from professionals is certainly necessitated.

Types and qualities of support within and beyond families

In the main there are specific types and qualities of support available to families (Cutrona 2000) and these are as follows.

Types of social support:

- *Concrete support* relates to practical acts of assistance between people, for example, childminding a sister's young baby while she goes shopping. It has been noted that too often a family's need for basic practical help is either missed or underestimated by professionals (Cochran 1993; Dolan and Holt 2002; Jack 2001).

- *Emotional support* comprises acts of empathy, listening and generally 'being there' for someone when needed (Cutrona 2000). There is a need to be discreet in how one offers emotional support, but it has particularly strong currency in that even if offered as an alternative to other types of need it is generally perceived as helpful (Cutrona 1996).

- *Advice support* can be more complicated and is often sought within families for its comfort and reassurance rather than the actual nature of the advice itself (Cotterell 1996). For example, in dealing with a family member with an illness such as cancer, other family members often seek advice which reassures them that they are doing their best for the sick person (Aymanns, Sigrun and Klaur 1995).

- *Esteem support* centres on how one person rates and informs another in terms of personal worth. For families, it is the foundation stone of their personal system (Burleson 1990).

Qualities of social support:

- *Closeness* – within family and other contacts, a person is more likely to access support from those that he or she sees as responsive and those with whom there is a shared sense of closeness. For example, research in Ireland and the US (Cutrona and Cole 2000; Riordan 2002) shows that this is particularly the case in respect of teen parents.

- *Reciprocity* involves acts whereby help is exchanged between people, ensuring that a person does not feel beholden to another. Very often within families this occurs automatically and its value lies in the comfort of knowing that the exchange of support is ready made and available if and when it is needed.

- *Durability* relates to the contact rates and length of time people are known to each other. Ideally reliable members are those who are known for a long period, are nearby to offer help, and typically are in no way intrusive (Tracy and Biegel 1994).

Thus, social support theory draws on a considerable body of research to clearly identify the types and qualities of relationships that provide support in a way that can be concisely demonstrated and easily understood. As such, it can be directly applied in the field of family support.

A model, definition and set of principles for family support

Using social support theory as a linchpin, it is possible to take a coherent view of family support in a way that is applicable across a range of contexts. This perspective allows the ultimate goal of achieving the rights of children and young people through meeting their needs within the family to be modelled within a set of levels of support, as set out in Figure 1.1 below. The emphasis on levels of support contained within the cupped model is consistent both with the social support and with wider family support literature. Beyond the nuclear family, there are extended family and friends, then the school and community, which in turn are supported by wider organisational networks, and finally, national policy and legislation.

Achieving rights/Meeting needs

Child/young person
Nuclear family

Wider family/friends

School/neighbourhood

Community/voluntary/statutory
Agencies/services/organisations

National policy/legislation

Figure 1.1: A cupped model of family support

This model has been used within the Irish context to help distil a clear and detailed definition for family support as follows:

> Family support is recognised as both a style of work and a set of activities that reinforce positive informal social networks through integrated programmes. These programmes combine statutory, voluntary, community and private services and are generally provided to families within their own homes and communities. The primary focus of these services is on early intervention aiming to promote and protect the health, well-being and rights of all children, young people and their families. At the same time particular attention is given to those who are vulnerable or at risk.

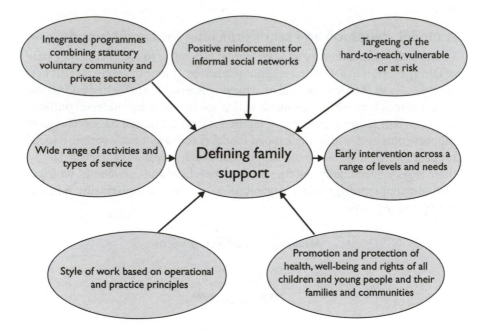

Figure 1.2: Defining family support

This definition can be presented figuratively as having seven distinct and equally related components.

A set of ten practice principles accompanies the definition. These principles all have a strong resonance for reflective practice.

1. Working in partnership is an integral part of family support. Partnership includes children, families, professionals and communities.

2. Family support interventions are needs led and strive for the minimum intervention required.

3. Family support requires a clear focus on the wishes, feelings, safety and well-being of children.

4. Family support services reflect a strengths-based perspective which is mindful of resilience as a characteristic of many children's and families' lives.

5. Family support promotes the view that effective interventions are those that strengthen informal support networks.

6. Family support is accessible and flexible in respect of location, timing, setting and changing needs and can incorporate both child protection and out of home care.

7. Families are encouraged to self-refer and multi-access referral paths will be facilitated.

8. Involvement of service users and providers in the planning, delivery and evaluation of family support services is promoted on an ongoing basis.

9. Services aim to promote social inclusion, addressing issues around ethnicity, disability and rural/urban communities.

10. Measures of success are routinely built into provision so as to facilitate evaluation based on attention to the outcomes for service users and thereby facilitate ongoing support for quality services based on best practice.

An approach to reflective practice

Practitioners involved in the various aspects of family support captured in the definition and principles above are all constantly trying to make sense of what they do. In various ways they are all putting words to what happened, how they and the other people involved felt about it and what it all meant. Mastering the daily routines and surprises of family support practice prompts a constant questioning of both individual actions and the structural constraints and opportunities that frame the action. In a range of ways, each chapter in this book shows how doing family support requires a mixture of description and questioning informed by action. It is that mixture which provides the basis for reflective practice.

There is an extensive literature based on a long tradition of studying how we learn about our worlds in this experiential way. This has been influential in adult education generally and in social work training in particular with its emphasis on placement-based practice learning (Clegg *et al.* 2000; Gould and Taylor 1996; Ruch 2002; Schon 1983). This perspective on adult learning takes the individual who is engaging in reflection as the starting point. 'Reflection is grounded in the personal foundation of experience of the learner, that is, those experiences which have shaped the person and have helped to create the person he or she now is and their intent' (Boud and Knights 1996, p.27).

It has been argued that the increasingly bureaucratic context in which most of the helping professions now work has created environments which are 'intrinsically antagonistic to thoughtful practice' (Pietroni 1995, quoted in Houston and Wilson 2005). For the front-line practitioner, competency-led training and narrow performance management have undermined effective developmental supervision and support, and restricted the time and opportunities for reflection. There is a tendency towards 'typification' (Marsh and Fisher 1992) encouraged by agency procedures. This tends to reduce the relationship between practitioners and service users to routine responses based on both sides of the relationship being stuck in the rigidly fixed categories of 'service supplier' and 'service user'. However, the reality of the relationships between practitioners and the family members they work with constantly subverts this typification. Both the definitions of what it is that families want help with and the development of useful responses are negotiated via a complex series of transactions between the practitioner and family members.

The challenge for reflective practitioners grappling with service delivery, management and policy making is to understand what it is they are contributing to the negotiation of useful responses to families' needs. The contribution must include not only skills and values but also knowledge. Indeed it is within the practitioners' knowledge base, their store of concepts, that the words will be found to identify their skills and values. It is difficult to match theory to practice in this way. Knowledge understood simply as the definitions, concepts and frameworks taught on courses or written in books is too limited to cover the diverse and complicated experience of practice. To be useful, knowledge needs to be transformed. As Gould (1996) points out:

> knowledge and formal theory are not neutral resources which can be drawn down and directly applied, but are only of use when mediated through the complex filters of practice experience. In order to become a tool for practice, the practitioner has to transform theory in the light of learning from past experience (reflection-on-action) and through improvisation during the course of intervention (reflection-in-action). (p.3)

There is a range of ways of detailing the process of reflective practice with a number of variations presented in different chapters in this book. One that usefully illustrates what is meant by the term is a four-step model that has been developed as an aid for front-line practitioners (Houston and Wilson 2005). The purpose is to get practitioners to describe and analyse a critical incident, evaluate the outcome, identify learning points and then act on them. For the first step it is important that a single, time-limited event is selected that can be described in detail, in terms of the physical environment in which it took place, what exactly was done and said, in what sequence, who was involved, and what was the emotional content. What has been described is then analysed in terms of the knowledge, skills and value components brought to it by the practitioner. Attention is given to what was the meaning of the incident to the practitioner who led to it being selected. The feelings which it prompted in the practitioner are also considered.

The second step evaluates the incident against what the practitioner had intended to achieve in the situation. Consideration is given to both what worked well and what did not work out as intended. This is used to highlight strengths, weaknesses or gaps in the practitioner's knowledge, skills or values. In that way the practitioner becomes the focus for reflection and the bridge is made to the third, prescriptive step – what does the practitioner need to understand and do differently in the future and how can that be achieved? Through these three steps, practitioners are encouraged to get perspective on situations they are deeply involved in. This is not so that they can distance themselves from what occurred, but rather to incorporate it into their pool of experience and understanding, in ways that will inform the fourth step – acting in a different way.

Understanding reflective practice in this staged and grounded way makes it clear that its aim is to inform and change individual behaviour. Change at any level is threatening. Recognising the link between change and reflective practice is to identify a major block to engaging in it. A natural wariness of change can be compounded by anxiety and fear of failure and admitting weakness and mistakes. Gambrill warns that asking questions of your own and others' practice can prompt defensiveness, hostility and anger. Dealing with that requires self-awareness and sensitive handling of others.

> Without emotion management skills for handling negative reactions to critical enquiry (your own as well as others), you may have a lapse of spirit and may not challenge fuzzy thinking... Concentrating on helping clients attain outcomes they value will give you the courage and focus you need. (1997, p.138).

Whilst recognising the individual as the starting point for reflective practice, it also needs to be stressed that development of personal knowledge is a very social process. For example, class-based power structures, organisational hierarchies and gender relations all frame the individual's opportunity to engage in reflective practice. Such social phenomena also provide the subject matter of much reflective practice. So it is not surprising that the link has been made between reflection and critical thinking (Adams, Dominelli and Payne 2002; Gambrill 1997). Gambrill, citing Brookfield, argues that reflection becomes critical when it has the purpose of unmasking how power underpins, frames and distorts processes and interaction. She also argues that critical thinking questions assumptions and practices that seem to make our lives easier but actually work against our long-term best interest. Adams takes this further by stressing that adopting a critical perspective links reflective practice to a more far-reaching transformation agenda.

> Reflective practice contributes to critical practice but of itself is not sufficient. Refection on its own views the situation unchanged, whereas critical practice is capable of change. Reflection on the situation *as it is* does not achieve transformation. Critical practice offers the prospect of transformation by not being bound by the status quo. (2002, p.87).

Reflective practice is based on a mixture of description and questioning informed by action leading to change – for the individual and the social context. The aim of this book is to stimulate and resource that process.

Format and content

It is important to meeting the goals of this book that reflective practice informs readers' engagement with the knowledge and experience shared by the authors in the chapters that follow. They are set out in three parts:

1.   engaging with policy and organisation

2.   using concepts, frameworks and tools

3.   advancing evaluation.

Engaging with policy and organisation

The general theme of the first part is that policy and organisational issues are as critical to family support as the direct face-to-face work that it involves. Reflective practitioners need to focus on themselves in the context of both policy and organisation. The first three chapters explore family support policy implementation in different settings. Writing in the UK context, Ilan Katz explores the potential role for schools to be a key site in which to deliver family support. The main messages from his chapter are the need for flexibility for families in accessing services, the importance of full engagement of school staff and the importance of engaging all significant family members. Rob Chaskin discusses the implications for family support of what we know about the community context of child well-being and family functioning from an American perspective. He draws attention to the possibilities offered by community capacity building. Rene Junker and Peter Steen-Jensen return us to the task of providing family support through state services. Drawing on their experience of a Danish municipality, they trace the significant shift of policy within their services for children and families towards family support.

The two remaining chapters in this part are policy focused. In the first of them Alex Wright stresses the importance of recognising the role played by practitioners in the development of policy through how it is implemented. She offers a conceptual framework to help practitioners and managers get to grips with how organizational structure and individual agency affect the policy implementation process. In the second policy chapter, Michelle Millar advocates the use of international comparison to find ways of understanding and influencing 'the policy space' occupied by family support. She presents the experience of family support within four countries in the Anglo-Saxon tradition of public administration.

Using concepts, frameworks and tools

Part 2 comprises eight chapters which cover a mix of theoretical knowledge and direct advice for practice, focusing on different areas of need. It begins with a chapter by Ruth Gardner which links family support, reflective practice and protecting children. Gardner argues that a reflective practice approach will enhance family support approaches to safeguarding children. Next, in their case-study of the Youth Advocacy Programme, Jeff Fleischer and Judy Warner demonstrate what an intervention for high-risk young people looks like when built on a family support strategy and principles.

Focusing on disabled young people and their families, Rosemary Kilpatrick makes a strong case for the value of a reflective approach in learning for service development. Using a case-study of a small-scale, parent-initiated intervention to meet the leisure needs of children with mild learning disabilities, she operationalises a reflective practice model to establish critical learning for practice and policy. Following this, Pat Dolan and Brian McGrath address the role of natural networks in the practice of family support. In respect of supporting adolescents experiencing difficulties through community-based approaches, Dolan and McGrath emphasise the role of natural networks with key messages for professionals.

In one of two chapters focusing on cultural issues, Fatima Hussain offers a theoretical framework within which to reflect on the challenge of cultural competence in working with families. Built around the triad of cultural knowledge, cultural sensitivity and cultural awareness, the chapter argues for a flexible, transformative and dynamic view of this aspect of practice. In his chapter, John Pinkerton shows how the content and style of work changes when it reframed as family support. He illustrates his argument by drawing on what is known about young people leaving care and a Preparation for Adulthood group-work programme.

Next, Pat Dolan focuses on what is needed for good practice. He describes practice tools in respect of social support, intervention programmes which focus on resiliency building, and a model for individualised reflective practice enhancement. In contrast to the more theoretical orientation of Hussain's earlier piece, Monit Cheung and Patrick Leung focus on culturally appropriate tools for practice. The chapter usefully brings together in a single analysis the challenge of cultural competence and evidence-based practice.

Advancing evaluation

The final set of chapters focus on issues of evaluation. While different in their focus and style, each reinforces a clear message about the importance of evaluation for all those working in family support. Charles Bruner exhorts practitioners to become key players in formulating the evaluation frameworks used to assess the services they provide. Taking responsibility for identifying core expectations for the process and outcomes of intervention and building these into programme practice is the key message. Todd Abraham and his colleagues argue for rigorous randomised control trial research as key to the development of efficacious family support interventions. Their chapter is a detailed account of experimentally based, highly policy-significant research on family support. From the other side of the world, Jackie Sanders and Robyn Munford adopt a similar stance to Bruner. Built on their experiences of research in Aotearoa / New Zealand, they propose an inclusive approach to the evaluation of family support services in which critical reflection is embedded at all levels.

In the book's final chapter, John Canavan reconsiders the definitional and theoretical base provided in this introduction, in light of reflections and insights contained in the subsequent chapters. In reflective mode, he details the initial intent of the book, assessing to what extent this has been achieved, leading on to an assessment of key issues for future efforts at framing and consolidating family support.

References

Adams, R. (2002) 'Developing Critical Practice in Social Work.' In R. Adams, L. Dominelli and M. Payne *Critical Practice in Social Work*. Basingstoke: Palgrave.

Adams, R., Dominelli, L. and Payne, M. (2002) *Critical Practice in Social Work*. Basingstoke: Palgrave.

Aymanns, P., Sigrun, H. and Klaur, T. (1995) 'Family Support and Coping with Cancer: Some Determinants and Adaptives Correlates.' *British Journal of Social Psychology 34*, 107–124.

Boud, D. and Knights, S. (1996) 'Course Design for Reflective Practice.' In N. Gould and I. Taylor (eds) *Reflective Learning for Social Work*. Aldershot: Ashgate.

Belsky, J. (1997) 'Determinants and Consequences of Parenting: Illustrative Findings and Basic Principles.' In W. Hellinckx, M. Colton and M. Williams (eds) *International Perspectives on Family Support*. Aldershot: Ashgate.

Burleson, B. (1990) 'Comforting as Social Support: Relationship Consequences of Supportive Behaviours.' In S. Duck (ed) *Personal Relationships and Social Support*. London: Sage.

Canavan, J. and Dolan, P. (2000) 'Refocusing Project Work with Adolescents towards a Family Support Paradigm.' In J. Canavan, and J. Pinkerton (eds) *Family Support: Direction From Diversity*. London: Jessica Kinglsey Publishers.

Canavan, J. and Dolan, P. (2003) 'Policy Roots and Practice Growth: Evaluating Family Support on the West Coast of Ireland.' In I. Katz and J. Pinkerton (eds) *Evaluating Family Support: Thinking Internationally, Thinking Critically*. Chichester: Wiley.

Canavan, J., Dolan, P. and Pinkerton, J. (2000) *Family Support – Direction from Diversity*. London: Jessica Kingsley Publishers.

Clegg, S., Tan, J. and Saeidi, S. (2002) 'Reflecting or Acting? Reflective Practice and Continuing Professional Development in Higher Education.' *Reflective Practice 3*, 1, 131–146, February.

Cochran, M. (1993) 'Parenting and Personal Social Networks.' In T. Luster and L. Okagaki (eds) *Parenting: An Ecological Perspective*. Mahwah, NJ: Lawrence Erlbaum Associates, Inc.

Cotterell, J. (1996) *Social Networks and Social Influences in Adolescence*. London: Routledge.

Cutrona, C.E. (1996) *Social Support in Couples – Marriage as a Resource in Times of Stress*. London: Sage.

Cutrona, C.E. (2000) 'Social Support Principles for Strengthening Families: Messages from America.' In J. Canavan, P. Dolan and J. Pinkerton (eds) *Family Support: Direction From Diversity*. London: Jessica Kingsley Publishers.

Cutrona, C.E. and Cole, V. (2000) 'Optimizing Support in the Natural Network.' In S. Cohen, L.G. Underwood and B.H. Gottlieb (eds) *Social Support Measurement and Intervention: A Guide for Health and Social Scientists*. New York: Oxford University Press Inc.

Dolan, P. and Holt, S. (2002) 'What Families Want in Family Support: An Irish Case Study.' *Child Care in Practice 8*, 4, 239–250.

Eckenrode, J. and Hamilton, S. (2000) 'One to One Support Interventions.' In S. Cohen, L.G. Underwood and B.H. Gottlieb (eds) *Social Support Measurement and Intervention: A Guide for Health and Social Scientists*. New York: Oxford University Press Inc.

Gambrill, E. (1997) *Social Work Practice: A Critical Thinkers Guide*. Oxford: Oxford University Press.

Gardner, R. (2003) *Supporting Families: Child Protection in the Community*. NSPCC. Chichester: Wiley.

Gould, N. and Taylor, I. (eds) (1996) *Reflective Learning for Social Work*. Aldershot: Ashgate.

Hardiker, P., Exton, K. and Barker, M. (1991) *Policies and Practices in Preventive Child Care*. Aldershot: Ashgate.

Houston, S. and Wilson, G. (2005) *Class Notes: Child Care Award Reflection-on-Action Groups*. Queens University Belfast: School of Social Work, unpublished.

Jack, G. (2001) 'Ecological Perspectives in Assessing Children and Families.' In J. Horworth (ed) *The Child's World: Assessing Children in Need*. London: Jessica Kingsley Publishers.

Jack, G. and Jordan, B. (1999) 'Social Capital and Child Welfare.' *Children and Society 13*, 242–256.

Marsh, P. and Fisher, M. (1992) *Good Intentions: Developing Partnerships in Social Services*. York: Joseph Rowntree Foundation/Community Care.

Pinkerton, J. (2000) 'Emerging Agendas for Family Support.' In J. Canavan, P. Dolan and J. Pinkerton (eds) *Family Support: Direction From Diversity*. London: Jessica Kingsley Publishers.

Pinkerton, J. and Katz, I. (2003) 'Perspective through International Comparison in the Evaluation of Family Support.' In I. Katz and J. Pinkerton (eds) *Evaluating Family Support: Thinking Internationally, Thinking Critically*. Chichester: Wiley.

Pinkerton, J., Dolan, P. and Percy, A. (2003) 'Family Support in Ireland: Developing Strategic Implementation.' *Child Care in Practice 9*, 4, 309–321.

Riordan, S. (2002) *Final Evaluation Report of the Teen Parents Support Initiative*. Dublin: Dublin Institute of Technology for the Department of Health and Children, Stationery Office.

Ruch, G. (2002) 'From Triangle to Spiral: Reflective Practice in Social Work Education, Practice and Research.' *Social Work Education 21*, 199–216.

Rutter, M., Giller, H. and Hagel, A. (1998) *Antisocial Behaviour by Young People*. Cambridge: Cambridge University Press.

Schon, D. (1983) *Educating the Reflective Practitioner: How Professionals Think in Action*. New York: Basic Books.

Tracy, E.M. and Biegel, D. (1994) 'Preparing Social Workers for Social Network Interventions in Mental Health Practice.' *Journal of Teaching in Social Work 10*, 206–216

Tunstill, J. (2003) 'Political and Technical Issues Facing Evaluators of Family Support.' In I. Katz and J. Pinkerton (eds) *Evaluating Family Support: Thinking Internationally, Thinking Critically*. Chichester: Wiley.

Whittaker, J.K. and Garbarino, J. (1983) *Social Support Networks: Informal Helping in the Human Services*. New York: Aldine De Gruyter.

Part 1

Engaging with Policy and Organisation

Chapter 2

School as a Base for Family Support Services

Ilan Katz

Introduction

This chapter will discuss the role of schools in providing family support. Through a review of policy developments within Britain and two related service initiatives it will argue that there is enormous potential for schools to become a central resource to families through delivering a range of services. This might appear obvious, but traditionally there has been a great deal of reluctance to utilise schools to deliver services to families. Schools' primary role has been to educate children, and the challenge of producing good educational attainment, along with extra-curricular activities such as sport and societies, has left little resource within schools to go beyond that remit.

Parents are traditionally seen by schools either as a further source of stress for teachers, or, in younger classes at least, as a resource to help the teachers in the classroom. Relationships between school and parents are normally mediated through institutions such as the Parent Teachers Association and parent governors, and through 'set piece' events such as parents' evenings where teachers and parents discuss the academic progress (and sometimes behaviour) of children. When parents have been involved in the school it is usually when there are problems with attendance or behaviour, and parents are then contacted by Education Welfare Officers[1] or head teachers to get them to do something about the situation.

---

1   The Education Welfare Officer's task is to help schools improve pupils' attendance and reduce unnecessary absence and truancy. Education Welfare Officers work closely with schools, children and their parents, and with other statutory and voluntary agencies to promote, encourage and enforce regular school attendance of children.

However, in recent years there has been a greater recognition that the psychological and emotional wellbeing of children is key to their educational attainment. As a result a number of initiatives and programmes have been set up to address these needs. These have included school counsellors, peer mentoring, anti-bullying strategies and 'circle time'. But these school-focused programmes are themselves limited, as in order to fundamentally change children's attitudes to education, families and communities need to be engaged as well. The role of parents goes far beyond providing encouragement and helping with homework. The culture of learning created in the home is a crucial factor in determining how children will approach the task of learning and their attitude towards education and training.

A recent review of the research evidence conducted for the Department for Education and Science concluded that parental involvement in their children's education is the single most significant factor in determining educational attainment of children (Desforges with Abouchaar 2003). But many parents are not able to give this support, either because of their circumstances, for example work commitments, or because they do not have the skills or motivation to help their children attain at school or even to attend. In Britain there has been a two-track policy to address this issue: 'stick and carrot'. On the one hand there have been a number of measures which have placed increasing responsibility on parents to ensure that children attend school. The most recent is the Parenting Order, which can be imposed on parents who persistently refuse to ensure that their children attend school. On the other hand there have been a number of initiatives which are aimed at supporting parents to prevent children from truanting or being excluded from school and to achieve academically.

Thus there is developing recognition that schools themselves can do a lot more to become engaged with the local community and in particular can support vulnerable children and families. Schools have a unique role in society and within communities. Virtually every child attends a school, and so it is one of the very few public services which are truly universal. Schools are in touch with more parents than any other institution, and so they can reach out to parents in a way that no other agency can do. Schools already have a range of health and care professionals working within them, for example school nurses and doctors, education and welfare officers and educational psychologists. There is clearly potential for closer relationships between parents and schools, not only so that parents can become more engaged in helping their children achieve academically but, equally importantly, so that schools can play a part in supporting vulnerable families within the community.

Developments in school and family policy

Government policy towards families in Britain has evolved significantly over the past few years. The overarching goal of the Government is the commitment to end child poverty by the year 2020. There are several strands to this policy, but the main foci are the raising of educational standards, benefit reform, encouraging parents (especially lone parents) into work and targeting services on those most at risk. In the first term of the current government the focus of education policy was almost exclusively on curriculum and school standards. The developments in family policy can be seen expressed in the Green Paper *Every Child Matters* (DfES 2003)[2] which advocated both universal and targeted parenting support and a greater focus on the family and child care.

Family support was at this stage focused mainly on the early years, exemplified by Sure Start (www.surestart.gov.uk), early excellence centres and neighbourhood nurseries. These initiatives were aimed at supporting families with young children, but also helping children to become 'school ready' and helping the parents (especially lone mothers) back into work. However, two influential reports published by the Joseph Rowntree Foundation in the late 1990s (Ball 1998; Dyson and Robson 1999) advocated strongly for the introduction of extended (or 'full service') schools which could play a much more prominent role in supporting communities and families. The Government's Social Exclusion Unit's Performance Action Team (PAT) Report 11 on schools, published in 2000, put forward a range of proposals to reform schools, and committed the government to develop full service and extended schools. PAT Report 12 focused on children at risk, and proposed a range of new approaches to target children at risk of social exclusion.

The Government's spending review of 2000 resulted in the announcement of several new initiatives which were aimed at supporting school-aged children and their families, and preventing them from becoming socially excluded. Government policy moved decisively towards a more holistic view of the role of schools, and began to take much more seriously the link between education, family support and outcomes for children. The most significant of these new initiatives were the Children's Fund and Connexions. A further development was the announcement by the Government in 2002 of the setting up of the Parenting Fund, which is aimed at increasing the capacity of the voluntary sector to deliver parenting programmes.

The Children's Fund is a six-year programme (2001–2006) that provides funding to multi-agency partnerships in every local authority in England to set up preventive services for children aged 5–13. Local partnerships are required to consult with children and families in the setting up and running of the services. The Children's Fund incorporated On Track, a pilot programme set up by the Home Office in 2000 in 24 neighbourhood areas to provide intensive services for children at risk of crime. The Children's Fund places a great deal of

2   Available online at www.dfes.gov.uk/everychildmatters/

emphasis on both family support and school-based services, and more than 50 per cent of services funded are based in schools. The 2004 spending review extends the Government's commitment to using school as the basis for supporting families and improving the life chances of children in poverty (HM Treasury 2004). Connexions (www.connexions.gov.uk) is an initiative which provides personal advisers to children aged 13–18 to encourage them to participate in education and employment and to support their mental and physical health. In theory it is a universal service providing advisers to every teenager, but in reality it is targeted at those young people at risk of not being educated and employed.

However, the most significant policy development in the UK has been the publication of the Green Paper *Every Child Matters* (DfES 2003) which sets out the overall direction of Government policy towards children and families. The main focus is on structural change in the management, configuration and accountability of children's services. The Green Paper provides the framework for improving the outcomes for children by:

- encouraging early intervention
- joined-up working between different professionals
- better information exchange between agencies
- increased accountability
- workforce reform.

Specific proposals for service development include the development of:

- children's trusts, which bring together education and social services (and in some cases other children's services) into one overall structure
- children's centres, which will provide day care and a range of services for children and families in deprived neighbourhoods
- extended schools, which attempt to combine family and community services along with schools' traditional roles
- a common assessment framework for all agencies
- multi-disciplinary teams
- nomination of lead professional for children known to more than one agency.

The Green Paper contains a clear commitment to parenting and family support, and to the link between parents, schools and communities. A whole chapter is devoted to supporting parents and a number of developments are proposed, including family learning programmes, the national roll-out of home visiting services such as Home Start, and Parent Information Point sessions for all parents with children in transition phases.

Service developments

We will now consider two service developments intended to express the policy direction set out in *Every Child Matters*:

1. extended schools, a major new development currently being piloted by the Department for Education and Skills (DfES), which combine schools with a range of family and community services

2. Parent Information Point (PIP) a pilot initiative aimed at providing parents of children at key transition stages with information and advice about parenting.

Extended schools

An extended school is one that provides a range of activities and services, often beyond the school day, to help meet the needs of its pupils, their families and the wider community. There are many ways schools can do this, and no one method or model. For example, an audit by Wilkin and colleagues (2003) collated information on some 160 schools and identified six main types or 'arenas' of provision operating within the concept of the extended school. These were:

1. additional schooling provision offering curriculum and leisure opportunities to pupils beyond the traditional school timetable;

2. community provision offering learning and leisure opportunities, or general community facilities (e.g. drop-in or advice centres);

3. early years provision, such as crèches or pre-school facilities;

4. family and parent provision involving support relating to their child's learning or to a more general parenting or family role;

5. other agency provision (e.g. from health, youth or social services);

6. specialist provision, offering high-calibre facilities in areas such as sports, arts, IT or business.

The audit revealed there was great variety amongst schools in terms of the numbers of arenas covered and the degree of investment in them.

However, the Government has funded some schools specifically to become extended schools. The Extended Schools Pathfinder initiative provided additional funding to projects in 25 Local Education Authorities (LEAs) from November 2002 to August 2003. Interim findings from an evaluation of the pathfinders (Cummings, Dyson and Todd 2004; Dyson, Millward and Todd 2004) confirmed that there is no single model of 'the extended school' and there is considerable variation between projects depending on factors including community need, geography and access to other funding streams. The most popular activities within schools are breakfast clubs, after school and holiday activities for pupils, funding transport to community activities, adult education, activities bringing art into schools, and community use of school facilities. The 'full-service' school in which community services are located on the school site is less common, though many schools are working towards this.

Although there is no single model of the extended school, it is helpful to think in terms of three levels at which projects might choose to work. The boundaries between these levels are not hard and fast. Schools can and do move between them as needs and opportunities change. Nonetheless, those involved in planning extended schools might find them a helpful way to organise their thinking:

1. *Developing extended activities.* At this level, schools are simply concerned to undertake activities for pupils, families and community members which are valuable in their own right. These activities need not be closely related to each other but will meet particular needs or maximise particular opportunities.

2. *Developing an extended school.* At this level, schools are trying to develop a coherent approach to their relationships with pupils, families and community. They seek to establish a distinctive ethos and to link activities so that they can address in a sustained way underlying issues such as pupils' attainments and motivation, family support for schooling and community attitudes to learning.

3. *Developing a local strategy.* At this level, the work of the extended school forms part of a wider strategy to address community needs and wishes. The issues at stake – employment opportunities, community cohesion, health, crime and so on – are not simply school concerns. Schools therefore may well work in partnership with other agencies and within the context of policy that is developed at neighbourhood, local authority or even national level. This approach is exemplified by a Local Education Authority (LEA) which has a strategy and some LEA funding for school-based funding to co-ordinate extended activities.

Several of the Pathfinder schools understand the school as a resource for the whole community. Many schools work together in federations or patches to support activities across more than one school and to combine funding streams. Activities are focused on pupils, families and the community. Adult education is an important part of this but there are many other varied ways of meeting particular community needs. The latter includes a family link worker to target support to 'at-risk' families, a breakfast club run by young people, and a garden project where pupils who have been underachieving and/or in danger of exclusion work with disabled adults to grow plants for sale and to enhance the school environment. Benefits for pupils have included case study evidence of cross-generational awareness, increased confidence, motivation for learning and decreased exclusion.

The evaluation (Cummings, Dyson and Todd 2004) also found that extended schools impacted on pupils, families and communities in a range of ways generating positive outcomes for all three groups.

- For pupils, there was evidence that activities could have an impact on attainment, behaviour and attendance.

- For families, there was evidence that activities could have an impact on involvement in children's learning.

- For communities, there was evidence that activities could have an impact on community pride and involvement.

In regard to community consultation and involvement the key appeared to be a careful and sustained process of trust-building where partners seek to understand each other's aims, priorities and working methods. This is difficult given the pressures under which all agencies are working, so it is important that the process is given ample time and develops through a series of progressively more ambitious initiatives.

Parent Information Point

The Parent Information Point (PIP) is an example of how a fairly low-level and basic service can have a real impact on parents. PIP was designed by the National Family and Parenting Institute (NFPI) and was a response to the Green Paper pledge to provide information to all parents at key developmental stages in their children's lives. The intervention itself is relatively straightforward: to offer a universal service, consisting of the provision of relevant information about child development issues and local services. The PIP events offer single information sessions to parents on a brief, one-off basis.

Each PIP event was designed to incorporate four core features:

1. a presentation of ten key child development points

2. video clips about national and local parenting services of support

3. a specially designed 'Who Can Help Parents?' board game introducing representatives from local support services

4. an information exchange or 'market place' of stalls setting out for parents what local parenting and family support agencies exist.

The PIP events were primarily delivered at school-based meetings to groups of parents with children in one of three key development stages – parents with children in a reception class (ages 4–5), pre-teenagers (Year 7) and teenagers (Year 9) The events were piloted in three areas: two northern metropolitan boroughs and one inner-city London borough. One of the northern boroughs was situated in an affluent area. The other metropolitan borough was less affluent with a high proportion of parents dependent on benefits. A high proportion of parents from this area were from ethnic minority groups – predominantly Asian (Pakistani and Indian). The inner city London borough was the least affluent of the three areas, with a high proportion of Bangladeshi parents. The structure of PIP included central co-ordination by NFPI and local co-ordination by a nominated individual in each pilot area. The pilots were delivered in nine schools: three schools per pilot area (one secondary school and two of its feeder primary schools). The pilot was delivered over six months and a rigorous evaluation was built into the design (Ghate and Bhabra 2004).

There was a considerable degree of diversity in the way PIP was delivered in each of the three areas and nine participating schools. None of the areas or schools integrated all four core features of PIP. There appeared to be a number of key barriers and key enablers to smooth implementation. A major barrier was the speed at which PIP was introduced. This limited the time available for input from local areas into a central model and resulted in limited programme fidelity (consistency of delivery). It was also found to be more challenging for the pilot projects to work with secondary schools due to the schools' other commitments. In areas with high numbers of parents from ethnic minority backgrounds it was difficult to convey information and materials if they were not translated into the languages used in the home. Also, pupil-post was found not to be an ideal way to publicise events – many parents who did not attend PIP simply hadn't heard about it.

Successful implementation of PIP was dependent on a number of factors. To start with, a nominated local co-ordinator in each area to organise the events was crucial. Good team working between the local co-ordinator and the schools was a major asset, especially in primary schools. The support and endorsement of the school staff was a key determinant of successful implementation. It was found that PIP events were far better attended and more effective when delivered in a school as opposed to a community venue. It was also important to hold PIP events at a range of times throughout the day (morning, afternoon and evening). It helped if there was a good introduction to the event which made the purpose of PIP very clear to parents. The 'market place' was an important component that was enhanced by the actual presence at their stall of local agency representatives.

PIP users showed a significant increase in self-reported knowledge and awareness of family support services, and willingness to access them. The session also increased their knowledge of child development issues and parenting confidence. The greatest impact was found to be amongst parents often deemed 'hard to reach', for example, ethnic minority groups and parents on low income. PIP also had a significant impact on parents with children in the reception age group, though in that group it was not particularly successful in reaching fathers. It was more successful in reaching them in the pre-teenage and teenage groups. Local agencies benefited from their involvement in PIP in terms both of reaching a wider variety of parents for whom their services are applicable and of 'networking' and sharing information with other local agencies.

Challenges in providing school-based family support

Whilst the British policy direction and the experience of such initiatives as the extended school and PIP encourage the development of school-based family support, if this is to happen and be sustained it is essential that the challenges that go with it are also recognised. One of the key challenges in providing family support from schools is the question of who should 'own' the initiative. It has been well documented that schools have difficulties relating to professionals from other agencies, especially social services (Baginsky 2000). There are many reasons for this, including the different professional languages of education, health and social services staff, different understanding of roles (i.e. each agency expecting the other to handle situations), lack of appropriate mechanisms for information sharing, unwillingness of schools to get involved with areas that detract from their core business of delivering the curriculum, teachers' fear of alienating parents by informing on them to other agencies and lack of training in child protection and child development for teachers.

Services which are 'co-located' in schools can overcome some of these difficulties, because the school staff are able to establish personal relationships with the family support staff, and are therefore more likely to establish a degree of trust. However, co-location does not resolve all the issues. There still remain issues around, for example, whether social workers or other family support staff should be employed by the school or by another agency such as social services or a voluntary agency. Employment by the school is more likely to allow the family support staff to become part of the school staff team, and this will facilitate communication and referrals. However, the disadvantages are that families themselves sometimes value a certain distance between the family support staff and school staff, mainly because of concerns around confidentiality. Also, if the family support staff become too identified with the school staff this can alienate them from colleagues working in social services and other agencies.

Of course the details of who employs individual members of staff are less important than how the family support service and service providers fit into the ethos of the school. Ideally they will act as mediators between the school and the other agencies, maintaining the trust and respect of all agencies, and between school and families, where appropriate. They will also work with teachers and other staff to educate them about child protection and family support issues, and will therefore try to change the ethos of schools so that they become more holistic in their view of children and families. In order to do all these things the family support staff must have the support of the head teacher, senior staff in the school and the pastoral staff, and should have clear protocols around issues such as confidentiality and consent. They also need to be able to work closely with providers in other agencies, and to understand the multi-agency frameworks which govern such matters as referral and information exchange.

Of course the ideal situation described above does not often prevail, and family support staff may be confronted by a number of conflicts, either within the school, between the school and other agencies or between the school and families. Family support workers need to be aware of the difficulties and develop strategies to deal with them.

Barriers to accessing school-based services

Although schools are known to be good venues for delivering preventive services such as family support, there has been some concern expressed in the literature that this is not always the case. Research shows that some groups of service users find it very difficult to access services in schools. This can be the case because the children are not attending school or because the parents have a history of poor relationship with school. Fathers in particular can prove difficult to engage. There are particular problems for families depending on whether they are in a rural or an urban area. It is also more difficult for parents of children at secondary school to link with school-based services.

Whilst over 95 per cent of children attend schools, there is a small number who do not. Some of these children (e.g. children educated at home, children in hospital, children in jail) are either relatively well off or should be having their educational and welfare needs met in other ways. However the majority of children not at school are from the most vulnerable and hard-to-reach groups in society. Children excluded from school or truanting are known to be at high risk for a range of difficulties such as crime, mental health problems, teenage pregnancy, etc. Other groups of children who may not be at school include some asylum-seeking children or other children recently brought into the country.[3] Family support programmes based in schools are unlikely to reach out to these groups of children and their families, especially if families need to physically go into the school to receive the service. Some services may deploy

---

3   The case of Victoria Climbié, who came to the UK from West Africa with a great-aunt and was killed by the aunt and her boyfriend, caused a national outcry in the country and has led to a complete overhaul of the child protection system. Victoria was never in school, and this was considered to be one of the major failings of the system.

outreach workers who can provide a service in the family home, but these are restricted to services which operate on a one-to-one basis.

However, recent policy and research has resurrected the importance of fathers and positive male role models as being key to improved outcomes for children. There is a recognition that family support services should support not only mothers but also fathers. That said, the vast majority of service recipients of family support services are mothers rather than fathers. Parenting and parent training are actually somewhat misleading terms because in reality the services are aimed primarily at mothers and mothering. Attempts to involve fathers in family support have not proved to be particularly successful (Ghate, Shaw and Hazel 2000). This poses the question of whether the problem is one of engagement (i.e. making services more attractive to fathers, for example by making them feel more welcome in family centres and providing services in the evening) or whether altogether new modes of delivery need to be developed so that family support itself will look rather different.

School-based services are particularly affected by the challenge of engaging fathers because it is overwhelmingly mothers who come into school to bring and collect children, help in the classrooms, watch school plays and sports days, etc., so fathers tend to see schools as rather alien and perhaps threatening environments. Family support services co-located in schools need to be able to reach out to fathers, again by employing outreach workers or by providing some services at a different venue. There may also be a need to change some of the ways the services work, for example opening during evenings and employing male workers.

There is also a difficulty in access for families who are experiencing problems which occasion a high level of confidentiality or stigma. Although schools provide a generally non-stigmatising environment, and parents routinely go into schools to discuss their children's progress, most parents are not used to going into school to discuss personal problems or family issues beyond children's education. A particular concern for many parents (and older children as well) is that of confidentiality. Schools are generally not laid out for confidentiality, and parents may well feel that they are being watched or that the information they give will be passed on to teachers or others. In particular parents are sometimes resistant to seeing psychiatrists, police or child protection workers in a school environment. So the school can be a benign environment when parents are attending for 'normal' reasons such as discussions with teachers about their children's progress in school, but can become very threatening if the service offered is more stigmatising and implies poor parenting.

Another issue regarding confidentiality is that parents and/or children may discuss private matters with teachers, and request that they do not disclose to other agencies. Historically teachers have been very reluctant to engage with the child protection system because they are unwilling to breach confidentiality with parents, fearing that this will damage their relationships and may ultimately lead to difficulties for the children (see Jones *et al.* 1987). Over the past few years a lot of training has been delivered to teachers about the necessity of referring child protection cases to social services departments. Nevertheless there are many problems other than child protection issues which parents may discuss confidentially with teachers, and it is often very difficult for teachers to make a judgement as to whether to refer them on to other services. These issues are much more easily dealt with when there are social workers or other professionals based in the school, and the teachers can then approach them informally to discuss cases without giving names or making an official referral.

Confidentiality is a real issue for children as well. Like parents, some children may wish to discuss issues confidentially with teachers; conversely other children may not want their teachers to know about issues discussed with school counsellors or other professionals. Children, especially adolescents, are acutely aware of the stigma of being involved in the child protection system or with children and adolescent mental health services (CAMHS), and schools need to handle these issues very carefully. For example, children may resent being called out of class to attend conferences, because they have to explain to their classmates why they were absent, and this is acutely embarrassing for them. Some of these issues can be overcome by situating the service in a part of the school which is less open, or allowing families who wish to maintain anonymity to enter the school from a different entrance.

Many parents who face difficulties bringing up their children have a history of conflict or poor relationships with schools, either when they themselves were school students or as parents. These parents are far less likely to see the school as a non-stigmatising environment in which to receive services. In these cases school staff need to be extra careful that parents are engaged with sensitivity. This can sometimes be very challenging, for example if parents are in dispute with the school about their children's education. Where possible these families should be provided with the choice of receiving family support services which are not associated with the school. However, engagement with the school should be the ultimate aim in all cases – it can never be in children's interests for their parents to be disengaged from their schooling.

RURAL/URBAN ISSUES

Schools in rural areas face particular difficulties in relation to providing family support services. This is because the children attending these schools tend to come from a wide geographical area, and it is often difficult for parents to come to school to access services. In addition rural schools are often smaller than those in urban areas, and so services may be seen as being less cost-effective than in urban areas. Inner city schools have different problems; whilst they are physically easier to access, they often serve an ethnically diverse population in areas with multiple problems. Family support services in these areas need to be sensitive to the different groups of families who attend the school, and need to provide culturally sensitive and accessible information to all parents.

PRIMARY AND SECONDARY SCHOOLS

Parents are more likely to engage with services which are based in primary rather than secondary schools. This is because parents (especially mothers) are more likely to be familiar with the school whilst their children are in primary school. Most parents pick their children up from school, and virtually all parents attend parents' evenings, school plays, summer fairs and other events at primary schools. Parents are also more likely to feel part of the school 'community' and to know other parents, who will live close by, and through discussing children visiting each other. Parents of secondary school children are far less likely to know other parents or the teachers, and their relationship with the school is therefore likely to be more distant. Nevertheless, for many parents the school will continue to be a good location for services. Secondary schools also often have facilities such as sports facilities which can act as a conduit to more specialist services.

In conclusion: three messages

This review of policy developments in Britain and related service initiatives suggests that there is enormous potential for schools to deliver a range of services to children and families. It also suggests that it will be challenging to release that potential. In meeting the challenge there are three central messages that need to be heard.

One size doesn't fit all

The main lesson for practitioners is that different families will respond differently to services, and that no school-based service will be relevant for all families. Whilst schools have been shown to be excellent venues for a range of family support services, they do not reach all families. Over and above the obvious point that some children do not attend school, there is a number of different reasons why family members will be reluctant to access services in a school context. The best way of overcoming this is to offer families different ways of accessing the service – either through home visits or by holding some sessions in community settings outside the school. When services are in school it is important to make parents and children comfortable by offering privacy and confidentiality (depending on the nature of the service) and by providing adequate facilities for the service.

School staff must be engaged

The most tricky aspect of providing family support services in school is the relationship between the service and the school. Without the endorsement of staff, especially the head teacher, services are unlikely to get off the ground. But even when they are operating, it is important for the family support staff to develop good working relationships with teachers and other school staff. Teachers are likely to be the main source of referral, and it is important for them to be kept on board. Tension can arise over issues such as confidentiality, giving children time out of class to attend sessions, differences of opinion over what actions to take (e.g. to exclude children), and this needs constant dialogue and negotiation. For services that consciously want to demonstrate to families that they are not part of the school culture, these issues are even more salient.

Family must mean the whole family

One challenge to providing family support services in schools is that the service is much more likely to be accessed by mothers and pupils attending the school rather than fathers or other children. The disengagement of fathers from family support services generally is well documented, but some fathers have particular difficulty engaging with school-based services. Practitioners need to be aware of these issues and make special attempts to engage with fathers, including non-resident fathers, who may well play an important part in the child's life. Mothers are more likely to be familiar with the school (especially the primary school) and fathers are more likely to be engaged if mothers are on board first.

If these three clear messages are attended to by all those involved in developing and delivering school-based services, there is every reason to be confident that such provision has a future as a very important part of the range of services needed to support children and families.

References

Baginsky, M. (2000) *Child Protection and Education*. London: NSPCC.

Ball, M. (1998) *School Inclusion: The School, the Family and the Community*. York: Joseph Rowntree Foundation.

Cummings, C., Dyson, A. and Todd, L. (2004) *Evaluation of the Extended Schools Pathfinder Projects*. London: DfES.

Department for Education and Skills and HM Treasury (2003) *Every Child Matters*. London: The Stationery Office.

Desforges, C. with Abouchaar, A. (2003) *The Impact of Parental Involvement, Parental Support and Family Education on Pupil Achievements and Adjustment: A Literature Review*. London: Department for Education and Skills.

Dyson A. and Robson, E. (1999) *School, Family, Community: Mapping School Inclusion in the UK*. London: National Youth Agency.

Dyson, A., Millward, A. and Todd, L. (2004) *A Study of 'Extended' Schools Demonstration Projects. Research Report 381*. London: DfES.

Ghate, D. and Bhabra, S. (2004) *Meeting the Mental Health Needs of Children in the Child Protection System.* London: Policy Research Bureau.

Ghate, D. and Hazel, N. (2002) *Parenting in Poor Environments: Stress, Support and Coping.* London: Jessica Kingsley Publishers.

Ghate, D., Shaw, C. and Hazel, N. (2000) *Engaging Fathers in Preventive Services: Fathers and Family Centres.* York: Joseph Rowntree Foundation and York YPS.

HM Treasury (2004) *Child Poverty Review.* London: HM Treasury, available at www.hm-treasury.gov.uk/spending_review/spend_sr04/associated_documents/spending04 _childpoverty.cfm

Jones, D.N., Pickett, J., Oates, M.R. and Barbor, P.R. (1987) *Understanding Child Abuse,* 2nd. edn. Basingstoke: Macmillan.

Wilkin, A., Kinder, K., White, M. and Doherty, P. (2003) *Towards the Development of Extended Schools.* London: National Foundation for Educational Research, DfES.

Chapter 3

Family Support as Community-based Practice: Considering a Community Capacity Framework for Family Support Provision

Robert J. Chaskin

Family support has been described in many ways – as a 'perspective on child welfare', a method of service provision, an 'ethos' guiding the delivery of services, the services themselves, a 'movement' (Family Support America 1996; Gardner 2003; Pinkerton and Katz 2003; Weissbourd 1994). However described, a broad range of programs and activities has been supported in a number of countries under its banner. In the United States, for example, family support has commanded attention from both philanthropy and public policy (including the allocation of tens of millions of dollars in federal funding through the Omnibus Reconciliation Act of 1993), and has entailed the creation of a national membership organization (Family Support America) that seeks to promote family support principles and practices through publications, advocacy and technical assistance (Family Support America 1996; Layzer *et al.* 2001; Weissbourd 1994).

As a field of practice, family support has for the most part been characterized by the development and delivery of a diverse set of services provided by a broad range of practitioners and organizations (voluntary and statutory) in local communities. Service provision is meant to be flexible, responsive, and interactive. It includes programs focusing on, for example, parenting education and parent support groups; home visiting; information dissemination, referral, and case management; counseling and crisis intervention; life-skills, literacy, and employment training; youth development; and advocacy activities (Family

Support America 1996; Gardner 2003; Gilligan 2000; Layzer *et al.* 2001; Lightburn and Kemp 1994).

But the principles and assumptions behind family support practice also represent part of a broader shift in orientation regarding social policy and service provision – especially for families at risk or living in disadvantaged circumstances – that is increasingly recognized and shared by a range of other, often complementary, efforts. These include education reform efforts such as full-service schools, juvenile justice initiatives such as community-based mediation and 'restorative justice' schemes, youth development efforts such as community-based after-school programs, and broad-based community development efforts, such as comprehensive community initiatives. One key assumption that undergirds many of these efforts is the importance of community in the lives of families and its potential as an organizing principle for informing practice.

Reflecting this, family support practitioners and scholars frequently invoke the relationship between their program offerings and the contexts in which they are provided, in particular the local communities in which children and their families live. This may include considering community context when developing programs and addressing strategic implementation challenges; creating reciprocal links between family support workers and activities and other community actors and efforts (e.g., neighborhood associations, service agencies, schools, family-oriented events) and, potentially, gearing family support provision to contribute to broader community development and 'community building' (Family Resource Coalition 2003; Garbarino and Kostelny 1994; Lightburn and Kemp 1994; Weissbourd 1994).

Across a broad range of efforts, an emphasis on community building has focused fundamentally on the goal of strengthening the *capacity* of communities to identify priorities and opportunities, effectively support and provide for the individuals and families who live there, and work to foster and sustain positive community change (Chaskin 2001; Chaskin *et al.* 2001). This chapter explores the relationship between family support practice and the notion of community capacity, and investigates the ways in which considering a community capacity framework may inform the work of family support practitioners and organizations.

The chapter is organized in five sections. First, it briefly describes the shift in orientation represented by family support and outlines the central ideas that drive family support practice. Next, it explores the relevance of 'community' and some of the ways in which the local community may influence child and family functioning. Third, it investigates the relationship of family support practice to the communities in which family support programs are delivered and to community development practice more broadly. Fourth, it outlines a framework for thinking about the idea of community capacity and the ways in which some contemporary efforts are attempting to build capacity in poor communities in the United States. Finally, it offers a platform for reflection on implications of this orientation for family support practice and policy.

A paradigm shift: from remediation to support

Family support today builds on the foundation of prior movements shaping social welfare practice for families, from an emphasis on parenting education provided by early Maternal Associations, to the social settlements that were founded in the latter part of the nineteenth century in England and the United States, to the self-help and community-based movements that emerged to provide local, voluntary assistance to families in need (Kagan *et al.* 1996; Weissbourd 1987, 1994). Over the course of the past three decades, in particular, family support programs and approaches gained ground in light of growing concern about the systems in place to address the needs of children and families and to promote their well-being.

In particular, the growth of family support responded to frustration with categorical approaches to service delivery which, during its emergence as a field of practice in the 1970s, were both fragmented and deficit focused. Rather than responding to the ways in which the needs and circumstances of families – especially poor families – are often interrelated, the service system was organized around discrete program areas (and supported by discrete streams of funding) that attempted to respond to narrowly defined problems (Gardner 1989; Levitan, Mangum and Pines 1989; Schorr 1988). This orientation not only failed to take into account the interaction among particular needs (for example, poverty, substance abuse, domestic violence, and child abuse or neglect are often correlated), it was also fundamentally reactive; it focused on post-hoc remediation rather than attempting to prevent problems before they could negatively affect families. Further, it failed to recognize and work with (let alone seek to promote) the potential assets that families can bring to bear on their circumstances and that may contribute to their well-being. Finally, family support was responding to a lack of attention to context – to the ways in which the developmental trajectory of children and the needs and circumstances of individuals are embedded in and influenced by a broader ecology of actors and environments. These include the family, school, church, neighborhood, and influences of the larger society (e.g., the structure of economic opportunity; racial and ethnic dynamics) that operate at different levels. Related to this is the need to pay attention to the temporal dimension of family functioning within these contexts, including the changing needs of both children's and parents' developmental trajectories (Bronfenbrenner 1979; Norton 1994).

In responding to these circumstances, proponents of family support have drawn generally on a few key theoretical propositions or 'premises' (Dunst 1995), most notably ecological theories of human development, theories on the role of informal social support networks and, later, notions of social capital and social exclusion. But family support as a field of practice has been fundamentally guided more by an emerging set of principles than by a formal theoretical framework. Indeed, in seeking to define family support in ways that can help guide practice, inform policy, and establish defensible frameworks for evaluation, the literature on family support offers multiple versions of sets of core principles, characteristics, or guidelines (e.g., Dunst 1995; Family Support America 1996; Gilligan 2000; Layzer *et al.* 2003; Pinkerton and Katz 2003; Pinkerton, Dolan and Canavan 2003; Weissbourd 1994). These principles operate at different levels. Some reflect broadly held *values*, such as taking a 'strengths based' perspective or affirming cultural diversity. Some suggest *conceptual orientations* that are grounded in such values and serve as a general guide to practice, such as the importance of mobilizing formal and informal resources or the need to promote 'social inclusion'. Some promote particular kinds of *concrete practice*, such as flexibility and responsiveness in scheduling and types of supports provided or involving families in the planning and provision of services. These principles have not yet been shaped into a coherent theory of change that defines family support (attempting, for example, to link its component assumptions and practices to a set of posited outcomes within an ecological framework). They do, however, suggest an attempt to fundamentally shift the paradigm – from categorical to holistic and flexible; from remedial to preventive and promotive; from deficit to asset based; from hierarchical to transactional; from service centered to family centered; from centralized and bureaucratic to community based.

Although it is but one of the number of principles that guides family support practice, the invocation of 'community' as a fundamental component of family support is virtually universal, and can be seen to crosscut many of the other principles as either context, medium of exchange, or target of change. Indeed, in some cases family support is seen to be as much about community as about service. In the United States, growing as they did out of the work of small, neighborhood-based organizations, 'family support programs were notably ambivalent about whether they were either a form of social service or a new community institution' (Halpern 1999, p.187). Although in large part organized around particular programs and the work of particular practitioners and organizations, family support is often defined more broadly in terms of providing a range of supports, through multiple referral paths, by multiple organizations, and through leveraging informal relationships among kin, peers and neighbors (Gilligan 2000; Lightburn and Kemp 1994; Pinkerton *et al.* 2003; Warren 1997). Beyond program and organization, family support is for some proponents 'about mobilizing support *in all the contexts in which children live their lives*' and, more fundamentally, about 'counteracting the corrosive potential of poverty and other harm that can befall children in disadvantaged communities' (Gilligan 2000, p.13). In the service of this, some argue that family support practice is moving – and needs to move – to engage in different ways with the communities in which they work, from, in one formulation, 'community linking to community building' (Weissbourd 1994, p.39).

In what ways is family support practice situated within community contexts? How do family support practitioners engage in community practice? What might a community-building orientation mean for family support provision? Before returning to these questions, it is worth interrogating some of the assumptions behind the relevance of the local community and what we know about its importance for children and families.

Why community?

The current focus on community reflected by family support practice and a range of other efforts is not new. Urban neighborhoods in the United States, for example, have been a recurring focus of social policy and organized social action at least since the turn of the last century (e.g., Halpern 1995; Miller 1981). Although there has always been a level of ongoing effort in local communities, the degree of broader policy attention and the level of resources provided to community-based efforts waxes and wanes.

The current focus on communities and their relationship to child and family well-being has come about for several reasons. First, building on the recognition that the needs and circumstances of children and families – especially poor children and families – are often interrelated is the recognition that these circumstances are often concentrated geographically (Ricketts and Sawhill 1988; Wilson 1987). By way of example, Figure 3.1 shows how the relative concentration of three social problems – child abuse and neglect (represented by numbers of children in the child welfare system), teenage parenthood, and family poverty – tend to cluster in particular neighborhoods in the city of Chicago.

Second, there is increasing research focusing on the effects that living in particular neighborhoods has on child development and well-being, and increasing evidence that indeed, for children and youth, community context matters – although not necessarily in simple and direct ways (e.g., Blythe and Leffert 1995; Brody et al. 2001; Brooks-Gunn, Duncan and Aber 1997; Furstenberg et al. 1999; Garbarino 1992; Rankin and Quane 2002).

Finally, for operational purposes the community has come to be seen, once again, as an important unit of action because of the belief that local communities have particular assets to bring to bear on the problems they confront and that they can be mobilized to do so. Indeed, many funders of community-based social programs target local communities because they see them both as the place where the needs and circumstances of disadvantaged people come together *and* where they can be best addressed, given the potential that neighborhoods provide to be comprehensive, to foster civic engagement, and to work at a manageable scale that allows for the concentration of resources (Chaskin 1998).

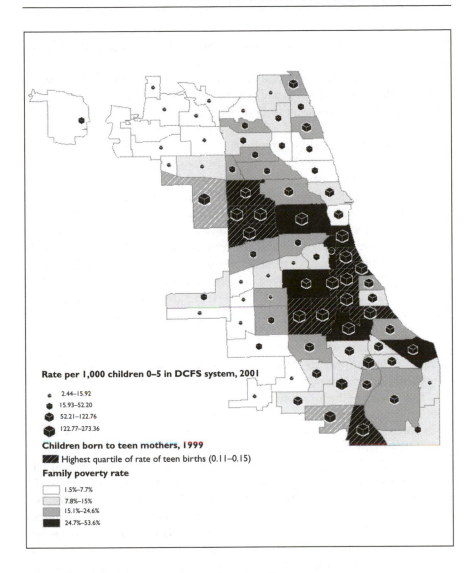

Rate per 1,000 children 0–5 in DCFS system, 2001

- 2.44–15.92
- 15.93–52.20
- 52.21–122.76
- 122.77–273.36

Children born to teen mothers, 1999
Highest quartile of rate of teen births (0.11–0.15)

Family poverty rate

- 1.5%–7.7%
- 7.8%–15%
- 15.1%–24.6%
- 24.7%–53.6%

Figure 3.1: Neighborhood concentration of social problems

Local communities provide an important context in which children, youth, and families grow, develop, and function. The built environment – housing, streets, parks, and the configuration of land use and facilities – can promote or inhibit a sense of safety, connection, and interaction among community members. Individual community members represent knowledge, skills and leadership that is either engaged in the community, focused beyond it, or left dormant. Formal organizations operating locally – neighborhood organizations, schools, service agencies, businesses – provide goods, services, and facilities for a range of activities that enrich or fail to support child and family functioning. Informal relationships, such as networks of association among neighbors, peers, and groups, provide or constrain access to information, opportunity, and collective endeavor.

The particular effects of local community context on family functioning and the well-being of children and youth are, however, difficult to disentangle. Although direct effects seem to be fairly weak when factors such as family poverty and mother's level of educational attainment are taken into account (e.g., Jencks and Mayer 1990), community context can have a significant effect on the social processes – such as parenting behavior, peer influence, monitoring and informal social control – that contribute to family functioning and child well-being (Furstenberg et al. 1999). For children and youth, such effects are generally mediated by parents, peers, and institutional environments (such as school), and the ways in which neighborhood influences are so mediated differ by the age of the child. For younger children, parents, family members and the home environment are critical mediating factors; as they enter adolescence, young people will be more heavily influenced by peers, school and neighborhood processes directly (Aber et al. 1997). There are also important interaction effects among community context, parenting behavior, youth behavior and child and family well-being (Furstenberg 1993; Furstenberg et al. 1999; Rankin and Quane 2002), and parents create and tailor family-management techniques in response to the opportunities and constraints provided by the neighborhood environment (Furstenberg 1993; Furstenberg et al. 1999).

The aspects of the local environment that seem to have an important influence on family functioning and the well-being of children and youth include both compositional and social organizational aspects. Compositional aspects include levels of concentrated poverty, crime, the concentration of single-parent families, housing quality, residential stability and the presence of relatively affluent families and professional and managerial workers. Poverty, for example, has been associated with high rates of child abuse (e.g., Coulton et al. 1995; Garbarino and Crouter 1978) as well as teenage births and delinquency (Coulton and Pandey 1992). The presence of relatively affluent neighbors seems to be related to child IQ (Brooks-Gunn et al. 1993) and school completion (Crane 1991). Aspects of social organization that seem critical include organizational participation, the number and quality of social ties, and a degree of 'value consensus' among community members. 'Collective efficacy,' for example – the extent to which neighbors share values and are willing to intervene in neighborhood affairs – has been shown to be strongly associated with lower levels of neighborhood violence, personal victimization, and homicide, and to partially mediate the effects of neighborhood social composition (e.g., poverty, race and ethnicity, residential stability) on violence (Sampson, Raudenbush and Earls 1997). Organizational involvement has been argued to foster democratic activism and community development (Putnam 1993), perceptions of personal efficacy (Zimmerman and Rappaport 1988), and to be associated with social control and lower levels of social disorganization (Sampson and Groves 1989; Shaw and McKay 1942).

It should be noted that the use and importance of the local community may differ for different populations and in different locations. More affluent individuals and those better integrated into the larger society (e.g., working men, adults, those with more education) often have more dispersed interpersonal networks and need to rely less on their neighborhoods. However, for those who are less affluent and less well integrated (e.g., children, women with young children, the elderly, ethnic minorities), the neighborhood is more likely to be both an important source of instrumental relational ties and to be relied on for many goods and services (Ahlbrandt 1984; Campbell and Lee 1992; Lee, Campbell and Miller 1991), except when these resources simply do not exist or where there are particularly serious barriers – such as high levels of violent crime – to engaging them (Furstenberg 1993).

Family support and community-based practice

Given the relevance of community for children and families, particularly for those living in disadvantaged circumstances, there are a number of different ways to think about community-based practice as it relates to family support. First, community may be seen as *context*, to be 'taken account of' in planning and providing support services to families. In this way, understanding community circumstances and dynamics and the ways in which they are likely to affect service users (e.g., what they need, the barriers they face, the resources and relationships upon which they may rely) may inform, among other things, the types of services provided, location and collocation strategies, approaches to outreach and engagement, and styles of interaction.

Second, community may be defined as a *target of intervention*, not merely taken account of, but in which particular aspects of the community environment are identified that are to be changed through planned intervention in support of families. This may include, for example, programs to provide housing, address issues of crime, or promote employment or commercial development in the neighborhood.

Third, community may be treated as a *unit of identity and action*, an organized social system with particular actors and capacities that can be brought to bear to support families and promote broader change. This may occur through the work of individual community members, organizations, and enacted relationships (formal and informal, interpersonal and interorganizational) both among them and between them and individuals and organizations beyond the community. In this case, beyond changing particular aspects of the community environment and attempting to promote discrete outputs in particular domains – more housing, safer streets, better jobs – the focus is on enhancing the 'capacity' of the community to manage, promote, and sustain particular kinds of change and to provide for the well-being of its members over time.

Another aspect of community-based practice concerns the ways in which community members *participate* in planning, decision making, oversight, use, and evaluation of services provided or action taken. In each of the approaches outlined above, community participation can be structured in different ways and with different emphases. The importance of participation is broadly invoked in family support (where users are to participate as 'partners' not clients) and community-building practice alike, though the assumptions and expectations for participation are often murky, and its implementation is often highly problematic (e.g., Briggs 1998; Chaskin 2005; Day 1997).

For the most part, family support programs have been 'community based' in at least three ways. First, they have been located and grounded in particular communities and have used local knowledge of those communities to design services that are responsive to local priorities and needs. Second, they have taken advantage of their presence and relationships within a community to facilitate outreach in order to engage more people who might benefit from the services available. Third, they have sought to use community connections as a way to link families to broader support systems that can be made available to them (Gardner 2003; Katz and Pinkerton 2003; Layzer *et al.* 2001). In particular, this has meant attempting to leverage social support resources existing within the informal networks maintained by users of family support programs, and acting as kind of broker – a 'point of entry' for a range of other services, including prevention services, early intervention programs, and crisis intervention (Lightburn and Kemp 1994; Nelson and Allen 1995; Weissbourd 1994, p.40). It should be noted, however, that a systematic review of evaluated family support programs in the United States suggests that fewer programs had components focused on community-level dynamics and strategies (peer support and network-building, connecting families to community resources, advocating on behalf of the community) than had components focused on child development, parent education, or child–parent relationships, separately or in combination (Layzer *et al.* 2001).

To date, then, family support programs have for the most part engaged in community largely as a critical context to understand and inform their strategic orientation to working with families, rather than as a target or medium of change. Increasingly, though, proponents of family support have sought to move beyond a community-as-context framework to argue for family support's role in promoting community change more broadly. Garbarino and Kostelny (1994, p.312), for example, suggest that 'social support must be part of a sweeping reform of the neighborhood and of its relations with the larger community,' addressing issues of social disconnection, social control, violence, poverty, and the psychosocial factors involved in both living and providing services in communities characterized by such disadvantage and social exclusion (Garbarino and Kostelny 1994; cf. Family Resource Coalition 1999). In the United States, this orientation has been met, from the other side, with an increasing focus on infusing or connecting community development and organizing activities – economic development, housing, grassroots mobilization, and policy advocacy – with family support. This has included, for example, expanding the purview of community development corporations and the creation of comprehensive community initiatives. Such efforts have sought to merge community development activities with the provision of social services, the promotion of service coordination, and the creation of community collaboratives for planning, development, and service delivery (e.g., Chaskin *et al.* 2001; Kingsley, McNeely and Gibson 1997; Knitzer and Adely 2002; Kubisch *et al.* 1997).

Community capacity and the capacity-building agenda

The growing (or renewed) recognition of links between aspects of community circumstances and social organization on the one hand, and outcomes for children, youth, and families on the other, has led to a range of efforts seeking to address the circumstances presented by communities directly. These efforts seek to invest in disadvantaged communities in particular ways in order to refine or recreate them as supportive environments for children and families.

To some extent, this has included moving beyond services to focus on the environmental and economic aspects of community life through the support of a range of community development activities, such as housing, infrastructure, transportation, and job creation. It has also included attempts to bridge community development and human service provision through 'comprehensive' planning approaches. But it has also looked *beyond* services, programs, and projects toward a goal of community 'capacity' building – developing a local capacity within communities to promote positive change, to manage change as it happens (i.e., to mediate between families and the effects of macro-level forces like economic restructuring or national policy changes), and to support individual well-being and family functioning.

But what is 'community capacity' and how is it built? The definition that I propose is that community capacity is 'the interaction of human capital, organizational resources, and social capital that can be leveraged to solve collective problems and to improve or maintain the well-being of a given community' (Chaskin 2001; Chaskin *et al.* 2001). By human capital (Becker 1975), I mean in this context the skills and knowledge of individuals that can be brought to bear on community circumstances. By organizational resources, I refer to the existence of organizations and institutions with the means to organize, plan, and produce goods and services for a community and to represent the community to outside actors. By social capital (e.g., Coleman 1988), I mean the instrumental relationships that exist among community members and organizations that can have an impact on community well-being; the 'resource potential of personal and organizational networks' (Sampson, Morenoff and Earls 1999).

But to operationalize this definition, and to use it as a way to better understand efforts that seek to build capacity in communities, it is useful to try to break down the concept into a set of component dimensions that relate to one another in particular ways (see Figure 3.2).

Essentially, the proposed framework suggests that communities with 'capacity' have some particular characteristics. They have enough of a sense of community that members recognize the ways in which they share circumstances and values, a threshold level of commitment among some members such that they are willing to act on the community's behalf, some way of solving collective problems, and access to resources within and/or beyond the community to bring to bear on community action. The framework also suggests that these characteristics operate through particular mechanisms or levels of agency – individuals, organizations, and networks of relations among them – in order to fulfill particular functions. This could be either in response to emerging problems (e.g., organizing in reaction to a sudden rise in violent crime), or to promote particular processes (e.g., facilitating voter turnout), or for the production of particular goods (e.g., childcare services or housing). When community capacity is engaged in these ways, it can both contribute to the strength of sense of community, commitment, problem-solving, and resource access *and* produce more discrete outcomes (e.g., crime reduction, influence on policy, improved services).

The framework also suggests that community capacity can be intentionally built though planned intervention. Efforts to do so have tended to focus in particular on four broad strategies. One is leadership development, which seeks to enhance the ability of individual community members (human capital) to take on particular change-agent roles on the community's behalf. Another seeks to strengthen the capacities of particular community organizations. The third focuses on community organizing and mobilization for purposes of advocacy or associational action. The fourth seeks to build the organizational infrastructure of the community by promoting collaboration and effective interorganizational relations. Finally, the framework recognizes that these processes are conditioned by a range of local circumstances (e.g., crime, residential stability) and macro-level influences (e.g., economic opportunity, migration patterns). These conditions may have important influences on existing community capacity and on the likely effectiveness of particular strategies to build it and promote different kinds of community change. (For an extended exploration of the idea of community capacity and approaches to building it, see Chaskin *et al.* 2001.)

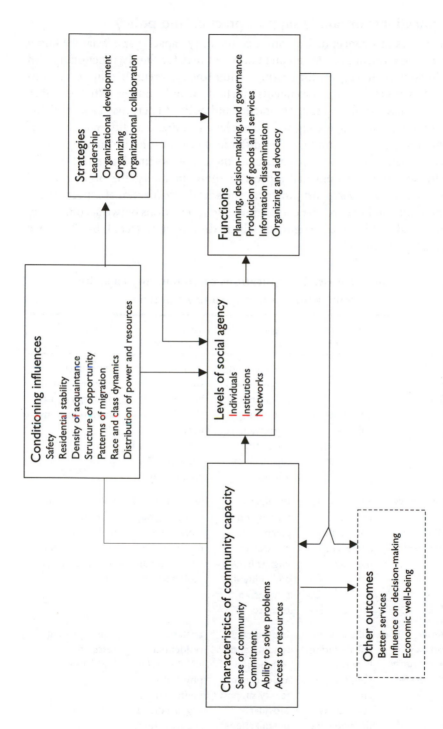

Figure 3.2: Community capacity and capacity building (Adapted from Chaskin 2001; Chaskin et al. 2001)

Implications for family support practice and policy

What does this conceptualization of community capacity and what we know about the influences of local community context for family functioning and child well-being suggest for gearing action toward strengthening local communities as supportive environments for children and families? What relevance does this have for family support practice and policy? There may be several different implications, operating at different levels, addressing different aspects of community capacity, and implying different kinds of roles for family support practitioners and policy. In particular, there are potential implications for addressing the environmental aspects of the community, the organizational capacities of family support providers, the social organizational aspects of the community, and the broader connections and interactions between community actors and the broader systems in which they operate (see Table 3.1 for a summary schematic).

Table 3.1 Possible implications of community capacity framework for family support practice

	Community environment	Organizational capacity	Social organization	Community connections
Possible component elements	Housing, crime, physical infrastructure, public space, employment	Strengthening organizations, expanding role of existing organizations, promoting organizational alliances	Individual social support networks, closed networks, 'weak ties' and bridging relationships	Government, business, policy makers, national and international NGOs
Family support practitioner potential role implications	Service array, service accessibility, approaches to outreach	Provider training on community assessment, engagement, and culturally responsive practice	Social-network focused group work, case management, organizing and mobilization	Political action, advocacy, mobilization, cross-community and cross-sectoral alliances
Broader possible policy or intervention implications	Alliances/ collaborations between family support and community development organizations	Unrestricted funding and technical assistance to family support provider organizations	Foster residential stability, safety, physical revitalization, organizational infrastructure	Policy planing, research, legislation

Community environment

First, there may be implications for addressing the environmental aspects of the community such as housing, public space, safety, and employment opportunity. Local conditions can influence the ways in which social interaction among community members occur, the extent to which assistance and opportunity are accessible to residents (and whether they choose to use them), and the basic health and well-being of community members. Concentrated poverty, crime, residential stability, housing quality, and socioeconomic diversity, in particular, are critical aspects of the local environment that seem to have important influences on child and family well-being. They may condition in important ways the possibilities for service provision, the strategies for engaging families to take advantage of such services, and the likely degree of impact they will have on families living under different community circumstances. One way of addressing these issues is by strategically responding to these conditions (in community-as-context mode) through attention to service array (both specialized and normative; for parents, children, and families; responding to psychosocial, physical, and economic needs), attention to service accessibility, and approaches to outreach and engagement. This dimension of the community capacity framework suggests, in addition, the potential for exploring the possible synergies between family support and community development practice and nurturing alliances between organizations and practitioners focused on each.

Organizational capacity

Second, there may be implications for focusing on the organizational capacity of family support service providers. Community capacity building approaches have focused on organizational development through some combination of strengthening existing organizations, helping existing organizations take on new functions or roles, creating new organizations, and changing the ways in which organizations relate to one another by promoting interorganizational alliances and collaborative arrangements (Chaskin *et al.* 2001). In the context of family support, this may include providing particular kinds of training for family support professionals. Such training might focus on enhancing their capacity to assess community circumstances and dynamics; engage with community members and with potential organizational partners; and provide flexible, culturally sensitive, community-responsive services. It may also include, at a policy level, providing flexible and unrestricted funding and technical assistance to existing organizations providing family support services in order to build these capacities, to foster and maintain interorganizational relationships, and to engage in community organizing and advocacy on behalf of families in the community.

Community social organization

Third, there may be implications for addressing the social organizational aspects of community. This may include fostering informal relationships and community support networks that can serve as a resource to families and support processes of collective socialization of children. The importance of such networks is increasingly recognized in both family support and community development practice and research. In thinking about social networks, however, it is important to recognize that they are not generic: they differ in their nature, structure, strength, use, meaning, and the extent to which particular individuals have access to them (Burt 1992; Coleman 1988; Mitchell 1969; Wellman 1988).

Three kinds of informal network configurations are particularly important in the current context. One is individual support networks, which provide particular individuals with access to people who provide them with some combination of emotional, instrumental (or tangible), informational, and companionship support (Cutrona 2000; Wills and Shinar 2000). A second kind of network, at the collective level, is sometimes referred to as 'closed networks' or 'bonding' relationships. These are the multiple, overlapping ties among members of a group or community that can promote solidarity and reciprocity as well as provide mechanisms for informal socialization and social control (Coleman 1988; Putnam 2000; Sampson 2001). A third kind of network configuration concerns the availability of 'weak ties' or 'bridging' relationships, which supply links to networks beyond one's intimate network and can provide important access to information, resources and opportunities not available through one's relationships with people within closed networks, particularly if they are members of disadvantaged or 'socially excluded' groups (Granovetter 1973; Putnam 2000; Room 1995).

Although the importance of these networks is well accepted, we know far less about how to foster and support their development. One approach is to bring people together for particular purposes in the hope that interaction will promote relationships that can have some staying power, and that can be re-engaged over time for a range of purposes. Various kinds of group work, some approaches to case management, organizing and mobilization around community problems, and efforts to provide opportunities for normative interaction among neighbors (e.g., through block parties or community festivals) are examples of this. Another approach is to address the structural and environmental factors that may promote or constrain interaction and relationship building. This may include efforts to increase residential stability (through home-ownership and tenant management programs), safety (through community policing and other efforts), physical revitalization (including the creation of safe and accessible 'civic space' such as parks, community centers, and libraries), and organizational infrastructure (promoting opportunities for participation in a range of clubs, associations, and community organizations).

Community connections

Finally, there may be ways to better connect communities to the broader systems and structures that have an influence on their well-being. This will build on the capacity of individual leaders, organizations, and organizational alliances within communities, and implies the need to get political and to think about working at different levels – both geographically (neighborhood, city, state) as well as strategically (through direct practice, planning, and policy advocacy). It also suggests the potential importance of fostering cross-community and cross-sectoral (public, private, voluntary) alliances that can leverage the resources, expertise, and connections of participants to increase the influence of disadvantaged families and communities on the policies and practices that affect them.

References

Aber, J.L., Gephart, M.A., Brooks-Gunn, J. and Connell, J.P. (1997) 'Development in Context: Implications for Studying Neighborhood Effects.' In J. Brooks-Gunn, G.J. Duncan and J.L. Aber (eds) *Neighborhood Poverty: Context and Consequences for Children.* New York: Russell Sage Foundation.

Ahlbrandt, R.S. (1984) *Neighborhoods, People and Communities.* New York: Plenum.

Becker, G. (1975) *Human Capital.* New York: Columbia University Press.

Blythe, D.A. and Leffert, N. (1995) 'Communities as Contexts for Adolescent Development.' *Journal of Adolescent Research 10*, 1, 64–87.

Briggs, X. (1998) 'Doing Democracy Up Close: Culture, Power, and Communication in Community Planning.' *Journal of Planning Education and Research 18*, 1–13.

Brody, G.H., Ge, X., Conger, R., Gibbons, F.X., Murray, V.M., Gerrard, M. and Simons, R.L. (2001) 'The Influence of Neighborhood Disadvantage, Collective Socialization, and Parenting on African American Children's Affiliation with Deviant Peers.' *Child Development 72*, 4, 1231–1246.

Bronfenbrenner, U. (1979) *The Ecology of Human Development: Experiments by Nature and Design.* Cambridge, MA: Harvard University Press.

Brooks-Gunn, J., Duncan, G.J. and Aber, J.L. (eds) (1997) *Neighborhood Poverty: Context and Consequences for Children.* New York: Russell Sage Foundation.

Brooks-Gunn, J., Duncan, G.J., Klebanov, P.K. and Sealand, N. (1993) 'Do Neighborhoods Influence Child and Adolescent Development?' *American Journal of Sociology 99*, 2, 353–395.

Burt, R.S. (1992) *Structural Holes: The Social Construction of Competition.* Cambridge, MA: Harvard University Press.

Campbell, K.E. and Lee, B.A. (1992) 'Sources of Personal Neighbor Networks: Social Integration, Need or Time?' *Social Forces 70*, 4, 1077–1100.

Chaskin, R.J. (1998) 'Neighborhood as a Unit of Planning and Action: A Heuristic Approach.' *The Journal of Planning Literature 13*, 1, 11–30.

Chaskin, R.J. (2001) 'Building Community Capacity: A Definitional Framework and Case Studies from a Comprehensive Community Initiative.' *Urban Affairs Review 36*, 3, 292–323.

Chaskin, R.J. (2005) 'Democracy and Bureaucracy in a Community Planning Process.' *Journal of Planning Education and Research 24*, 4, 408–419.

Chaskin, R.J., Brown, P., Venkatesh, S. and Vidal, A. (2001) *Building Community Capacity.* New York: Aldine de Gruyter.

Coleman, J. 1988. 'Social Capital in the Development of Human Capital.' *American Journal of Sociology 94* (supplement), 95–120.

Coulton, C. J. and Pandey, S. (1992) 'Geographic Concentration of Poverty and Risk to Children in Urban Neighborhoods.' *American Behavioral Scientist 35,* 3, 238–257.

Coulton, C.J., Korbin, J., Su, M. and Chow, J. (1995) 'Community Level Factors and Child Maltreatment Rates.' *Child Development 66,* 1262–1276.

Crane, J. (1991) 'Effects of Neighborhoods on Dropping Out of School and Teenage Childbearing.' In C. Jencks and P. Peterson (eds) *The Urban Underclass.* Washington, DC: Brookings Institution.

Cutrona, C. (2000) 'Social Support Principles for Strengthening Families.' In J. Canavan, P. Dolan, and J. Pinkerton (eds.) *Family Support: Direction from Diversity.* London: Jessica Kingsley Publishers.

Day, D. (1997) 'Citizen Participation in the Planning Process: An Essentially Contested Concept.' *Journal of Planning Literature 11,* 3, 421.

Dunst, C. (1995) *Key Characteristics and Features of Community-Based Family Support Programs.* Chicago: Family Resource Coalition.

Family Resource Coalition (1999) 'Towards a Comprehensive Approach: A Community Economic Development Primer for Family Support Groups.' Chicago: Family Resource Coalition, unpublished manuscript.

Family Support America (1996) *Making the Case for Family Support: An Essay with Supporting Documents.* Chicago: Family Support America.

Furstenberg, F.F. (1993) 'How Families Manage Risk and Opportunity in Dangerous Neighborhoods.' In W.J. Wilson (ed) *Sociology and the Public Agenda.* Newberry Park, CA: Sage Publications.

Furstenberg, F.F., Cook, T.D., Eccles, J., Elder Jr, G.H. and Sameroff, A. (1999) *Managing to Make It: Urban Families and Adolescent Success.* Chicago: University of Chicago Press.

Garbarino, J. (1992) *Children and Families in the Social Environment.* New York: Aldine de Gruyter.

Garbarino, J. and Crouter, A.C. (1978) 'Defining the Community Context of Parent–Child Relations.' *Child Development 49,* 604–616.

Garbarino, J. and Kostelny, K. (1994) 'Family Support and Community Development.' In S.L. Kagan and B. Weissbourd (eds) *Putting Families First: America's Family Support Movement and the Challenge of Change.* San Francisco: Jossey-Bass Publishers.

Gardner, R. (2003) *Supporting Families: Child Protection in the Community.* Chichester: John Wiley & Sons.

Gardner, S. (1989) 'Failure by Fragmentation.' *California Tomorrow* (Fall), 18–25.

Gilligan, R. (2000) 'Family Support: Issues and Prospects.' In J. Canavan, P. Dolan and J. Pinkerton (eds) *Family Support: Direction from Diversity.* London: Jessica Kingsley Publishers.

Granovetter, M. (1973) 'The Strength of Weak Ties.' *American Journal of Sociology 78,* 1360–1380.

Halpern, R. (1995) *Rebuilding the Inner City: A History of Neighborhood Initiatives to Address Poverty in the United States.* New York: Columbia University Press.

Halpern, R. (1999) *Fragile Families, Fragile Solutions.* New York: Columbia University Press.

Jencks, C. and Mayer, S. (1990) 'The Social Consequences of Growing up in a Poor Neighborhood.' In L.E. Lynn Jr and M.G.H. McGeary (eds) *Inner-City Poverty in the United States.* Washington, DC: National Academy Press.

Kagan, S.L., Cohen, N., Hailey, L., Pritchard, E. and Colen, H. (1996) *Toward a New Understanding of Family Support: A Review of Programs and a Suggested Typology.* Washington, DC: Administration on Children, Youth and Families.

Katz, I. and Pinkerton, J. (eds) (2003) *Evaluating Family Support: Thinking Internationally, Thinking Critically.* London: John Wiley & Sons, Ltd.

Kingsley, G.T., McNeely, J.B. and Gibson, J.O. (1997) *Community Building: Coming of Age.* Washington DC: The Urban Institute.

Knitzer, J. and Adely, F. (2002) *The Role of Community Development Corporations in Promoting the Well-Being of Young Children.* New York: National Center for Children in Poverty.

Kubisch, A., Brown, P., Chaskin, R.J., Hirota, J., Joseph, M., Richman, H. and Roberts, M. (1997) *Voices from the Field: Learning from Comprehensive Community Initiatives.* Washington, DC: The Aspen Institute.

Layzer, J.I., Goodson, B.D., Bernstein, L. and Price, C. (2001) *National Evaluation of Family Support Programs, Volume A: The Meta-Analysis.* Cambridge, MA: Abt Associates.

Lee, B.A., Campbell, K.E. and Miller, O. (1991) 'Racial Difference in Urban Neighboring.' *Sociological Forum 6*, 3, 525–550.

Levitan, S.A., Mangum, G.L. and Pines, M.W. (1989) *A Proper Inheritance: Investing in the Self-Sufficiency of Poor Families.* Washington, DC: Center for Social Policy Studies, George Washington University.

Lightburn, A. and Kemp, S.P. (1994) 'Family Support Programs: Opportunities for Community-Based Practice.' *Families in Society: The Journal of Contemporary Human Services 75*, 16–26.

Miller, Z. (1981) 'The Role and Concept of Neighborhood in American Cities.' In R. Fisher and P. Romanofsky (eds) *Community Organization for Urban Social Change: A Historical Perspective.* Westport, CT: Greenwood Press.

Mitchell, J.C. (1969) 'The Concept and Use of Social Networks.' In J.C. Mitchell (ed) *Social Networks in Urban Situations.* Manchester: University of Manchester Press.

Nelson, K. and Allen, M. (1995) 'Family-Centered Social Services: Moving Toward System Change.' In P. Adams and K. Nelson (eds) *Reinventing Human Services: Community- and Family-Centered Practice.* New York: Aldine de Gruyter.

Norton, D. (1994) 'Education for Professionals in Family Support.' In S.L. Kagan and B. Weissbourd (eds) *Putting Families First: America's Family Support Movement and the Challenge of Change.* San Francisco: Jossey-Bass Publishers.

Pinkerton, J. and Katz, I. (2003) 'Perspective through International Comparison in the Evaluation of Family Support.' In I. Katz and J. Pinkerton (eds) *Evaluating Family Support: Thinking Internationally, Thinking Critically.* London: John Wiley & Sons, Ltd.

Pinkerton, J., Dolan, P. and Canavan, J. (2003) 'Towards a Working Definition of Family Support.' A draft paper for the Department of Health and Children, Republic of Ireland.

Putnam, R. (1993) *Making Democracy Work: Civic Traditions in Modern Italy.* Princeton, NJ: Princeton University Press.

Putnam, R. (2000) *Bowling Alone: The Collapse and Revival of American Community.* New York: Simon & Schuster.

Rankin, B.H. and Quane, J.M. (2002) 'Social Contexts and Urban Adolescent Outcomes: The Interrelated Effects of Neighborhoods, Families, and Peers on African-American Youth.' *Social Problems 49*, 1, 79–100.

Ricketts, E.R. and Sawhill, I.V. (1988) 'Defining and Measuring the Underclass.' *Journal of Policy Analysis and Management 7*, 316–325.

Room, G. (1995) 'Poverty and Social Exclusion: The New European Agenda for Policy and Research.' In G. Room (ed) *Beyond the Threshold: The Measurement and Analysis of Social Exclusion.* London: The Polity Press.

Sampson, R.J. (2001) 'Crime and Public Safety: Insights from Community-Level Perspectives on Social Capital.' In S. Saegert, J.P. Thompson, and M.R. Warren (eds) *Social Capital and Poor Communities.* New York: Russell Sage Foundation.

Sampson, R.J. and Groves, W.B. (1989) 'Community Structure and Crime: Testing Social-Disorganization Theory.' *American Journal of Sociology 94*, 4, 774–802.

Sampson, R.J., Morenoff, J.D. and Earls, F. (1999) 'Beyond Social Capital: Spatial Dynamics of Collective Efficacy for Children.' *American Sociological Review 64*, 5, 633–660.

Sampson, R.J., Raudenbush, S. and Earls, F. (1997) 'Neighborhoods and Violent Crime: A Multi-level Study of Collective Efficacy.' *Science 277*, 918–924.

Schorr, L.B. (1988) *Within Our Reach.* New York: Anchor Books.

Shaw, C. and McKay, H. (1942) *Juvenile Delinquency and Urban Areas.* Chicago: University of Chicago Press.

Warren, C. (1997) 'Family Support and Empowerment.' In C. Cannon and C. Warren (eds) *Social Action with Children and Families.* London: Routledge.

Weissbourd, B. (1987) 'A Brief History of Family Support Programs.' In S.L. Kagan, D.R. Powell, B. Weissbourd and E.F. Zigler (eds) *America's Family Support Programs: Perspectives and Prospects.* New Haven, CT: Yale University Press.

Weissbourd, B. (1994) 'The Evolution of the Family Resource Movement.' In S.L. Kagan and B. Weissbourd (eds) *Putting Families First: America's Family Support Movement and the Challenge of Change.* San Francisco: Jossey-Bass Publishers.

Wellman, B. (1988) 'Structural Analysis: From Metaphor to Theory and Substance.' In B. Wellman and S.D. Berkowitz (eds) *Social Structures: A Network Approach.* Cambridge: Cambridge University Press.

Wills, A. and Shinar, O. (2000) 'Measuring Perceived and Received Social Support.' In S. Cohen, L.G. Underwood and B.H. Gottlieb (eds) *Social Support Measurement and Intervention: A Guide for Health and Social Scientists.* Oxford: Oxford University Press.

Wilson, W.J. (1987) *The Truly Disadvantaged.* Chicago: University of Chicago Press.

Zimmerman, M.A. and Rappaport, J. (1988) 'Citizen Participation, Perceived Control, and Psychological Empowerment.' *American Journal of Community Psychology 16,* 5, 725–750.

Chapter 4

Supporting Families through Local Government: A Danish Case Study

Peter Steen Jensen and René Junker

Introduction

This chapter traces the efforts of the Municipality of Odense in restructuring services for children and young people, using family support as a key strategic focus. It illustrates the reflective approach through which the Municipality identified key problems in its service provision, the basis of these problems in risk-focused work with vulnerable children and families and the solutions to these problems. We discuss four examples of the solutions it has adopted:

- developing clear policy and practice guidelines for staff
- implementing a common language for defining needs
- focusing on building protective factors in the child's environment
- linking more effectively with universal services.

Critically, the chapter highlights the planned, evidenced nature of the service restructuring.

Transformation of the family

From a sociological perspective, the institution of the family constitutes the most important target group for the exercise of authority by the municipal segment whose core services are support for vulnerable members of society (i.e., children, adolescents and families). Although the family is viewed as one of society's principal institutions, it does not constitute a social problem in itself. Yet because of its importance, it can serve as the point of departure for understanding some social problems, especially those related to the issue of socialisation, family background, social inheritance, etc. However, the family is a difficult entity to study.

This is because it is so dynamic. In the long-term, the family is constantly transforming and at the same time – in the short term – it constitutes one of society's most enduring, leading institutions.

The family is indisputably undergoing major changes – as it probably always has. To a large extent, these changes emanate from two sources: first, the structural changes in society to which the family has to adapt; and second, the changes in the basic normative orientation of society. Important qualitative changes in the family include the following:

- Children are now planned. This gives a totally different outlook on issues regarding responsibility for children and children's rights.

- We are experiencing 'social rapidisation', i.e., everything is changing at ever-greater speeds. This means that in most situations the childhood and adolescence experienced by the parents is useless as a model for their own parenting. Standards and ideals are totally different. This makes it difficult for parents to make the right choices with regard to childrearing and in preparing their child for his or her future adult life. Parents do not serve as role models for their child to the same extent that they used to.

- Children are increasingly viewed as autonomous individuals with individual rights separate from their parents. This is partly due to increasing individualisation and partly to parent–child disengagement – there is no such thing as a coherent family any more, but a group of autonomous legal entities. Modern children have legal rights. Consequently, the institution of the family is headed towards increased differentiation – it is no longer a unit.

- Parents working outside the home means that most children also spend much of their childhood and adolescence outside the home. Parents' working conditions and public child-care schemes thus play a decisive part in the child's general living conditions (Berger and Luchmann 1996; Jørgensen and Dencik 1998).

In parallel with this trend, the welfare state has enlarged the range of services offered to families with young children. Nowadays the institutions of the welfare state are an integral aspect of the daily lives of most families with children. Consequently, the family's role in the child-rearing process has changed. Many functions are no longer performed by the family alone but through interaction with public 'rearers' and childminders. Accordingly, this trend can be interpreted as leading to the functional demise of the family because the time set aside for being together, among the extended family, has also been reduced.

Child and youth policy of the Municipality of Odense

The family is the central target group of the Municipality of Odense. This implies the continued belief that the family's essential task is to serve as an agent of socialisation. Such a family outlook is the key basis of child and youth policy and implicitly guides the choice of theoretical and methodological frames of reference. In practice, this means that the professionals who have primary contact with the family base their work on the following values:

- making the child's current situation, development and growth clear to the parents

- supporting the parents in appreciating and exploiting their own resources in the parenting process

- supporting the demands and responsibility of the parents for being the primary persons in their child's life

- cooperating with vulnerable families for the purpose of prevention and earlier intervention.

The organisational framework for supporting the families in the Municipality is based on two integrated systems: the *normal system* and the *special system*. The normal system includes the school department, the department of recreation and the department of day care institutions. The special system has only one department, with the purpose of helping the three departments in the normal system give the children and adolescents with special needs the best possible help from within the normal system. Excluding the children and adolescents from the normal system is therefore viewed only as a last option.

Characteristics of social problems

Some socio-political solutions involve a greater degree of uncertainty than others, making them more complicated to implement. In conjunction with categorising the solutions to social problems, a distinction is made between regulatory and interventional solutions. Regulatory solutions are established by law, and are either not open to any interpretation at all or open to only limited interpretation when it comes to implementation. This involves aspects such as pension payments or other regulated rights and duties pursuant to the Danish Social Services Act.

Interventional solutions are typified by situations in which a public authority seeks to influence user behaviour by means of its own organisations. This involves 'human processing' and is highly prevalent in the social sector. An analysis of regulatory and interventional solutions conceptualises social problems as *tame* and *wild* problems respectively. Tame problems are typified as being relatively easy to define: they can be differentiated from other problems by the fact that their solutions are obvious and thus the proper solution has relatively obvious criteria.

Solutions to wild problems are fundamentally different from their tame counterparts, and are typified by the opposite characteristics. Wild problems cannot be clearly defined or dissociated from other problems. The goals of their solutions defy precise definitions and as a result there are no clear strategies for achieving an ideal solution. Whereas tame problems have an objective, quantifiable 'best solution', wild problems also have a 'best solution', but an assessment of whether this best solution has been achieved is normative (Krogstrup 1997). Most of the core social services offered by the Department of Child, Youth and Family Services are regarded as interventional solutions to wild problems.

Over the years, traditions of basic social work approaches have been based on process-oriented and relational approaches, for the purpose of adjusting inappropriate behaviour without having the end product in view. The 'wild' problem areas remained wild, making them managerially and financially difficult to manage. This has had some significant consequences for Denmark's social sector, affecting every municipality in the country. These are described in more detail below.

Rise in social-intervention cost levels

The costs of out-of-home placement and preventive measures for vulnerable children and adolescents are rapidly growing. From 1995 to 2000, costs have risen by 35 per cent to DKK 6 billion nationwide in 2000. The cost increase is due partly to more recipients and partly to an actual growth in unit costs. This means that Denmark is spending millions of DKK on developing, intensifying and strengthening prevention and intervention at all levels – day-care centres, recreation centres, schools, after school centres, administration units, etc. Despite all the endeavours, the number of children at risk does not seem to have declined. The increasing number of incoming reports, recommendations for special actions and other initiatives speak for themselves. And this is occurring in spite of the fact that interest in the child's family conditions has never been greater (Skaarup 2000).

In the area of services for children, an increasing volume of Nordic research has taken a critical look at social work principles and effects. The research challenges the extent to which social work manages to handle its 'classic' task: to integrate and normalise deviant sections of the population (Bømler 1998; Egelund 1998). It is interesting to note that cost levels continue to rise because more children and adolescents are being referred to special services at the same time that the intervention does not reduce the number of children 'at risk'. The tendency towards self-fulfilling prophecy is emerging: the more actions it is possible to implement, the greater the number of children who become encompassed by the special services. In this context, we social workers should rightfully reflect on whether social work has counterproductive effects and occasionally defeats its own ends by causing marginalisation and ostracism, instead of integrating and normalising the deviant sections of the population.

Almost no other area can be allocated funding legitimately without demanding that the area documents the effect of the measures to be implemented. This is because social work exclusively legitimises itself by virtue of the fact that its purpose is, after all, to help children, and some childhoods would be considerably worse if steps weren't taken to help. Traditionally, social work is – quite legitimately – retrospective and process-oriented and not very oriented towards the future or the product (Egelund 1998).

Increasing demands for action

Reports published by the National Association of Local Authorities in Denmark and the Danish National Institute of Social Research call attention to the rise in the potential demand for services and to the fact that more and more children and adolescents are being referred to special services. Is this a genuine indication that more children and adolescents are living a life that worries professionals and that ways of life in Denmark have deteriorated to such an extent that societal factors are producing greater numbers of deviant sections of the population? An unequivocal reply to this is not readily available, but here, too, the social work profession plays a part.

Several studies conclude that children are more likely to have problems if they grow up in disadvantaged social circumstances, but that there is no unambiguous correlation between living under disadvantaged circumstances and becoming a 'problem child'. Problem children come from other types of family as well, and children who live under disadvantaged circumstances do not always turn into 'problem children'. In this regard, the studies make a break with the otherwise staunch concept of 'social inheritance' and emphatically downplay the tradition that legitimises intervention based on the significance of social inheritance. They show that the vast majority of children are capable of coping with deprived family conditions without having problems later on in life (Hessle and Wåhlander 2000; Jørgensen et al. 1993).

Even so, there is a widespread belief that children cannot live under relatively unsatisfactory circumstances without impairing their development, despite the fact that research in the field shows that many children are capable of coping like everyone else, despite difficult family conditions. In addition, the backgrounds of some children and youths are so deprived that the customary individualised social intervention has little chance of normalising or integrating them. These children have endured all types of social measures with little effect.

A debate has arisen regarding many of these children – and could have taken place a century ago when lock-and-key and other incarceration-like treatment forms were also discussed. As a result, many severely deprived children and adolescents have to expect to live life as ostracised members of society. We lack documentation for and a discussion of what it means to be left out and what it means to 'return' from the ranks of the outcasts and become integrated into ordinary ways of life (Becker 1963; Egelund 1998). As far as these children are concerned, we lack adequate information as to how to implement sustainable measures. Experience shows that if we believe we can base our professional efforts on habitual approaches, we are risking a boomerang effect in which the activation of greater numbers of measures leads to continued cost increases – without any effect.

This calls into question the very legitimacy of social work. On the one hand, unnecessary measures are put into operation aimed at children with various types of problem, which should actually be handled by the normal system. Although these children and adolescents demand many resources, they are not children 'at risk'. We have many human resources in our day-care centres, schools and clubs that we cannot afford to overlook. In this context, we argue in favour of supporting all inclinations for care, closeness, human responsibility and direct solidarity found in our immediate surroundings, thereby reducing the target group of children who come in contact with the special services system.

On the other hand, social work has lost its grip on some groups of children who lack the potential to form the relationships that generate change. This leaves a large middle group where the effect of social work is difficult to prove. We have to believe that the interventions we set into motion work, but we don't really know whether they do as the measurements of the effects of the interventions are scarce and the ones that do exist do not exactly glorify the effectiveness of the social intervention measures.

Using risk factors as a yardstick

Social work has shifted from safeguarding basic rights and meeting needs to identifying groups or persons who are at risk or endangered. Modern social work has turned into 'damage control' and avoiding the worst. In this context, assessments of high risk become a yardstick for determining who can remain in familiar surroundings and who can't (Bømler 1998).

The assessment of risk factors usually entails four factors as yardsticks:

1. physically and somatically conditioned burdens such as disabilities, illnesses and retarded development

2. socio-cultural circumstances, such as low social class, unemployment, poverty and lack of cultural integration

3. dynamic, family-related circumstances such as family conflicts, crime and substance abuse

4. school situations where children have poor social relations, learning difficulties and behavioural problems.

We know that these factors have an undermining effect and that they also affect vulnerability in general (Jørgensen et al. 1993). However, other circumstances are important to the relationship between undermining factors and individual reaction patterns (abnormal development). Some children develop greater staying power than others, such as being better at holding onto a positive self-image. The Mønsterbryderprojektet [Mould-breaker Project] at the Danish University of Education draws attention to the importance of secure, harmonious personal relationships with parents, families and friends, and to the importance of a feeling of self-control, the presence of potential supporters and the ability to implement realistic problem-solving strategies (Elsborg, Hansen and Hansen 1999).

It is concluded that the human ability to counteract various hardship factors differs too greatly to permit the use of traditional risk factors in making individual predictions. This is not a question of children who are exposed to disadvantaged living circumstances or who develop abnormally, but involves hardship factors or degrees of exposure to hardship circumstances, compared to protective factors and the child's vulnerability. Examples of protective factors include contact with an understanding teacher at a day-care centre, the establishment of rewarding contacts, and many other factors in social contexts. The overall effect of these protective and resource-oriented circumstances can compensate for the hardship factors and hereby safeguard sound development, even if the childhood and adolescence were spent under disadvantaged conditions (Jørgensen et al. 1993).

It should be noted that modern social work devotes very little attention to protective aspects and to the resources available in a child's network. The use of hardship circumstances as risk measurements is given top priority in professional assessments of a child's situation, with the greatest emphasis given to the family circumstances. As a result, action is taken on the basis of the hardship circumstances, resulting in almost permanent emergency preparation, which paradoxically may lead to a situation in which no one dares to take a risk, using the original meaning of the word, i.e., to perform a professional act whose result is not a foregone conclusion. This does not mean knowing the effect of an action, but rather having an overly pessimistic view of the child's fate if nothing is done and, in return, being overly optimistic about the result of intervention.

The risk-as-yardstick approach goes hand in hand with the dwindling confidence in social workers as experts who help to work out social problems. Increased professionalism and the fostering of an identity as professional therapists – who endeavour to become skilled psycho-social clinicians and who can compensate for social shortcomings and also generate growth and development in their clients by entering into a direct, therapeutic relationship with these individuals – has reduced the focus on resources. This exerts a great influence on the increasing costs and cements the fact that modern social work involves 'damage control' and avoiding the worst, thus downplaying the attention to protective factors.

The social worker's basis for decision-making

The Danish National Institute of Social Research has published two new studies on how social workers handle children's services cases (Christensen 2002; Egelund 2002). The studies show that case processing is very dissimilar in the municipalities, with regard to preventive efforts as well as out-of-home placement. A chief conclusion of the study is that the caseworkers' assessments of children's situations vary greatly as do the choice and degree of the intervention. The variations are so great that the same family can be assessed differently and be given different services by two different caseworkers from the same administrative unit.

As a result, there is a risk the focus will shift from the problems confronting the child and the family, perceived on the basis of objective theoretical and empirical knowledge, to the social worker's subjective and individual perceptions as the bases on which to make an assessment and select the measures to be taken. This is underpinned by the study of the Institute of Social Research (Egelund 2002), which concludes that many of the indications noticed by social workers in their assessments of families do not refer to the children or the parents but to the social workers' requirements of being a 'good client'. This means that the relationship between the social worker and the family has a big influence on which measure the social worker chooses.

On the one hand, the family's life must change by means of these relational efforts that require the establishment of a sustainable relationship. On the other hand the cooperation difficulties are often perceived as a characteristic of the family, not as difficulties resulting from the interaction between social worker and family. This leads to great variation in the professional assessments. The ideal decision-making situation must be a professional assessment that takes into account the individual peculiarities as well as a certain degree of uniformity.

New demands on the municipal organisation

Social work is straddling the fence between being retrospective and process-oriented on the one hand and oriented towards the future and the product on the other. The need to include both elements in the professional approach has never been greater than it is today. This requirement of social work in the future entails changes in a wide variety of areas within the municipal management of practical implementation.

Four examples below show how the Municipality of Odense has organisationally planned its administrative management and leadership in one area whose core services are exclusively interventional by nature and are regarded as solutions to wild problems.

Implementing the basis for a decision

In order to integrate a family approach within the basis on which assistance measures are chosen, the policy committee has adopted a basis for making these decisions that is substantially more specific and subtle than Danish social services legislation in general. The basis for the decisions was drawn up in the light of theoretical frames of reference and empirical knowledge and its purpose is to minimise each professional's subjective attitudes to the choice of the measure to be implemented. The out-of-home placement scheme of the Municipality of Odense is used by way of illustration.

The basis for out-of-home placement implicitly includes the Municipality's level of service, local policies and financial scope. These fixed policy statements constitute the external political framework. These elementary policy decisions can be adjusted according to political priorities. The basis for out-of-home placement derives from an extensive study arising from the efforts of the interdepartmental committee on children, which has charted and reviewed research reports on vulnerable children. This is the theoretical foundation for the basis for out-of-home placement.

The policy decisions and the theoretical foundation jointly constitute the complete basis and establish highly specific guidelines for the part played by each specialist in relation to children placed outside their own home. The basis is very specific in the following areas:

- It specifies the guidelines for which children can be placed outside the home. For instance, adolescents between the ages of 16 and 18 cannot be placed out of the home, but must be offered in-home and network support as an alternative.

- It specifies the expected duration of the out-of-home placement. This makes it possible to establish a financial framework/ management and to prioritise resources. It occurs within the following framework: short-term placement (less than two years), long-term placement (more than two years) and permanent placement (up to 18 years of age).

- It specifies the child's or adolescent's primary need for the intervention. In this context, it distinguishes among three types of need: care, training and specific treatment.

- It specifies the type of placement. Several types are traditionally used in Denmark. They include placement in a shared housing facility, family care, boarding schools, continuation schools, 24-hour care centres, residential institutions, private residences and secure wards.

The guidelines are specified based on age groups, in terms of where children and adolescents can reside. For instance, it specifies that, initially, children aged 0–6 should be placed in family care, whereas children and adolescents between the ages of 7 and 14 should be placed in a residential institution.

The basis is a tangible instrument for the administrative management of practical implementation, which disengages the subjective approaches of the individual caseworker from the decision-making process, and which implicitly includes the Municipality's level of service and local policies, including a focus on the family approach. Similar administrative guidelines have been drawn up for other areas, such as for those involving persons with disabilities and preventive intervention. In these cases, the wild problem areas are 'tamed', in a sense.

Implementation of a common language for defining children at risk

Every normal service unit, residential institution and school has socially at-risk children and professional staff who are unsure of whether they can accommodate or consider the needs of these children. Usually, this leads to a discussion on whether the children at risk should remain within the normal service unit and whether the scope of possible assistance measures available to the day-care centre, for instance, is sufficient. Most of these discussions result from uncertainty and varying notions of what characterises children at risk and thus what automatically triggers an assistance measure.

In a society with increasingly varied ways of life and a decay of normative perceptions leading to changes to the institution of the family it becomes essential to establish a common perception of the children who are actually at risk. For this reason, a common language has been introduced making a distinction among three types of children at risk:

1. particularly vulnerable children with one or more traits indicating abnormal development

2. endangered children who have difficulties in several areas

3. problem children who have previously been exposed to social and mental hardships (Jørgensen et al. 1993).

The essential point is that the special system is solely responsible for characterising whether a child is at risk and, if that is the case, the category in which the child belongs. Though it will not be possible to offer special intervention to children who are not at risk, their needs must be handled by the normal service unit in which the child participates. Thus, the special system makes very specific demands on the normal service units regarding which children these normal service units must continue to accommodate – either with or without support measures.

From trouble-shooter to resource scout

The child and youth policy of the Municipality of Odense stipulates that wherever possible, the child's problems must be resolved within the child's own sphere and in cooperation with the parents. This means that the professional must insist on the parents' responsibility for their child by making them aware of the resources they themselves possess. In this way a resource-oriented parlance, in contrast with trouble-shooter parlance, will give access to personal resources and those of others, thereby generating more of these effective means. This underscores a positive approach to children and families, which contrasts with the culture of diagnosticians and trouble-shooters and is based on the resources already present in the sphere of each child.

The strategic choice to implement a resource-oriented approach and a deliberate shift of the approach methods applied in social work make it possible to put more focus on the 'protective' factors in the child's surroundings and provide greater freedom to act when establishing social measures for the purpose of keeping at-risk children in their familiar surroundings.

Cooperation with the normal service units

Most parents do not want themselves or their children to develop a need for special support. The ideal picture of a 'good childhood' is still a child who grows up in a nuclear family and attends a 'normal' day-care centre, school and after-school centre. In spite of the debates and normative perceptions, a specific daily reality exists in the municipalities where efforts are being made to find the best solution for a number of children and adolescents within the municipality's own framework.

This is frequently a complicated, subtle task entailing many considerations, interests and relationships with the child, etc. We know that there are at-risk children in almost every day-care centre, school, after-school centre and special service; and we know that the professionals who work in these units are unsure whether the service has the capacity to meet these children's needs. The number of children and parents who receive some form of aid is on the rise. Similarly, many of the professionals in the normal service units talk of how their work has become increasingly burdensome.

The normal service units play a key part in the ongoing debate about efforts made on behalf of children and adolescents at risk. This brings into focus the responsibility and potential of normal service units to provide services for children at risk. After many years of researching into and identifying the problems and factors that come into play in the everyday situations of children and adolescents, several researchers have recently started to show an interest in identifying the factors that produce an ambition to succeed. 'Mould-breakers' and 'dandelion children' are terms used to describe children who – despite a terrible upbringing – grow up to lead 'normal' lives devoid of a negative social inheritance. Similarly, it is interesting to examine the factors that generate success in our day-care centres, clubs and schools when a threatening situation is overcome – when we have indeed been preventive.

At a local municipal level, therefore, it is important to ask some key questions regarding the efforts of the normal service units for children at risk.

- Is the adult/child's environment sufficiently open and accommodating? Is the child being given the right development opportunities?

- Are we creating a daily existence and fellowship where everyone contributes and participates – or are we ostracising the underprivileged, those who are unable to live up to our standards?

- Is each of us good enough at doing the right thing at the right time – do we have the knowledge, the intuition and the energy to commit, to react and to act?

- Are we good enough at participating in interdisciplinary teamwork?

The first two items deal with accommodating and allowing for diversity. It is an old discussion about how to define a good life and who holds the right yardstick. When a teacher is concerned about a child's upbringing, is it because the teacher's middle-class norms are unable to grasp the child and family's way of life, or is it because something is really not quite right about the child's family environment? Who is right?

Normal service units and special service areas share the common task of giving each child opportunities and challenges in an environment based on a culture of caring, learning and development. At the same time, however, the fact that we even think in terms of underprivileged children and adolescents puts us in a dilemma. By naming and pointing out the disadvantaged children – the children at risk – we have also removed them from our 'normality', because we have defined them by virtue of their dissimilarity to the norm. The fact that we are simultaneously absorbed in explaining the cause of the phenomena we are observing doesn't make it any better.

All the same, we obviously must also prepare ourselves for the last two items: it is important that the professionals, the specialists, are good at getting involved with the children and cooperating with the parents, are capable of reacting and acting at signs of suffering, and capable of advising families on how to get proper assistance. This means that we have to acquire the willingness and expertise to participate in difficult interdisciplinary teamwork. This not only involves cooperation among the professions involved, but also cooperation between the normal service units and special services.

The political committee has therefore adopted the following fundamental values for social intervention within the Municipality of Odense:

- Social intervention must be implemented in the local community in close interaction with the normal system (day-care centres, schools and after-school centres).

- The intervention has to be implemented as early as possible.

- The intervention wards off placement in the 24-hour care system.

- Coordination and development occur across the departments.

These fundamental values guide the way in which social interventions and collaboration are organised. The purpose is to give every child and adolescent with special needs in the Municipality the opportunity to receive local intervention in his or her own normal environment.

Conclusion

Modern society, including the institution of the family, is in a state of transformation. New problems are emerging in parallel with a paradigm shift of fundamental values and methodological approaches in social work. The way in which the municipality organises social intervention aimed at vulnerable families is therefore currently being modified. This has been triggered by the changes stated above at structural and normative levels. In this area of municipal social services, which exclusively involves intervention solutions and where the social effort revolves around the family, it has turned out to be far more necessary than tradition has dictated in the past to 'tame' wild problems by applying specific guidelines and political objectives to the implementation of the social intervention. The Municipality of Odense's reorganisation of social work is moving away from being exclusively retrospective and process-oriented to an orientation towards the future and the product.

References

Becker, H. (1963/1995) 'Outsiders.' In E. Rubrington and M.S. Weinberg *Study of Social Problems, Seven Perspectives.* 186–191. New Yor: Oxford University Press Inc.

Berger, L. and Luchmann, T. (1996) *Den samfundsskabte virkelighed* [Society's Reality]. 2nd edn, Viborg, Denmark: Lindhart and Ringhof.

Bømler, T. (1998) *Fra integration og normalisering til social omsorg og støtte: i sammenhold eller sammenbrud* [From Integration and Normalisation to Social Care and Support: Unity or Breakdown?] København: Akademisk Forlag.

Christensen, E. (2002) *Børnesager – Evaluering af den forebyggende indsats* [Children's Cases: an Evaluation of the Preventive Effort]. København: Socialforskningsinsituttet.

Egelund, T. (1998) 'Efter socialt arbejde' [After Social Work]. *Social Kritik, issues 57–58.*

Egelund, T. (2002) *Tærskler for anbringelse – En vignetundersøgelse om socialforvaltningernes vurderinger i børnesager* [Placement Threshold: a Vignette Study on the Evaluations Performed by Social Services Administrative Units in Children's Cases]. København: Socialforskningsinstituttet.

Elsborg, S., Hansen, T.J., and Hansen, V.R. (1999) *Den social arv og mønsterbrydere* [Social Inheritance and Mould-Breakers]. København: Danmarks Pædagogiske Institut.

Hessle, S., and Wåhlander, E. (2000) *Högriskbarn – Livskarriär och livskvallitet som vuxna* [Children at Risk: Careers and Quality of Life]. Edsbruk, Sweden: Akademistryck AB.

Jørgensen, P.S. and Dencik, L. (1998) *Børn og familie i det postmoderne samfund* [Children and Families in Postmodern Society]. København: Hans Reitzels Forlag.

Jørgensen, P.S., Ertmann, B., Egelund, N. and Hermann, D. (1993) *Risikobørn. Hvem er de – hvad gør vi?* [Children at Risk: Who Are They – and What Should We Do?] Copenhagen: SIKON.

Krogstrup, H. (1997) *Brugerinddragelse og organisatorisk læring i den sociale sektor* [User Involvement and Organisational Learning in the Social Sector]. Århus: Forlaget Sytime.

Skaarup, P. (2000) 'Risikobørn i søgelyset' [Spotlight on Children at Risk]. *Pædagogisk og psykologisk tidsskrift 6,*

Chapter 5

Implementing Family Support Policy: Empowering Practitioners

Alex Wright

Introduction

This chapter aims to assist practitioners, supervisors and managers develop a greater understanding of the policy process through analysis, reflection and self-awareness. In particular the chapter focuses on policy implementation. Understanding how policy is implemented at the operational level is 'essential to improve social service delivery' (Brooks and Miljan 2003). At the same time, and this is often not recognised, implementation is a key aspect of the policy making process itself (Wharf and McKenzie 1998). Making policy and implementing it are not two distinct sets of activity. They need to be regarded as part of a single process. If family support is to be successfully implemented as a new policy direction, this unified process needs to be understood by those responsible for implementing it – operational managers and front-line practitioners.

Policy implementation has generally been considered from a manager's perspective, with very little focus on the front-line worker's viewpoint (Gummer 1990; Lewis *et al.* 2001; Rapp and Poertner 1992; Weinbach 1990). While awareness of the importance of the practitioner's role in policy implementation is not a new development (see for example Lipsky 1980; Smith 1965), there is now a growing interest in this aspect of the policy process. For example, in setting a future direction for family support, Pinkerton (2000) notes that practitioners have a key role in the implementation of policy through their practice. He advocates for a 'transparent, rigorous and self-critical approach to detailing their work' (p.223). The conceptual frameworks presented in this chapter should help in achieving that goal.

The chapter sets out two linked frameworks that help to describe and analyse the role of individual staff in the implementation of policy and how that is enabled or constrained by organisational structures. They draw attention to the central social science concerns of 'structure', 'agency' and 'power'. The first framework presented is the Integrated Power Approach (IPA). The IPA presents a multifaceted view of power which integrates the location and source of power with the process of exercising power. The second approach is the Policy Implementation Framework (PIF). It provides a means to deconstruct the policy process through the examination of organisational structure and the methods used to implement policy.

The following section provides a summary of the theoretical underpinnings of the IPA. The second section provides an overview of the PIF within which front-line practitioners, as well as managers, can situate, analyse and evaluate their role in the policy implementation process. The third section considers from an IPA perspective examples of policy implementation based on research findings on how the concept of 'children in need' was operationalised as part of promoting the policy of family support in Scotland. The fourth section then suggests what the implications of IPA and PIF are for organisational policy formulation, definition, implementation and evaluation. It lists six recommendations for an inclusive and reflective policy process. The chapter concludes with a call for creating organisational contexts that promote and enable reflective policy processes in the interests of children and families.

Power, policy and organisations

Organisational theories tend to be polarised regarding sources of power (Reed 1996). Traditional theories of organisation argue that power is embedded in the structure of an organisation and granted to the organisational elite due to the authority assigned to their position (Hardy and Clegg 1996; Morgan 1986). This is a one-dimensional view of power which identifies the powerful as the one 'who prevails in cases of decision-making where there is an observable conflict' (Lukes 1974, p.11). Power is getting someone 'to do something he [sic] would not otherwise do' (Dahl 1957, p.82).

At the start of the last century Michels (1915) asserted that power in organisations always centralises to a limited few and coined the phrase the 'iron rule of oligarchy'. Based on this rule, policy decisions will always be made by an organisational elite, those positioned at the top of the organisation's structure. No matter how democratically formed, organisational process eventually results in a formal hierarchical structure. 'Who says organisation, says oligarchy' (Michels 1915, p.418).

Within that tradition, policy planning and implementation is considered a hierarchical top-down process with the organisational policy determined by staff in senior positions directing the implementation of policy through subordinate staff (Gummer 1990; Van Meter and Van Horn 1975). From this perspective, policy formulation is considered distinct and separate from policy implementation. Discontinuities between the formal policy and its implementation are blamed on problems with policy design or 'management of inter and intra organizational linkages' – in particular excessive amounts of worker autonomy (Gummer 1990, p. 93). Solutions to difficulties in policy implementation often focus on motivating subordinates to achieve the agency's goals. 'In its most general form, an inquiry about implementation...seeks to determine whether an organisation can bring together men [sic] and material in a cohesive organisational unit and motivate them in such a way as to carry out the organisation's stated objectives' (Van Meter and Van Horn 1975, p.448).

Social service organisational structure

Modern social or human services organisations generally take the form of a bureaucratic structure as originally studied and labelled by Weber (1947). While organisational contexts have changed to include unionisation, professionalism, the use of complex technology, a decentralisation of tasks, and less rigidity in authority-based boundaries (Clegg and Hardy 1996; Gummer 1990), the bureaucratic structure nevertheless continues to dominate. Bureaucracy can be figuratively illustrated as a pyramid, in which organisational power is situated at the top with supporting units filling out the base of the pyramid (Gummer 1990). In other words a bureaucratic structure would seem to be in keeping with the traditional perspective on power.

However, in addition to being bureaucratic social service organisations today are characterised by other key features. They suffer from a chronic lack of resources (Gummer 1990) and increase in supply only leads to more service demand (Lipsky 1980). Many of their service users are involuntary (Lipsky 1980). They pursue complex, multiple goals which are often ambiguous, vague and conflicting (Gummer 1990; Hasenfeld 1983; Lipsky 1980; Smith 1979). These goals are inevitably difficult to measure and evaluate (Hasenfeld 1983; Lipsky 1980). Staff in different organisational positions do not necessarily share the same goals which can become expressions of the interests of various groups in the organisation (Smith 1979, p.8). Far from the neat top-down pyramid of Weber's model of bureaucracy or Michels' 'iron rule of oligarchy', the conditions of today's social services organization create a much more fluid and contested context.

Worker discretion as an alternative source and location of power

In contrast to the top-down view of organisational power, an alternative perspective argues that power is not only located in the organisation's structure and associated authority, but also in the agency of individual actors by way of their capacity for discretion (Gummer 1990; Hardy and Clegg 1996; Lipsky 1980; Smith 1965). Agency can be defined as the 'actions' and 'micro-practices' of individuals (Reed 1996, p.46). There is always the potential for individuals, wherever located in an organisational hierarchy, to decide to what extent they will submit to the instructions of those above them. This capacity to exercise discretion, through the practitioner's agency, creates an additional source of power to that which comes from position in an organisational hierarchy.

Of particular relevance for social service organisations for understanding this alternative source of power is Smith's (1965) seminal study of a state psychiatric hospital. In contrast to Michels' 'iron rule of oligarchy', Smith believed that power is often dispersed away from the organisational elite to those at the lower levels in the organisation structure in order to meet organisational goals. This decentralisation of the executive process locates organisational initiative in front-line units and recognises the individual worker's autonomy associated with the division of labour and differentiated tasks (Smith 1965, pp.389–390). In effect, practitioners' day-to-day work is what creates organisational policy – whether or not formally condoned by managers.

Lipsky (1980) further developed this understanding of the role of practitioners in creating policy through implementation with his theory of 'street-level bureaucracy' and 'street-level bureaucrats'. Similar to Smith's front-line workers, street-level bureaucrats are workers who 'interact directly with citizens in the course of their jobs, and who have substantial discretion in the execution of their work' (p.3). The relationship between management and subordinate workers is both 'intrinsically conflictual' and one of 'mutual dependence'. There is a paradox of power evident in social services organisations. Managers are dependent on practitioners to implement formal policies but are not able to directly supervise that implementation. As a result, front-line workers are 'de facto policy makers' (Lipsky 1980, p.25).

From this perspective policy needs to be seen to be as much about the action and verbal statements of front-line staff as the top-down promotion of published policy documents (Fulcher 1989). Policy includes both the formal and the informal. Formal policy includes written goals, objectives, mechanisms, rules and roles. In contrast informal policy includes goals, rules and roles as embodied in everyday interactions. 'The decisions of street-level bureaucrats, the routines they establish, and the devices they invent to cope with uncertainties and work pressures, effectively become the public policies they carry out' (Lipsky 1980, p.xii).

In effect, the agency perspective argues that practitioners hold a strategic position in relation to operational policy due to the discretion inherent in their role (Lipsky 1980; Smith 1965; Wyers 1991). Practitioners have to be granted substantial autonomy in their daily work because of the skills and knowledge required to do their jobs and this discretion allows practitioners to 'deviate from prescribed agency policies' (Gummer 1990, p.104). As a result, the process of formulating and implementing policy needs to take account of discretion as a source of power which is located with front-line practitioners.

Dimensions to the process of exercising power

Lukes (1974) analysis of power contributes further to understanding the complexity of policy implementation. He was interested in why workers' use of their discretion is limited and why resistance within organisations occurs infrequently. Rather than focusing on the locations and sources of power, Lukes considered the processes used to exercise power and presented a 'three-dimensional view' of this. He built on the definition of power 'A exercises power over B when A affects B in a manner contrary to B's interests' by identifying societal and class mechanisms that prevent conflict through 'shaping...perceptions, cognitions and preferences in such a way that they [those in position B] accept their role in the existing order of things' (1974, p.24). This presents the status quo as 'natural', 'divinely ordained' and 'mutually beneficial'. Power is thus employed through both overt and covert processes.

Lukes (1974) identified three dimensions in the exercise of power used to ensure submission of organisational actors: episodic, manipulative and hegemonic (Reed, 1996, p.41). The episodic dimension of power concentrates on observable conflicts of interest between identifiable social actors with opposing objectives in particular decision-making situations. For example, open disagreement between two programme managers over service provision priorities would be an episodic power struggle. Manipulative power by contrast is the behind-the-scenes activities through which already powerful groups manipulate the decision-making agenda to screen out issues which have the potential to disturb or threaten their domination and control. The introduction by a programme manager of an intake form which defined need primarily by existing services, rather than by what families were asking for, thereby controlling demand on resources, would be an example of manipulative power. The third of Lukes' dimensions is that of hegemonic power. It emphasises how existing ideological and social structures constitute and limit the interests and values available to social actors and thereby determine their action. Sexism, racism and professional identity exemplify the hegemonic dimension. Within a social service agency, systemic sexism, racism or the dominance of a professional perspective may set the parameters of service provision.

An Integrated Power Approach

From the discussion above it is clear that to understand policy making within social service organisations requires recognition of the different types of policy, formal and informal, and of how power relationships, based on different location, source and types of process, determine the ways in which policy is made and implemented. All can usefully be drawn together into a single perspective – an Integrated Power Approach (IPA). The IPA provides a multifaceted view of power which integrates the location and source of power with the process of exercising power. It recognises that power in organisations is located in both structure and agency. Authority is the source of power within structure and discretion is the source of power for individual agency. Whatever its source and wherever it is located, power has to be exercised and the IPA uses Lukes' three-dimensional view of power to identify the types of process involved.

The implications of taking an IPA perspective on the analysis of policy are to break with the traditional view of top-down policy implementation con-trolled solely by staff in management positions. It allows for a much more fluid and contested process of defining what policy is and how it is implemented. It accepts that there can be both competing and unified, cohesive and contradic-tory, policies co-existing within an organisation at any given time, and that policies are constantly being transformed as a reflection of the organisation's internal and external power contexts. Policy making and policy implementation reflect conflict over and within the process of defining, formulating, implementing and evaluating organisational goals (Gummer 1990; Reed 1996; Smith 1979).

Policy Implementation Framework

In this section the perspective provided by the IPA is developed into a Policy Implementation Framework (PIF), which provides a means to examine and understand the specific power dynamics involved in any particular situation where a policy, such as family support, is being implemented. The PIF provides a basis for reflective analysis of policy implementation as it enables anyone involved in the policy process to understand the experience better and to make choices about their own activity through the examination of agency, organisa-tional structure and the way in which power is being used to implement policy. There are two steps involved in the application of the PIF. The first is to clarify the locations and sources of power involved – agency/discretion or struc-ture/authority. The second is to identify which of the dimensions of power is dominant: episodic, manipulative or hegemonic. In the following discussion examples of implementing family support policy in Scotland are provided, drawing on research into front-line social workers' and their managers' experi-ences of operationalising the core concept of 'children in need' (Wright 2003).

The Scottish study showed that during the early stages of implementing new family support policy there was considerable debate within social work departments as to how best to operationalise the core concept of 'children in need'. Findings identified considerable divergence between formal and informal policy and revealed that implementation of the formal policy was generally limited to activity by managers. This was not surprising given that the organisa-tional division of labour made implementation of formal policy an integral part of managers' jobs. Managers reported the highest rate of engagement with the policy and saw themselves as being key formulators of how 'children in need' was understood in the local authority. Managers were more likely to demonstrate knowledge of the formal policy than front-line social work staff. Social workers reported much less involvement in the formal policy implementation process and when they were included, their involvement was of a temporary nature. 'Children in need' policy implementation was prominent in service planning at the strategic management level, but not particularly consciously employed at the service provision level. The structural division of labour within the organisation separated front-line staff from engaging in formal policy making. It created a division between formal and informal organisational policy.

Findings also suggested that the difference in engagement in the structure was reflected in how the implementation of the policy was pursued. Most effort seemed to be focused on encouraging other departments in the local authority and other agencies to take on a greater responsibility for service provision and the associated resources. In this way pursuing a policy based on 'children in need' primarily took on the form of advocacy by managers for a corporate approach to providing and resourcing children's services. Policy implementation did not in the main mean identifying a particular group of children for receipt of services from front-line staff in accordance with the new legislative mandate. That said, there were other expressions of the implementation of the 'children in need' policy closer to practice. These included using it to widen eligibility criteria for families to access services and to advocate for additional resources for those families. In these ways the policy was used by front-line practitioners as a basis to improve the quantity and quality of direct service delivery.

Understanding the way in which the new policy is based on the core concept of 'children in need' is helped by application of PIF. Findings are presented in Table 5.1 to exemplify the intersection of the policy's power location (structure/authority or agency/discretion), the 'where', and the power dimensions (episodic, manipulative or hegemonic), the 'how'. This intersection of location and dimension expresses the specification of policy, the resultant 'what'. Each section within the table presents examples of analysed responses reflecting power locations interconnecting with power dimensions. These responses (not exhaustive) exemplify different agency and structural locations as well as episodic, manipulative and hegemonic power dimensions. They show which is the dominant power set. Completion of such a table by anyone involved in the implementation of policy would provide clarification as to the power context in which they were operating at any particular point in time.

Policy examples within the Policy Implementation Framework

An example of 'agency-episodic' policy implementation was an open disagreement between two social workers and their decisions related to service quality and quantity for service users identified as 'children in need'. The distinction

Table 5.1 The Policy Implementation Framework

Power Dimensions (How)	Power Location (Where)	
	Agency	Structure
Episodic	Conflict between practitioners regarding eligibility requirements, specific services or resources. Open disagreement between managers setting policy priority areas.	Formal authority for policy decisions granted to managers (role restriction) in conflict with practitioners. Conflict between departments regarding responsibility for services.
Manipulative	Policy made during a closed-door, restricted membership meeting. Practitioner going behind supervisor's back regarding service provision. Practitioner presenting case plan to Children's Hearing without manager's approval.	Program resource distribution decisions such as funding, staffing made by local authority management.
Hegemonic	Individual professionalism and moral influence on service planning, assessment and provision. Experiences with oppressive factors (racism, sexism) affecting practice. Application of targeted versus universal services, to individuals/families.	Legislation regarding corporate service responsibility for children in need. Institutional/residual focus of service provision on corporate level. Targeted versus universal service legislation on a programme level. Oppressive factors (racism, sexism) affecting organisational division of labour, rewards system. Gender differences in practitioner and management positions.

between the agency and structural location in this situation is that no authority was granted to either practitioner to determine a universal outcome and so the practitioners formulated the policy through their individual practice. The practitioners were in control but with different results.

In contrast 'structure-episodic' policy implementation was frequently evident when managers used their formal authority to define and determine a service quality or quantity issue in the face of a different view being taken by the social worker involved. Another example of 'structure-episodic' implementation was where local authority departments other than social services debated and at times rejected their responsibility for 'children in need'.

An expression of 'agency-manipulative' policy implementation by a front-line worker was the provision of services without a manager's knowledge or consent. For example, one social worker described 'going behind her supervisor's back'. She continued to provide services to a family whom she considered to have 'children in need' contrary to her manager's instruction. Another social worker described presenting a case plan which she knew to be opposed by the manager in the formal setting of a Children's Hearing.

However, in most cases policy implementation took a 'structure-manipulative' form. Most social workers reported exclusion from the formal policy planning process, and those who did participate reported limited input. For example practitioners' input to policy documents was often solicited in the form of feedback on a draft document with no formal mechanism to question the very basis of the document. Practitioners were also never granted reduction in work load to participate in policy planning. The system acted as a disincentive for workers to participate and there was little motivation to participate in the process as any time spent on policy planning resulted in overtime work to 'catch up' with their caseload.

Hegemonic dimensions expressed through assumptions based in gender, socio-economic status, professional perspective and law were also evident as influences in the implementation of 'children in need' policy. 'Agency-hegemonic' influence was evident when a practitioner spoke of acting in accordance with the view that the role of social welfare was to meet human needs on a universal level. She provided services for 'children in need' based on that conviction. More apparent however was the 'structure-hegemonic' combination which reinforced aspects of the legislation which were consistent with a technical administrative approach compatible with the gendered assumptions of management.

Operational policy process: discussion and recommendations

The PIF provides a basis for reflective policy implementation. It is best suited to organisations which are open to continuous learning, through the systematic employment of transparent, inclusive policy planning and evaluation. While there is a finite amount of funding available for public resourcing, planning and responding to need requires a thoughtful, collaborative and co-ordinated response by service providers to ensure that resources allow children and their families to realise their potential. Ultimately, the PIF is a method that practitioners can use to facilitate the implementation of successful family support services to meet the needs of children and families.

Agencies that are structured based on top-down hierarchies 'usually fail to produce the changes they espouse' (Cohen and Austin 1994, p.2) unless policy initiatives take into account the many views within an organisation. An implication of regular exclusion of front-line staff from the formal policy process is that these staff will feel removed from the resulting formal policy. This can ultimately contribute to feelings of 'powerlessness and isolation' within the organisation (Davies 1989, p.196). This can also result in practitioners having no sense of ownership of the policy and so lead to their own personal policy formulation.

In order for practitioners to provide family support and become 'supporters' to families (Robinson 1996) organisations require organisational change to allow for this type of support. Within an organisational context, structural flexibility and service delivery should encourage a more diverse, inclusive and integrated approach to planning for, and responding to, families' needs. Changes in policy initiatives should take into account the many views within an organisation; otherwise ignorance or a general lack of commitment to formal policies may occur. Processes should be in place to allow for staff to provide input in the policy process and to raise issues regarding informal policy formulation. Channels of communication can open between organisational actors to allow for pertinent information to be shared between hierarchical levels: upwards, downwards and sideways within the organisation.

As McGrath and Grant (1992) advocate, greater involvement of front-line staff, and also consumers, in the planning process would encourage inclusive needs-based rather than resource-based services and planning. In order to foster innovation in organisational change, Cohen (1999) recommends the inclusion of workers in all aspects of organisational improvement as a necessary part of their job description. This inclusiveness should be broadened to all policy levels. Organisations should mandate membership by all levels of staff on policy planning committees as a job requirement. Support must also be provided to ensure that all staff are able to take part in the process. Wharf and McKenzie propose a policy making process that is built up from practice and as a result incorporates 'the knowledge not only of practitioners but also of the people they serve' (1998, p.3).

Under the use of regular and ongoing training, social service agencies could become 'learning organisations', encouraging the perspective that learning is an ongoing process, both on a personal and organisational level (Lewis *et al.* 2001, p.318). Organisational learning is defined as:

> ...the process through which an organisation continuously improves its performance over time and through experience. The learning process is interactive and purposeful, not simply the receiving of information or ideas from a

central source. Learning takes place as the parts of an organisation struggle to make sense of current practices or conditions that are considered problematic, and to invent more effective practices. (Cohen and Austin 1994, p.13)

Operational policy process recommendations

Organisational operational policy process which takes account of both the IPA and PIF should include the following six points.

1. The organisation should incorporate an inclusive policy planning process. This includes policy formulation, definition, implementation and evaluation. This process should involve both managers and front-line social workers (as well as other stakeholders and, especially, service users).

2. Staff should have a conceptual and practical knowledge of specific policy. Formal policy should be defined and shared through systematic and systemic dissemination in organisational contexts such as: supervision and training; electronic delivery modes; regular and planned dialogue within and between staff/teams/programmes. Practical knowledge should address the realities of practitioners (resource access, community support, rules/regulations and tradition) when planning policy implementation.

3. There should be an accepted organisational position that policy implementation reflects power locations and dimensions. Whenever possible planned policy should be assessed regarding challenges/opportunities to policy implementation (in structure and agency arenas, as well as dimensions) in a 'pre-engagement' phase. Solutions to foreseeable problems should be incorporated whenever possible.

4. During the engagement phase with operational policy (policy implementation) all staff, especially practitioners, should be aware of their authority and discretion and methods of implementation, and the effects they have on the policy.

5. During the post-engagement phase policy analysis and evaluation should occur. This should include discussions regarding challenges/opportunities to policy implementation (in structure and agency arenas as well as dimensions). Additionally, the identification of the frequency of the operational policy; the context of its implementation (i.e. planning; assessment; advocacy; intervention, staff training); the agent who implemented the policy (i.e. who uses the policy); and the quality (i.e. efficient, effective, delivering

improvement, problematic) should assist in understanding the policy and suggest future policy directions.

6. The implementation of policy and the evaluation of operational policy should reflect a shared organisational goal of a commitment to serving the best interests of service users.

Conclusion

This chapter has attempted to encourage greater awareness and understanding of the operational policy process. The Integrated Power Approach argues that, partly due to the very nature of social service agencies, organisational policy reflects power locations and dimensions. The analysis of policy using PIF provides a useful and insightful theoretical framework for understanding policy formulation in organisations. The Policy Implementation Framework allows for the examination and evaluation of policy situated within organisational power positions and dimensions. It does not assign a positive or negative judgement regarding the benefits or limitations of the operational policy. Rather it allows for understanding through analysis and reflective practice based on a theoretical perspective on power embedded in policy implementation. Analysis and reflective practice empowers staff to increase self-awareness of their role as change agents, as well as the organisational structures that support and/or challenge operational policy. Through the identification of the intersection of position and dimension, practitioners and managers should be better able to analyse, evaluate and contribute to operational policy.

In concluding the chapter, recommendations for an inclusive organisational policy process were presented and suggested as necessary to empower and provide practitioners with an organisational context that promotes and enables a reflective policy process. It is that process which can empower family support practitioners in their daily work of implementing and creating policy and ensure that the best interests of children and their families remain the overarching organisational goal of all policy.

References

Brooks, S. and Miljan, L. (2003) *Public Policy in Canada.* 4th edn Don Mills, Ontario: Oxford University Press.

Clegg, S.R. and Hardy, C. (1996) 'Introduction to Organizations, Organization and Organizing.' In S.R. Clegg, C. Hardy and W.R. Nord (eds) *Handbook of Organization Studies.* London: Sage Publications.

Cohen, B.J. (1999) 'Fostering Innovation in a Large Human Services Bureaucracy.' *Administration in Social Work 23,* 2, 47–59.

Cohen, B. and Austin, M. (1994) 'Organizational Learning and Change in a Public Child Welfare Agency'. *Administration in Social Work, 18* (1) 1–18.

Dahl, R.A. (1957) 'The Concept of Power.' *Behavioral Science 2,* 201–205.

Davies, L. (1989) 'Professional Autonomy Revisited. The Case of British Social Work Practice in Child Abuse.' *Canadian Social Work Review 6*, 2, 186–202.

Fulcher, G. (1989) *Disabling Policies? A Comparative Approach to Education Policy and Disability.* London: The Falmer Press.

Gummer, B. (1990) *The Politics of Social Administration. Managing Organizational Politics in Social Agencies.* Englewood-Cliffs, NJ: Prentice Hall.

Hardy, C. and Clegg, S.R. (1996) 'Some Dare Call it Power.' In S.R. Clegg, C. Hardy and W.R. Nord (eds) *Handbook of Organization Studies.* London: Sage Publications.

Hasenfeld, Y. (1983) *Human Service Organizations.* Englewood Cliffs, NJ: Prentice Hall.

Lewis, J., Lewis, M., Packard, T. and Souflee, F. (2001) *Management of Human Service Programs.* 3rd edn, Scarborough, Ontario: Thomson Learning.

Lipsky, M. (1980) *Street-level Bureaucracy. Dilemmas of the Individual in Public Services.* New York: Russell Sage Foundation.

Lukes, S. (1974) *Power: A Radical View.* London: Macmillan.

McGrath, M. and Grant, G. (1992). 'Supporting Needs-led Services: Implications for Planning and Management Systems (A Case Study in Mental Handicap Services).' *Journal of Social Policy 21*, 1, 71–97.

Michels, R. (1915) *Political Parties.* London: Jarrold & Sons.

Morgan, G. (1986) *Images of Organization.* Newbury Park, CA: Sage.

Pinkerton, J. (2000) 'Emerging Agendas for Family Support.' In J. Canavan, P. Dolan and J. Pinkerton (eds) *Family Support: Direction from Diversity.* London: Jessica Kingsley Publishers.

Rapp, C. and Poertner, J. (1992) *Social Administration: A Client Centered Approach.* New York: Longman.

Reed, M. (1996) 'Organizational Theorizing: A Historically Contested Terrain.' In S.R. Clegg, C. Hardy and W.R. Nord (eds) *Handbook of Organization Studies.* London: Sage Publications.

Robinson, J. (1996) 'Social Workers – Investigators or Enablers?' In D. Cullen and E. Batty (eds) *Child Protection the Therapeutic Option.* London: British Agencies for Adoption and Fostering.

Smith, D.E. (1965) 'Front-line Organization of the State Mental Hospital.' *Administrative Science Quarterly 10*, 381–399.

Smith, G. (1979) *Social Work and the Sociology of Organizations.* Rev. edn, London: Routledge & Kegan Paul.

Van Meter, D.S. and Van Horn, C.E. (1975) 'The Policy Implementation Process. A Conceptual Framework.' *Administration & Society 6*, 4, 445–488.

Weber, M. (1947) *The Theory of Social and Economic Organization,* (trans. A.M. Henderson and T. Parsons). New York: Oxford University Press.

Weinbach, R. (1990) *The Social Worker as Manager.* New York: Longman.

Wharf, B. and McKenzie, B. (1998) *Connecting Policy to Practice in the Human Services.* Toronto: Oxford University Press.

Wright, A. (2003) 'Children in Need: An Examination of Policy Formulation in Scottish Social Work.' PhD thesis. Glasgow: University of Glasgow.

Wyers, N.L. (1991) 'Policy-practice in Social Work: Models and Issues.' *Journal of Social Work Education 27*, 3, 241–50.

Chapter 6

A Comparative Perspective: Exploring the Space for Family Support

Michelle Millar

Introduction

In developing family support services many practitioners and policy makers are motivated by questions such as: 'Is this the most efficient and effective way of providing our services?'; 'Do our policies tackle the problems they aim to address?' Moreover policy, like time, does not stand still and what was once the solution to a problem can itself become a quandary or obsolete prompting policy actors to seek new remedies. In their quest for new ideas, policy actors increasingly look to how other states have managed similar problems and what lessons there are to learn from those experiences (Adshead and Wall 2003; Rose 2004). No country's problems or policy responses are unique. Rose, one of the first writers on 'lesson learning' from international comparison, argues that it is 'the politics of the ostrich' to claim that the problems of a single country are unique (Rose 2004, p.3). Faced with uncertainty as to what constitutes family support and how best to develop it, both policy makers and practitioners would do well to reflect on how countries other than their own are tackling the issue.

There is a growing public and social policy literature on international 'lesson learning' or 'policy transfer': 'the process by which knowledge about policies, administrative arrangements, institutions etc in one time and/or place is fed into the policy making arenas in the development of policies, administrative arrangements and institutions in another time and/or place' (Dolowitz and Marsh 1996, p.1). A well recognised example of such cross national lesson learning in the field of family policy is the widespread implementation of Family Group Conferencing (FGC). This approach to engaging the wider family network in devising their own solutions to problems that have been identified in the lives of some family members came out of the experiences of the Maori people of New Zealand. It was a response to Maori concerns about the over-representation of their children in the care system and a desire to use traditional forms of family support to find alternative solutions (Featherstone 2004; Marsh and Crow 1998). Despite these very specific origins FGC has been taken up by a range of other countries including Australia, Canada, Ireland, Israel, Norway, South Africa, Sweden, the UK and the USA (Brown 2003; Sundell, Vinnerlijung and Ryburn 2001). The application and implementation of FGC in these other countries has involved its modification to suit domestic requirements. Policy transfer does not involve the wholesale 'copying and pasting' of legislation, policy and practice from one country to another but rather 'lesson learning' and adapting policy and practice to correspond with cultural, institutional, and administrative arrangements.

Taking a comparative perspective on family support is not easy because, as Featherstone has pointed out, the remit of family support can be 'infinitely elastic' (2004, p.2). However, rather than abandon the quest for a common understanding of family support, Featherstone advocates that 'what is necessary is to unpack the spaces it occupies at both policy and practice levels in particular periods' (2004, p.2). This chapter recommends that view to anyone attempting to incorporate international comparison in their reflective practice and attempts to illustrate what it means by sketching out the policy space of family support in Ireland, England, Australia and New Zealand.

Making comparisons

There are many ways of exploring the policies of other countries for the purpose of comparison and lesson learning. The traditional library-based literature search is one (Higgins and Pinkerton 1998). Through the use of electronic bibliographic databases this is becoming increasingly sophisticated (Taylor, Dempster and Donnelly 2003). But for those practitioners who wish to reflect on their practice through comparing the policies and programmes of other countries with that of their own, the internet is perhaps a more accessible starting place. Focused web-based searching, using a search engine such as Google, can identify, and increasingly also provide access to, research, policy analysis and practice advice. It enables access to state documents, reports and investigations which provide important background information to specific policy programmes and projects. Keeping abreast of developments in journal articles and conferences is now made easier thanks to the internet. For example, in this chapter much of the background information on Australian policy came from conference papers posted on the web. The reflective practitioner should also utilise the contacts he or she may have with colleagues in other states who are working in similar organisations as undoubtedly they will have experienced analogous difficulties or problems.

However, it is important to have realistic expectations about what will be found. It needs to be recognised that there is still relatively little published about family support policy from a comparative perspective. Available information tends to be largely focused on exploring the legislative and policy frameworks within a particular jurisdiction. It is left to the reflective practitioner to consider the relevance to his or her own situation. In trying to make the comparisons it soon becomes apparent that the cultural and moral expectations about family life in different societies considerably influences the appearance of family support policy. Moreover the general character of particular welfare states with regard to redistribution also shapes the scope and context of family support policy. The national case studies sketched out in this chapter highlight the need for practitioners and policy analysts alike to go beyond legislative measures supporting family support and unpack the policy space by considering the wider social and economic goals of government – many of which are found in strategy documents, conference papers, programmes for government and related social policy measures.

Ireland

A reasonable starting place for describing family support in Ireland would seem to be the Family Support Agency Act 2001. Section 4 of the legislation details the functions of the Family Support Agency (FSA) as being to provide a family mediation service; to support, promote and develop the provision of marriage and relationship counselling and family support services; to support, promote and develop the Family and Community Services Resource Centre programme and to undertake research on family issues. The Act provides for the FSA to finance voluntary bodies engaged in delivering services within the agencies' remit. It would appear then that family support in Ireland is primarily about mediation and counselling. In fact the FSA is only one small part of the picture of family support in Ireland.

Since the 1990s commitment to family support has emerged in a number of Government reports and legislation. In particular the Child Care Act 1991 places a statutory obligation on the public sector Health Boards to identify and promote the welfare of children who do not attain sufficient care and attention. Section 3 of Part 2 of the legislation explicitly states that Health Boards should provide family support services. Whilst the Child Care Act 1991 laid the foundations for the expansion of family support services, it was by and large a child protection focus which informed the implementation of the legislation in response to the findings of the Kilkenny Incest Investigation (McGuinness 1993) and subsequent abuse inquiries (Murphy 1996; Pinkerton, Dolan and Percy 2003). It was the Report of the Kilkenny Incest Investigation that recommended the establishment of primary prevention and family support measures. That said, it was only with the publication of the report of the Commission on the Family (1998) coupled with the launch of the Springboard Programme (1998) that a more family support focused policy emerged which could be characterised as having both preventive and supportive measures to fortify family life.

The report of the Commission on the Family (1998) advocated a need to strengthen the coping ability of families by targeting support to those families that encounter adversity. The vision of family support as put forward by the Commission on the Family is one which is preventive in its orientation based on the community development principle of empowerment with an explicit focus on disadvantaged communities:

> [family support] is empowering of individuals, builds on family strengths, enhances self esteem and engenders a sense of being able to influence events in one's life, has significant potential as a primary preventative strategy for all families facing the ordinary challenges of day-to-day living, and has a partic- ular relevance to communities that are coping in a stressful environment. (Commission on the Family 1998, p.16)

Informed by the Commission on the Family, the Springboard Programme was launched in 1998 consisting initially of 15 family support projects which focused on families at risk of child protection and targeted disadvantaged and vulnerable families. Projects are delivered mainly by voluntary and community organisa- tions who are obliged to work in partnership with other agencies and families to develop family support programmes in order to provide care, intervention, support and counselling to targeted children and families.

Despite a proliferation of policy documents committing to family support in Ireland, in recent times there is little policy agreement as to what actually constitutes 'family support' in Ireland: 'Family support still does not seem to have one common understanding typified by a singular agreed national defini- tion within the arena of Irish social policy and child welfare practice' (Dolan and Holt 2002, p.245). There is, however, an inherent assumption in family support practice, if not policy, that informal and neighbourhood networks of support are crucial for vulnerable and disadvantaged families (Dolan and Holt 2002; Pinkerton *et al.* 2003). On the ground family support services incorpo- rate a wide range of interventions, including pre-school services, parental edu- cation, development, support activities, home visiting and educational youth projects. Whilst most family support initiatives are state funded the delivery of family services is largely provided by the community development and volun- tary sectors. This relationship is reinforced by the Family Support Agency Act of 2001.

The important point to note here is that in order to understand family support policy in Ireland it is essential to go beyond specific family support measures and consider other policy which incorporates family support. That includes the Government's commitment to tackling social exclusion, to part- nership and to promoting inter-agency collaboration. The introduction of the

Strategic Management Initiative as part of a much wider debate about governance is as important to the development of family support as the specifics of child welfare policy. Government commitment to the reduction of poverty levels, social partnership and inter-agency collaboration can be found in the National Anti-Poverty Strategy, the National Agreements and the National Development Plan as well as in the National Children's Strategy. A key theme of all these documents is the rejuvenation of disadvantaged communities and community empowerment. The publication of Green and White Papers on the Community and Voluntary Sector and its relationship with the State signalled the State's recognition of those sectors as having a significant role in the promotion of social cohesion and as active partners in the process. Family support in Ireland must be seen in this broader policy context. Only when that is done can family support be appreciated as the key measure it is in tackling social exclusion, delivered on a partnership basis with state funding for the provision of services offered by voluntary, community and non-profit organisations.

England

As with Ireland, context and terminology is an important issue when trying to get a picture of family support in England. Featherstone (2004) notes that until the 1980s 'prevention' as opposed to 'family support' was the concept employed to describe the activities of the statutory and voluntary sectors in England and the UK generally (note that it is important to recognise that there are a number of separate but related jurisdictions within the UK), which aimed to prevent children entering state care and to assist families. This was transformed in England with the introduction of the Children Act 1989, which struck a new balance between child protection and the promotion of family life: 'The advent of family support was designed to signal the desirability of a broader focus, a signal which was strengthened by its use in the guidance associated with the Children Act 1989' (Featherstone 2004, p.3).

Rather than being the main focus of child welfare, child protection was to be integrated with family support services. The Children Act placed a requirement on local authorities to provide a range of services to support families whose children are 'in need'. The importance of the legislation was that for the first time specific services to support children in need and families in the community were named. Such services include advice, guidance and counselling; day care and family centres and home helps.

However, policy commitments to family support also emerged in an era of Conservative government which transformed the management and implementation of social policies. As Tunstill explains, the reduced role of local authorities, reduced government expenditure, the introduction of market conditions to public and social services coupled with the rediscovery of the family as central to the New Right ideology all contributed to the philosophy underlying the Children Act 1989 (Tunstill 1995, 1997).

Since taking power in 1997, the Labour government has attempted to create a 'Third Way' in social and welfare policy, a middle ground between the traditional ideologies of the right and left. Two of the guiding principles of the 'Third Way' are the desire for 'a strong civil society with strong communities' and 'modern government based on partnership and decentralisation'. These principles have been operationalised in a series of community-based social policies which are complex partnership programmes designed to bring together service providers in the public, private and voluntary sectors to work towards targets of area improvement by reducing inequalities. These programmes operate on the underlying assumption of devolution of authority and responsibility to the community level and are based on the premise of the community development orientation of empowerment and partnership.

Gardner (2003) explains that contemporary family support policy in England can be seen as an element of social capital and a means to social inclusion, a way of reinforcing economic measures to end child poverty. Such policy initiatives attempt to target resources on those parents and children who are or could become socially excluded, 'in particular those affected by poverty, crime and poor educational achievement giving them access to social capital and life chances' (p.3). Recent policy commitments to family support in England reflect the Government's commitment to tackling social exclusion in a community setting. A good example of this is Sure Start. It is a nationwide, area-based programme whose goals are to improve social and emotional development, improve health, improve the ability to learn and strengthen families and communities. As community building is seen as key to tackling social exclusion, family support services are perceived as imperative in regenerating local communities. The programme is targeted at children and families in disadvantaged areas and offers a wide range of supports and services from pre-natal care until the age of four.

Even under New Labour, however, the direction of child welfare is driven in part by the need for a political response to high profile child protection tragedies. In conjunction with the Government's formal inquiry into the death of child abuse victim Victoria Climbié, a Green Paper *Every Child Matters* (Dept. for Education and Skills 2003) proposed four areas of service development for improving outcomes for children and families: early intervention and protection, supporting parents and carers, accountability and integration and workforce reform (Gardner 2003). Following from the Green Paper a Children Bill was introduced in March 2004 which provides for the establishment of a Children's Commissioner and a statutory framework which imposes a duty on local authorities to make arrangements for inter-agency co-operation between local authorities, key partner agencies and the voluntary and community sector. Thus family support in England as in Ireland is seen to have a history that is both restrained and promoted by its wider political and policy context.

Australia

In Australia the federal and state/territory governments fund family support services which are provided by the voluntary, community and private sectors. As with other countries, family support in Australia reflects the premise that services are a mechanism for protecting children but not a substitute for child protection (Fernandez 2004). The background to contemporary family support policy in Australia stems from the establishment of the Family Services Committee in 1975 whose mandate was to examine the needs of families and recommend the future role of government in delivering those services. In 1977, the Committee proposed the funding of services aimed at preventing family breakdown. This resulted in Commonwealth pilot funding of projects under the Family Support Services Scheme, provided by the voluntary and community sector. In 1985, the administrative responsibility for the funding of such projects shifted to the Commonwealth and States engaged in a 50/50 cost-sharing arrangement. By 1987, in the wake of a State Working Party report on the future of the Family Support Services Scheme, the Family Support Program (FSP) was launched, based on bilateral Commonwealth–State agreements with National Program guidelines including neighbourhood-based family support services, home management assistance and parent support as services eligible for funding (Family Support Australia 2000).

By 1998, the Commonwealth Government, whilst committed to the FSP, claimed that such services were essentially a State welfare responsibility. It was decided that the Commonwealth would maintain funding and State government would control program management. In practice this meant that the States received general revenue in which they could allocate funds to family support services on the basis of their own priorities. This transition of responsibility for FSP to the States was not due to any formal evaluation of the FSP, nor is there any official agreement which outlines the responsibility between the Commonwealth and the State governments regarding family support. This has resulted in considerable variation in the nature and scope of family support services. Some states, such as New South Wales, Queensland and Tasmania, continue to provide family support services as they were under the original Family Support Services Scheme. For example, Families First is an initiative of the NSW Government to support parents and carers bringing up children through the provision of co-ordinated services which focus on prevention and early intervention. Other states have diffused family support services across numerous departmental programmes, making it difficult to determine the nature and scope of services, as well as funding, across Australia (Family Support Australia 2000).

Family support in Australia at a federal level is being incorporated into wider social policy goals of welfare reform, social capital and the reinvigoration of local communities. Family support is therefore one component of a larger strategy whose overarching aim is to reinvigorate disadvantaged communities with initiatives to recognise and encourage volunteering and the value of community leadership as well as to provide additional family support through community identification and management of support programmes (Commonwealth of Australia 2002, p.35). The 'Stronger Families and Communities Strategy' was announced in April 2000 by the Prime Minister and is a Commonwealth initiative which signified a major shift in Australian social policy to early intervention and prevention responses.

The strategy is a component of a much wider policy initiative in Australia which bases social policy in the framework of what is known as the 'Social Coalition'. That is, the belief that social policy is best developed and delivered in partnership with communities, business and individuals (Commonwealth of Australia 2004, p.3). This derives from what would appear to be the Government's desire to foster community development, partnership and social capital. Indeed, a group of leading civil servants told an audience that there exists:

> a basic belief that governments alone cannot build capacity or trust i.e they cannot create social capital…at best governments can help to contribute to the supports and policy settings needed to strengthen the social fabric…at worst governments may actually erode community capacity and diminish trust through policies and programs that lead to dependency…pre-packaged program responses are often inappropriate to meet the diverse range of family and community needs. (McKay *et al.* 2000, p.3)

Underlying Australia's contemporary family support strategy is what Smith and Davies describe as a strong theme in Australian social policy, that is, 'that individuals have responsibilities and obligations to society and that they should plan and respond to problems in a self-reliant manner' (Smith and Davies 2002, p.10). The strategy is linked to a programme of welfare reform which aims to reduce the number of jobless families and households, reduce the proportion of the population relying on income support and build stronger communities. The activities of the strategy are in keeping with welfare reform and focus on areas of disadvantage to build community and family capacity in order to create a platform for economic and social participation for community members (Smith and Davies 2002, p.10). As with the two previous national case studies, to understand Australian family support requires an understanding of a wider and changing policy environment.

New Zealand

Sanders and Munford assert that family support services in New Zealand 'can be broadly defined as intensive home based support for families wanting to make changes in various aspects of family life, such as family relationships and parenting' (2003, p.169). As with the other countries considered in this chapter, family support services in New Zealand are provided within communities by a variety of non-governmental agencies funded by the Department of Child, Youth and Family. Within this context, the family support strategy 'Strengthening Families' is a component of a wider strategy 'From Welfare to Well Being', which aims to alleviate the intergenerational transmission of disadvantage within families. The 'Strengthening Families' strategy promotes co-ordination and collaboration to achieve health, educational and social outcomes for children and young people.

The strategy arose from awareness amongst public sector managers that a large proportion of spending in health, education and welfare was going to the same communities and within them to the same disadvantaged families. Yet the services were fragmented and families were receiving assistance from various service providers without any co-ordination. This lack of inter-agency co-ordination was said to be a consequence of the widespread state sector reforms including funding pressures and the introduction of the Privacy Act 1993, which was deemed as inhibiting the willingness of staff to share information across agencies.

In 1993 a pilot programme of Family Service Centres was introduced based on early intervention and inter-sectoral delivery model of social services to pre-school and primary school children and their families. However, the greatest impetus for contemporary family support services in New Zealand emerged in 1994 with the publication of the Christchurch Health and Development study (Fergusson *et al.* 1994) which highlighted the relationship between the presence of early risk factors in individual families and later more negative life outcomes. In October 1995 the New Zealand Cabinet required that a long-term strategy to strengthen families at risk be developed and that officials undertake a stock-take of existing programmes and policies which support and strengthen families. This exercise established that there was a lack of programmes which focus on intensive intervention with at-risk families.

In December 1997 the government agreed to establish a Targeted Family Service (now called Family Start), a home-based early intervention service to families in need of support, which aims to identify children in high-risk families at the birth of the child. The programme aimed at engaging with the families' informal and formal networks using a strengths-based perspective. Family workers would identify all the needs of all family members and create with them a strategy which drew on the families and their communities' strengths to meet those needs. Moreover, Family Start was not intended to replace services already in existence; rather it builds on work already being undertaken and complements services that now operate collaboratively.

There are four key Strengthening Families programmes: Family Start; Social Workers in Schools; Local Co-ordination; the Strategy for Children and Young People with High and Complex Needs. While the Ministries of Health, Education, Social Development and the Department of Children and Young Persons work together on policy development at the local level, a Strengthening Families Local Management Group is established in order to bring the service providers and community groups together and develop collaborative case management.

Whilst there is undoubtedly a need for greater collaboration between agencies supporting vulnerable families, as with other jurisdictions, New Zealand's family support policy needs to be understood in the context of the State's ideology surrounding welfare and governance. Contemporary family support policy is shaped by what Craig depicts as New Zealand's core economic and social policies. These send clear Third Way signals which he unequivocally describes as being 'hard nosed fiscal prudence, an open economy, wedded to a polysemous development of rubrics of "imagined inclusion"' (Craig 2003, p.336). He characterises the Labour government as one which seeks to manage economic constraints and promote social inclusion in the context of partnership with communities (Craig 2003).

In July 2004, the new Families Commission was established in New Zealand following The Families Commission Act 2003. The Commission is aligned to the Ministry of Social Development and its primary and legislative function is advocacy. The role of the Families Commission is to act as an advocate for families as social institutions at the government level and in the public sphere in general; the Commission also has a research on family and parenting issues responsibility and policy development function. Within the legislation establishing the Commission is a far-reaching definition of the family in order to adopt a broad and inclusive approach to families including: groups of people who are related by blood, adoption, extended family, two or more living together as family, *whanau* (family) or other recognised group. It excludes groups with common objectives such as gangs, flatmates, and professional or social organisations. At the time of writing the Commission has just been established and is in the process of getting up and running, yet its establishment has been well received in most quarters.

Lessons to be learned?

What lessons can be learned by comparing the family support policies of these four relatively similar jurisdictions from different sides of the globe? First, it is clear that one has to consider both history and context to uncover what family support as a policy is at any one moment in time. Specific legislation errs on the side of vagueness (and possibly caution) in categorically defining the concept and can be misleading. Therefore, any attempt to understand family support in a particular jurisdiction must go beyond legislation specifically addressed to family support. Other child welfare concerns need to be considered. In particular it should be recognised that family support primarily emerged in the context of policy moves in the wake of child abuse scandals. In addition it is the wider social policy goals of the late 1980s and early 1990s that dictated the way in which family support policy was conceived and implemented in individual countries. The wider social policy and economic trends reveal much about the role of family support and its delivery in the countries considered in this chapter.

Family support appears to be directly influenced by the general welfare and governance ideologies held by governments. The provision of services by voluntary and community groups funded by government typifies a new shared public management culture of purchaser/provider split, coupled with the view that governance by partnership is more effective in assisting the vulnerable and disadvantaged. Within the four jurisdictions there is a shared climate of Third Way partnership. As in many other areas of social policy, family support takes shape in local initiatives provided by the voluntary and community sector on behalf of the state. The relationship between these third sector groups and the state changed in the 1980s and 1990s with governments embracing family support services and incorporating them into wider social policy goals.

Voluntary and community bodies which were already providing support services to vulnerable and disadvantaged families were contracted by the state to provide such services on its behalf. Community and voluntary bodies are in effect implementing 'top-down' strategy objectives in a bottom-up approach, as partners with the state in solving local problems. Furthermore, in all four jurisdictions family support was found to be an area-based intervention in keeping with the Third Way focus on social inclusion measures aimed at promoting community regeneration and building social capital. Family support is deemed as having a key role to play in this process. It is officially recognised in key policy documents and strategies as having a pivotal role in key policy areas including not only child welfare but also education and health and, not least, the promotion of social inclusion.

Conclusion

The national case studies sketched out in this chapter highlight the need for practitioners and policy analysts alike to go beyond legislative measures supporting family support and unpack the policy space that promotes and constrains it. This involves considering the historical development of wider social and economic goals of government – many of which are found in strategy documents, conference papers, programmes for government and related social policy measures that family support practitioners may not immediately see as having relevance to them. By recognising that this breadth of perspective is necessary to explore what constitutes family support policy in other jurisdictions it becomes apparent that the same process must be followed by reflective practitioners in relation to their own countries. By exploring the space family support occupies in other countries reflective practitioners gain a better understanding of how to see what is possible in their own.

References

Adshead, M. and Wall, O. (2003) 'Policy Transfer in the Irish University Sector.' In M. Adshead and M. Millar (eds) *Public Administration and Public Policy in Ireland: Theory and Methods*. London: Routledge.

Brown, L. (2003) 'Mainstream or Margin? The Current Use of Family Group Conferences in Child Welfare practice in the UK.' *Child and Family Social Work 8*, 4, 331–340; *Child and Family Social Work 6*, 4, 327–336.

Commission on the Family (1998) *Strengthening Family for Life*. Dublin: Stationery Office.

Commonwealth of Australia (2002) *Australia's Background Report on Family Friendly Policies: OECD Review of Family Friendly Policies*. Canberra: Commonwealth of Australia.

Commonwealth of Australia (2004) *Stronger Families and Communities Strategy: National Agenda for Early Childhood*. Canberra: Commonwealth of Australia.

Craig, D. (2003) 'Reterritorialising health: Inclusive partnerships, joined-up governance and common accountability platforms in Third Way New Zealand? *Policy and Politics 31*, 3, 335–352 (18), 1 July.

DFES (2003) *Every Child Matters*. London: HMSO

Dolan, P. and Holt, C. (2002) 'What families want in family support: An Irish case study.' *Child Care in Practice 8*, 4, 239–250.

Dolowitz, D.P. and Marsh, D. (1996) 'Who Learns What from Whom? A Review of the Policy Transfer Literature.' *Political Studies 44*, 3, 343–357.

Featherstone, B. (2004) *Family Life and Family Support: A Feminist Analysis*. Basingstoke: Palgrave Macmillan.

Fergusson, D.M. Horwood, L.J., Lynksey, M.T. (1994) 'The childhoods of multiple problem adolescents: A 15-year longitudinal study.' *Journal of Child Psychology and Psychiatry 35*, 6, 1123–1140.

Fernandez, E. (2004) 'Effective Interventions to Promote Child and Family Wellness: A Study of Outcomes of Intervention through Children's Family Centres.' *Child and Family Social Work 9*, 1, 91–104.

Gardner, R. (2003) *Family Support: NSPCC Information Briefings*. London: NSPCC.

Higgins, K. and Pinkerton, J. (1998) 'Literature Reviewing: Towards a More Rigorous Approach.' In D. Iwaniec and J. Pinkerton (eds) *Making Research Work: Promoting Child Care Policy and Practice*. Chichester: Wiley.

Marsh, P. and Crow, G. (1998) *Family Group Conferences in Child Welfare*. Oxford: Blackwell.

McGuinness, C. (1993) *The Report of the Kilkenny Incest Investigation*. Dublin: Stationery Office.

McKay, R., Emerson, L., Delahunt, R. and Gifford, J. (2000) 'The Stronger Families and Communities Strategy: Prevention and Early Intervention Strategies in Family Policy.' Paper presented at Family Futures: Issues in Research and Policy. 7th Australian Institute of Family Studies Conference, Sydney, 24–26 July 2000.

Murphy, M. (1996) 'From Prevention to "Family Support" and Beyond: Promoting the Welfare of Irish Children.' *Administration 44*, 2, 73–101.

Pinkerton, J., Dolan, P. and Percy, A. (2003) 'Family Support in Ireland: Developing Strategic Implementation.' *Child Care in Practice 9*, 4, 309–321.

Rose, R. (2004) *Learning from Comparative Public Policy: A Practical Guide*. London: Routledge.

Sanders, J. and Munford, R. (2003) 'Lessons from the Evaluation of Family Support in New Zealand.' In I. Katz and J. Pinkerton (eds) *Evaluating Family Support: Thinking Internationally, Thinking Critically*. Chichester: Wiley.

Smith, B. and Davies, A. (2002) 'The Stronger Families and Communities Strategy: A Government Approach to Supporting Stronger Communities.' Paper presented at The Cutting-edge of Change: Shaping Local Government for the 21st Century, University of New England/ University of Western Sydney Armidale NSW, 15–17 February 2002.

Sundell, K., Vinnerlijung, B. and Ryburn, M. (2001) 'Social Workers' Attitudes Towards Family Group Conferences in Sweden and the UK.' *Child and Family Social Work 6*, 4, 327–336.

Taylor, B.J., Dempster, M. and Donnelly, M. (2003) 'Hidden Gems: Systematically Searching Electronic Databases for Research Publications for Social Work and Social Care.' *British Journal of Social Work 33*, 423–439.

Tunstill, J. (1995) 'The Concept of Children In Need: The Answer or the Problem for Family Support.' *Children and Youth Services 17*, 5/6, 651–664.

Tunstill, J. (1997) 'Implementing the Family Support Clauses of the 1989 Children Act: Legislative, Professional and Organisational Obstacles.' In N. Parton (ed) *Child Protection and Family Support: Tensions, Contradictions and Possibilities.* London: Routledge.

Part 2
Using Concepts, Frameworks and Tools

Chapter 7

Safeguarding Children Through Supporting Families

Ruth Gardner

Introduction

This chapter considers those aspects of reflective practice that are most relevant to family support and safeguarding children. Specifically, it gives detailed examples from the author's research of ways in which reflective practice, as described here, offers the potential to enhance family support practice. The chapter falls into two parts, one exploring reflective practice itself and the other considering this learning across family and service case examples. Key issues covered include:

- the role of learning, including error, in reflective practice

- the nature of expertise as distinct from expert knowledge

- the role of interpersonal skills in reflective practice

- the pay-off for children and families from reflective practice.

Ultimately the aim of preventive support is that concerns about children's welfare are addressed effectively, 'in a timely and sensitive way, with as little damage to the family as possible' (Gardner 1998, p.2). The approach described is positive and inclusive wherever possible, rather than defensive and risk-averse. The chapter uses both the terms 'child protection' and 'safeguarding children'. In England (whose policy and practice is used as the main reference base for this chapter) 'safeguarding children' conveys the general responsibilities of agencies, groups and individuals, without their necessarily having a statutory duty to act in cases of possible harm to children. The term 'child protection' tends to be reserved for interventions, usually by social services and the police, under Section 4 of the Children Act 1989 and its associated guidance. But, as always, there are overlaps and grey areas. Statutory agencies have a responsibility to develop strategies to keep *all* children in the community safe; this is a potential role for the new Safeguarding Children Boards. At the other end of the spectrum, agencies working in the community, such as schools and voluntary organisations, come into contact with specific child protection concerns and increasingly have formalised procedures to deal with them, and training in the use of these procedures.

Learning and reflective practice

Active learning is central to reflective practice, for example, 'the worker's capacity for appraisal and self-appraisal, and the ability to learn constructively from significant experiences' (adapted from Morrison 2004, p.41). Brockbank and McGill (1998, p.84) comparing the processes of learning and reflective practice, quote Harvey and Knight's description of the reflective practitioner as one 'who consciously engages in a dialogue between the thinking that attaches to actions and the thinking that deals in more propositional (abstract) knowledge'.

Our actions inevitably test and modify theory and derived understanding, as we contextualise them to our specific circumstances. This process brings with it the risk of failure to address those circumstances adequately. Brockbank and McGill suggest that without such constant reality testing, solitary reflection can become self-confirming. Even reflective dialogue between colleagues can be collusive, simply reaffirming received ideas: 'part of the skill in facilitating reflective learning through reflective dialogue is to grapple with that tendency for inter-personal collusion…if I do receive feedback about that of which I am unaware, I now have, at least, a choice. I may resist…but I am no longer ignorant' (1998, p.85).

Perhaps controversially, one could argue that all policy and guidance invite a degree of intellectual collusion because they imply that best practice can somehow be 'copied' from a text. In fact practice has constantly to be re-invented, to make adjustments in the light of current risks and opportunities, and it is this that constitutes real skill.

Active or critical reflection, it is argued here, is a vital constituent of practice that goes beyond learning about best practice or even hearing feedback on our own. It is a skill in the difficult process of internalising that feedback, then externalising and acting on it. It is about engaging with new realities, and this includes acknowledging the compromise between retaining consistency and adapting to a changing context. In learning theory terms this is 'deep learning'.

Most importantly, reflective practice uses poor outcomes and criticisms as constructive learning. As in all areas of endeavour, 'mistakes' are sources of discovery, effective adaptation and refinement of detail. The fact that in human services they can be very costly in every sense should not lead us to pretend they can be entirely eliminated – this denial can result in the collusion referred to above and a failure to give the feedback that can lead to improvement.

Brockbank and McGill (1998) argue that without engagement, teaching becomes purely 'transmittive' of data rather than truly informative, or transformative, of the recipient's learning. The analogy with child care practice seems to be good. Any amount of scanning and recording, however accurate, will be fruitless without a real interest in both the data and the people (colleagues, families) who have to use it, and a sense of why and how this data can improve a child's life.

Learning in a risky environment

The paradox of learning is that when we need to draw on it quickly, in a new or demanding situation, we may be too stressed to apply it creatively. Work with vulnerable children, who may or may not be at risk, presents just such pressure to be 'right first time'. Certainty is at a premium, the consequences of a misreading are potentially very serious, while those closely involved are often distressed and/or distressing. At such times the power of absorbing and synthesising information may be stimulated or else impaired by stress, depending on its degree and type and the individual's circumstances. Here, self-knowledge is just as important as other types.

Active reflection needs to be a matter of course and a natural way of thinking on task, rather than only in response to a crisis. Difficult situations can then be seen more as a challenge than as an insurmountable obstacle or threat. The practitioner's working environment and support structures make the difference between a difficult situation being a challenge or a threat. This framework includes personal and professional support, guidance both written and personal and constructive critique. Habitual and rehearsed reflection improves judgement of the nature of the challenge, and appraisal of what resources are needed to provide an adequate response, not only from the practitioner but from those (including family members, managers and whole organisations) who are party to the reality that has to change.

Specialists working with risk (surgeons, pilots or fire-fighters) are asked to simulate or enact the high pressure situation repeatedly, so that reflection for action is their immediate response to critical moments of stress, and all technical knowledge comes as 'second nature'. Munro (2002) describes reflective practice as 'holistic reasoning' that draws on both analytical and intuitive thought processes, arguing that in social welfare these two aspects of learning have been separated into a false dichotomy: 'intuitive reasoning can be more or less steered by explicit ideas or structured guidelines, and analytical methods may rely to varying degrees on intuitive skills in collecting and organising the necessary information' (p.3). She adds that practitioners should be prepared to use formal tools such as risk assessment as an evidence base, rather than a substitute, for their own judgement.

A supportive work environment allows the development of *expertise* – defined by Klein (2000, p.168) not as 'knowing more' but 'learning how to perceive': 'to spot patterns (that are invisible to a novice) and anomalies – things that do not fit the typical picture, and to have an overall picture of the situation; past, present and future'. Munro (2002, p.169) also quotes Klein's helpful definition of expert (in this context, fully reflective) practice. To paraphrase, such practice is:

- structured and deliberate, with clear goals and means of evaluation

- based on feedback checked for its accuracy, timeliness and use for diagnostic or assessment purposes

- based on an extensive bank of experience, both direct and indirect, that is regularly reviewed for learning and insight.

These are skills the individual can perfect and practise to some extent by him or herself. But as 'feedback' suggests, expertise in social care, particularly with vulnerable children, includes people skills, such the ability to *listen and communicate*, to *motivate* – in order to overcome obstacles to action, and to *act* in a timely way. An analytical approach to emotive experiences requires a structure and systems that support individual *and* group reflection.

The attributes of such an approach can be seen graphically in (thankfully rare) situations presenting critical choices in response to potentially life-threatening circumstances. One example is provided by the reported reactions of one individual during freak floods in Cornwall in August 2004, when many lives were saved by his getting people out of a hotel where they had taken shelter from the storm. His action, and theirs, in leaving an apparently sound building to face horrendous conditions – was, on the face of the evidence, unreasonable; but he persuaded them, correctly, that they were at much greater risk staying where they were.

Some accounts suggest such actions are purely intuitive, making 'heroism' a nearly magical phenomenon, rather like a hitherto ordinary person putting on Superman gear. Closer inspection indicates that 'heroic' actions result from a combination of (many different kinds of) knowledge and experience, reflection and effective communication, that in more mundane circumstances are collectively termed 'expertise'. What is special is the ability to act on these in both unexpected and highly stressful circumstances. In the case in question, the 'hero' had:

- *special and detailed knowledge of the context for the decision that was needed* – he had worked at the hotel ten years previously. This was a necessary but not a sufficient qualification; in addition, he was able to *recall the specific piece of relevant information* about that context, namely that the hotel was positioned directly over a culvert.

- *ability and motivation to put past and present evidence together*, to suspect the possibility that the unusual weather might cause the culvert to present a structural risk, then to go out and check that risk for himself.

- *ability, motivation and confidence to assume responsibility for taking action* based on his informed assessment. At this stage many people would have looked to share, debate or pass on responsibility.

- *authority with those he had to influence.* The components of this authority may have included: mutual knowledge, respect or trust; the urgency he communicated; the evidence he drew on to persuade them to do something counter-intuitive.

Such an account presents an extreme example of the ability to combine thinking that deals in knowledge with thinking that attaches to actions. We should not forget the elusive element of chance in such volatile situations; or 'luck' when applied to the individual. A different outcome might well have led to a different view of actions that appear well judged in the light of a given set of events. In the context of work with vulnerable families, the practitioner has to combine timely knowledge and reflection with judgement, persuasion and ultimately personal responsibility for their own and sometimes for others' actions.

Munro concludes (2002, p.170) that 'poor thinking tends to be characterised by a blinkered approach, considering few options, reaching conclusions too hastily, and then not paying attention to information that tells against that conclusion'. This refers both to over-reliance on external systems without regard to the context or unique features of a case, and also to over-hasty intuitive responses without the use of checks. A sense of individual and collective timing is all-important. Poor thinking applied to the above example would have been on the one hand to undertake a safety check (no time) and on the other to panic and create a stampede for the door.

Learning, reflective practice and family support

Family support services provide a good environment for learning about reflective practice in safeguarding children. Practitioners can work with a range of families, often with more time, choice of strategies and potential for positive feedback than is usually possible when working solely with crises. The work often requires close collaboration with family members, i.e. children, parents and other carers such as grandparents, parents' partners etc., and with other professionals such as health visitors and teachers.

There is thus a potentially wide spectrum of feedback to be obtained. This involves the challenge of reflection, negotiation and action, both individually and jointly. At best, collective dialogue and continuous evaluation are the outcome, taking account of difference rather than simply looking for common themes. While there is not usually the degree of stress and antagonism that child protection work can generate, preventive work often exerts long-term pressure of sustaining focus on individual and joint goals in the work and preventing loss of momentum. This is especially true of chronic low-level depression, child neglect or relationship problems.

Two (anonymised) illustrations of such practice are provided here from research commissioned by the National Society for the Prevention of Cruelty to Children (Gardner 2005). They concern family support services in the community where safeguarding children is a particular concern. While these real-life examples do not fit neatly into theoretical categories, they demonstrate evidence of the key elements discussed above, including continuous deliberation, seeking feedback, analysing and applying experience and developing a learning cycle.

Case example 1, reflective family support: Metropolitan Suburbs – seeking and using feedback as evidence of needs

In the 1990s, a handful of NSPCC workers in metropolitan suburbs were engaged in community development, action research and service delivery, in equal proportions. Rather than one survey or pilot study followed by a single funding process, there have been numerous smaller studies in partnership with various local groups and agencies. This process has meant an investment of time and funding in work on the joint local strategy, in parallel with direct work with families.

It could be argued that this diverts resources from helping children in need. However, project workers and other local staff thought that the involvement of families in research and planning led to services with greater impact relative to resources, because they were more relevant to local needs. Certainly it was the only project we studied, other than those specifically aimed at black families, which had succeeded in providing services to a diverse cross-section of local communities. The project's action research and strategic activity includes surveys of access to childcare and adult education opportunities for black and ethnic minority families; work to build a family support strategy for the city; and research into child safety in the project area, involving parents, workers and academics.

This effort to gain an overview of the needs of children and families locally was partly due to the community development experience of the project manager:

> ...she is prepared to ask the uncomfortable questions and is very clear – the excellence of the project is that it has developed services with others and in response to the changing needs of this area

> (Education Worker)

Practitioner research of this type contributes greatly to reflective practice in family support, identifying methods of safeguarding children more effectively in their own communities and thus preventing rather than responding to instances of harm. Fuller and Petch (1995, p.184) note that, depending on effective dissemination and implementation strategies, such work has the potential to impact on wider agency practice. It can raise awareness of feedback such as that of service users and can develop research-mindedness both in the researcher and in colleagues. Service users can also acquire research skills in collecting and organising evidence, increasing their skills and influence.

In the case of Metropolitan Suburb, a wide range of service developments has followed, some of which are described below. For a fuller account of the project's work, the reader is referred to Baldwin and Carruthers (1998). They found an apparent relationship between areas of deprivation and levels of child protection registration in the city. The current research also found a tendency for rates of child protection referrals and conferences to be higher, and child protection registration lower, where community family support is well developed, providing some evidence for effective preventive work at the stage when concerns have been identified.

The Metropolitan Suburb project has explicit aims, including:

- to work with parents to define their own needs and problems in bringing up children, to identify resources needed and parents' preferred solutions

- through collaborative work, to improve the sensitivity and effectiveness of local services for children and families

- to help parents provide written accounts of their experience which can be used in training professionals

- to identify and promote preventive initiatives to reduce child protection concerns

- to demonstrate the usefulness of self help and family support programmes as a major priority in child protection.

Parents who had been consulted thought this approach had made a difference to attitudes, increasing both their self-respect and respect from others. Parents quoted by Baldwin and Carruthers said:

> ...we have the same fears as professionals have for our children – we also have the same expectations for them as everyone else does. We have found that people do care about our children, but we need support to carry on caring. We all have a responsibility to keep children safe. Since we began talking to policy makers, attitudes about parents living on this estate have changed. Two years ago we were told that it would be impossible to have a safe play area on the estate. Now the local authority has identified £200,000 to build one, in consultation with local parents and children. The local authority has also shown a commitment to providing childcare and to ensure that their meetings are scheduled at times that parents can attend. The NSPCC has responded positively to our views by providing our area with co-ordination and administration time for the project...and providing support to local parents, particularly those more likely to be isolated, through a network of trained 'parent volunteers'. (Baldwin and Carruthers 1998, p.156)

Applying reflective learning

The project has developed sustainable interventions based on reflective practice. For example, it has combined professional knowledge, particularly in the fields of community development, adult education and child protection, to great effect by recruiting and training volunteers direct from the community to assist families. The benefits are multiple:

- The service is the result of a full and open consultation – it is therefore well known already and has a positive reputation.

- For most parents, there is less stigma in a volunteer service than in professionals visiting.

- The project had a more diverse group of service users and volunteers than others, as a result of its surveys and outreach services.

- The volunteers benefit from training and work experience and some go on to paid employment.

- Although volunteers are not a cheap option, there is cost saving in some cases – the cost of training volunteers and support to families was offset by savings on crisis services which in some cases were the only alternative.

Furthermore, the infrastructure that makes this scheme work is carefully planned and every volunteer is provided with a volunteer pack job description, person specification, self-assessment, police checks, training and regular supervision.

Parents' activities, social and educational opportunities

Other services run by the NSPCC Metropolitan Suburb project include parents' activity groups. A two-hour weekly lunchtime group offers a variety of sessions on subjects including art, decorating, child development and health. Parents can take part in more adventurous activities such as canoeing or climbing, while the children are in a crèche. The value of the activity group to parents lies partly in meeting others and having a break from the children. The educational, fun approach also had results for women who subsequently took up adult education, for which this authority has a strong reputation. Many were studying maths, computing or/and English and said their confidence had greatly increased as a result. Some had gone on to further education and/or employment.

'Together Into Play' sessions offered an activity-based approach for parents to learn about child development, child health, play and learning with their children. A bilingual parents' group with a pre-school children's play morning is held where workers are available who speak Hindi, Punjabi, Urdu and English. Through this group, held in their local health centre, mothers also learnt of and accessed other preventive services such as local authority services for children in school holidays. Ten-week courses are run on subjects such as stress management, how to help with counselling, and handling children's behaviour.

The project has tried to find creative ways to involve fathers, for instance, a male member of staff has used sports venues to try to get men's groups going. More investment is needed in developing these ideas, and since this research concluded, there has been an internal seminar to explore and develop family support for fathers. Many of these initiatives have since been funded and developed within central government's family support programmes such as Sure Start.

Views of the project and its work

The fact that the NSPCC project was based on the estate it served, and that the project manager showed energy and courage in speaking out about local issues, had earned respect from local workers:

> I think it's an excellent project because it has evolved with the needs of the area. The volunteer visiting helps with isolated parents, encourages them to use services. In adult education we have spent a long time promoting the service, knocking on doors, posting leaflets, and we researched the childcare and adult educational needs of the Black and Asian communities with the [NSPCC] project. That is paying off – we've got a lot of full courses running.
>
> (Community Education Officer)

Pauline aged 26, with one child, said:

> I do the mum's activity group and the group about playing with children, and I've done three ten-week courses. It has helped me not to get over-stressed and to deal with situations – money for instance – better. I wanted somewhere safe for the children, for their well-being; they get good care. Now, rather than shout at [three-year-old] I try to react calmly.

Adapting services on the basis of reflective practice

The Metropolitan Suburb's project is based on community development and systems theory. The project workers took the view that dealing with family crisis and stress by one-to-one case work *on its own* is ultimately insufficient. It can provide a clear framework and child-centred goals but may also reinforce a family's isolation and highlight problem behaviour. Group and educational approaches can be used to encourage mutual learning and combat social isolation, attracting resources to challenge poverty and poor environment, at least in local terms. For example, the project arranged the bulk purchasing of some household items. Such an approach has the enormous benefit of encouraging both personal *and* community growth. It does not pretend to cure all underlying structural ills, but it clarifies their nature and potentially gives service users more say in use of resources.

The project's evidence-based approach appears more structured and open to partnership than earlier models of community work. There is encouraging evidence that the project is meeting at least the short term support needs, over six months, of mothers and children, in a local authority where levels of children accommodated or on child protection registers are high. Numbers of service users and trained volunteers at the project have grown each year.

Case example 2, reflective practice and family support: Metropolitan Outskirts – seeking and using feedback as evidence of needs

As with the previous example, this project was developed on the basis of several years' analysis of referrals, identifying gaps in the response to families under stress. Reflective practice is used to continuously review and modify services in response to changes in demand. Local families can access a number of levels of support just by walking down the street and knocking on the project door. For instance, the project runs a weekly support group for parents and children as well as offering therapeutic and recovery work from the effects of trauma such as domestic violence or childhood abuse: practical advice and a safe place for children and families.

Clear goal-setting and monitoring effectiveness

The broad aims of the project are to support families, prevent abuse and to empower the local community. This combination of safeguarding children and supporting families is reflected in the service objectives for pre-school children. These are to provide:

- a facility where pre-school children can be left and cared for while parents attend workshops on issues which directly affect their parenting

- participating children with a 'high warmth, low criticism' environment in which they can feel free to play and learn

- a safe, nurturing and stimulating environment in which all children have an opportunity to advance their physical, intellectual, emotional and speech development in order for them to achieve their full potential.

Similar objectives apply to two after-school clubs run for older children on a weekly basis, with all these services being provided by two full-time workers with the support of volunteers. The parents' support group acts as a drop-in, so that visitors can find out more about the other services being offered without necessarily referring themselves. It provides the opportunity to obtain information about child development and about local services for children and adults, well as support to access other services if they are wanted.

Applying reflective learning

The workshops described below offer the additional opportunity for parents to use reflective learning themselves. The two staff members run cycles of three-day workshops, for children aged 8 to 15, for teenage girls aged 14 to 17, and for women. Each series of workshops addresses specific issues such as 'parents under stress', 'journey to recovery', 'the inner child'. Each has specific objectives set out below.

- *Parents under stress:*
  - to identify stresses and other factors in parenting
  - to develop new coping networks which facilitate positive relationships with children and promote listening to children
  - to help parents develop a positive future for themselves and a high warmth, low criticism environment for their children

- *Journey to recovery:*
  - to provide a group of women survivors of abuse in childhood and/or violence in adulthood with a 'safe place' to tell their own stories and witness those of others in a non-shaming group

- ○ to contribute to their own and others' safe parenting
- ○ to reclaim their own potential for recovery from abuse
- *Inner child:*
  - ○ to further develop the 'safe place' established within the previous workshops, using art materials and creativity
  - ○ to help parents develop positive experiences with their own children by experiencing childhood activities for themselves
  - ○ to enable parents to make positive choices about their own and their children's futures.

All these workshops are evaluated by exit questionnaires and all are oversubscribed. Some of the men we spoke to who had experienced abuse wanted a similar service. Service users can attend a cycle of workshops more than once, and a few are trained and supported to assist with running them. From the comments of the parents, children and referring agencies, the research identified the following elements in the perceived success of this model:

CLEAR STRUCTURE AND ETHOS

- providing an environment where all communication, including criticism, is as constructive as possible and participants are encouraged to support one another

- providing opportunity for exploring past or present experiences, whether damaging or otherwise, in a confidential, safe environment which will allow participants to stop blaming themselves and move on

- providing access to other opportunities, for example, specialist advice or support; adult education; training as a volunteer; employment.

CONTINUITY OF STAFFING, LOCAL KNOWLEDGE AND INTER-AGENCY TRUST

Staff had worked in the local authority area for some years, and a good level of trust existed between individuals and agencies. One of the project staff had worked in the local social services. Thresholds for referral were mutually understood. A menu or continuum of services existed on site, offering families some control over where and how they sought help and at what level of intensity.

There was an emphasis on recovery, skills and strengths, recognising that the majority of parents are both willing and able to be effective and safe carers. There were also clear professional boundaries and responsibilities in the project. These matters were explicit in policy documents, information leaflets, statements of values and conducts, and complaints procedures, which were posted up and readily available. For instance, because the project was located within the estate, it was seen as extremely important that staff were punctilious about service users' right to confidentiality and privacy, especially that of children and staff. Therefore, volunteers did not greet parents they met in the public areas until they were greeted. Another example is that the children interviewed knew, and told the researcher, how they could complain to NSPCC's regional office.

Children knew, and their parents agreed, that unless their immediate safety was at risk, anything they said would not be quoted outside, even to members of their own family. They said that this was part of the introduction to the project. Staff contacted service users and arranged to see them and explain the centre before a first visit. Staff returned phone calls, notes and messages. There were lapses and mistakes, but service users mentioned these in the context of a service that set and maintained a high standard of communication.

These strict 'rules of conduct', repeatedly stated and followed, might appear overly bureaucratic. However, the 'rules' gave many parents a sense of respect and safety within the project that was exceptional in their dealings with professionals, and for a few also exceptional in their personal lives. The project gave a clear message that individuals were valued and should value themselves.

Feedback on the project

Parents valued having a range of services readily available at, or through, the same access point. These included informal social drop-in; advice for their children and/or as a parent; and specialised intensive group work without lengthy referral to deal with past or present trauma. Most parents accepted that serious concerns about their own parenting might be reported by the NSPCC to social services and/or the police. Those who had this experience said that they had been supported by the NSPCC in improving their parenting, and continued to receive family support from the NSPCC throughout and beyond the child protection process.

In the context of our discussion of reflective practice, the amount of learning demonstrated by the service user feedback is impressive. We need to establish whether and, if so, how, such learning is consolidated and used by parents over the long term, but there is evidence that reflective practice in family support is also educative practice. It models self-awareness, constructive criticism and evidence-gathering to make the case for change or development on the personal and group levels. Where practitioners are reflective and applying their learning, parents are empowered to be the same.

Diana, aged 36, with two children, described experiences of serious assault as a child:

> We were strapped as children, the children were stood in a corner and told not to answer back; I remember my brother black and blue from it. I moved around with my husband's work for many years and he got violent. I left him with the children after 18 years and went into a refuge.

She thought that the project had allowed her the distance and support to seek alternatives to displaying anger to her very destructive nine-year-old: 'Many times I felt like hitting her, but I didn't; I thought "if I do that I'm no better than him". He hit me, not them, he was good with children generally, he just shouted at them. Now, I stop the children's treats rather than shout at them.'

In another example, Molly, a grandmother aged 56, described what she saw as the consequences of a family history of abuse, and an immediate experience of violence and insecurity, for her grandchildren:

> My grandchild Jane is nine years old and was in a Refuge for three months when she was five, and for three months last year. Her mother has had three violent partners and Jane is violent to her sister and brothers, and when she is restrained – she kicked the wardrobes in at the refuge. Even so, she is top of the class in reading. Her brother is seven – he has Oppositional Defiance Disorder, it's like ADHD but Ritalin doesn't work. He watched his mother being raped. He is in a special unit now – calming down a bit. These problems have been passed on I believe; I was abused as a child and I was so ashamed of myself, I married the first man who came along and he did the same to my daughters. Only one of my daughters did the same though. I think it can be stopped for my grandchildren, now they are getting help. It shocked me when my grandson came to the workshop and said 'What makes me sad? Seeing my dad strangling my mum'.

In order to support her daughter's family, Molly needed support herself, but the project allowed her to use her experience, including her mistakes, to assist other's reflective learning.

> Volunteering, supporting other parents, makes me feel better and I am putting something back for all the help NSPCC gave me. I get maintenance support from the project – keeping me on an even keel when I get low. For Jane – she can get her emotions expressed, her bad experiences, and it leaves room for her to have a normal life and be a little girl, to achieve more. It's the only place I know where children can get this out and it is not judged too horrible to hear – the only place you get affirmed as a good parent. It is about changing perceptions, recognising that people need help in a safe place without thinking your child might be snatched. Prevention sums it up. I go and help with social services' training for child protection workers now.

Summary

Family support work provides good opportunities for skills in observation, gathering of data and participative feedback with families and other practitioners. Safeguarding children requires abilities to sift information for patterns of concern, to assess risk, to communicate and act both authoritatively and sensitively. With the right configuration of skills and supports, it is possible to combine the learning from these areas. Such work has the potential to link observation and analysis, feedback and action, thus improving reflective practice at both ends of the service spectrum.

Reflective practice is primarily about *informed judgement and action based on evidence and feedback*. To paraphrase an earlier quotation, it requires the *ability to engage in a dialogue, both internally and with others, between the thinking that attaches to actions and the thinking that deals in ideas*. Learning about the views of service users, and applying evidence of service effectiveness, are equally important in trying to achieve best practice in preventive work. This should result in a *creative adaptation of what is known to be effective, to local needs and circumstances*.

At a strategic level these ideas are now built into the Best Value framework for local authority services, a framework that broadly reflects the principles of reflective practice. This framework identifies:

- the *challenge* in terms of unmet need
- national and local *comparisons* as to what is achievable
- the means of *consulting* with those most involved to create an action plan
- *collaborative or competitive strategies* to implement the plan.

There is thus a possibility of developing a learning ethos across whole organisations leading to better outcomes for children and families in need.

References

Baldwin, N. and Carruthers, L. (1998) *Developing Neighbourhood Support and Child Protection Strategies.* Aldershot: Ashgate.

Brockbank, A. and McGill, I. (1998) *Facilitating Reflective Learning in Higher Education.* Buckingham: Open University Press.

Gardner, R. (1998) *Family Support.* Birmingham: Venture Press.

Gardner, R. (2003/2005) *Supporting Families: Child Protection in the Community.* (2005 revised paperback) Chichester: Wiley.

Fuller, R. and Petch, A. (1995) *Practitioner Research: The Reflexive Social Worker.* Buckingham: Open University Press.

Klein, G. (2000) *Sources of Power: How People Make Decisions.* Cambridge, MA: MIT Press.

Morrison, T. (2004) *Staff Supervision in Social Care.* Brighton: Pavilion.

Munro, E. (2002) *Effective Child Protection.* London: Sage.

Chapter 8

Youth Advocacy: Programming Justice-focused Family Support Intervention

Jeff Fleischer, Judy Warner, Carla J. McCulty
and Michael B. Marks

Introduction: providing support for those who may have been forgotten

Youth justice and human service systems are responsible for children, youth and families requiring extensive support. Even the harshest critics of these systems concede that they provide beneficial services for many youth and families. Yet there are many others who do not seem to benefit from the services or make the positive changes the system expects. These are the persons labeled as 'not amenable to service', 'socially deviant', or some other negative designation. The final label applied by the system is that an individual is not 'community ready' and therefore needs to be treated in isolation. The end result is often recommendation and referral to an out-of-home placement or an institution such as a group home, high-support secure facility, psychiatric hospital, residential treatment center, detention center or correctional facility.

Not all human services providers accept the notion that out-of-home placement is the best or only alternative for extremely high-risk children and youth. Youth Advocate Programs, Inc. (YAP), an internationally recognized human services agency, exemplifies those dedicated to community-based alternatives to residential care. Since 1975 YAP has been demonstrating the viability of reduced reliance on institutional and other out-of-home placements. YAP's strength-based model has proven effective as an alternative to placement and as an aftercare program for those returning from institutions. This innovative model is distinguished by its ability to meet the needs of diverse and challenging target populations, including those 'forgotten' or lost in institutions.

This chapter examines key elements of YAP's Family Support programming for young people who have come to the attention of the justice and welfare systems, highlighting strategies to reduce the high costs – both monetary and in quality of life – that result from unnecessary out-of-home placement of 'difficult' or 'incorrigible' youth. The chapter is structured as follows:

- History, context and overview of the model

- Approaching 'difficult' youth and families

- Four pillars of community-based care

- Guiding principles of YAP's Family Support model

- Supportive evidence and outcomes of the YAP.

Using YAP as a case study, the chapter's key aim is to illuminate for the reader key elements of what Family Support interventions for extremely challenging target populations look like in practice.

History, context and overview of the model

YAP was founded in 1975 by Tom Jeffers, a leader in advocacy for system change. The agency's core mission is to provide community-based, community-safe alternatives to out-of-home placement of high-risk young people. YAP is a private, non-profit, charitable organization dedicated exclusively to non-residential services. The agency's first program served approximately 100 youths incarcerated in an adult state prison in the Commonwealth of Pennsylvania. Within three months of their referral to YAP, those youth had been returned to appropriate settings in their communities. With its strengths-based approach, YAP's initial reintegration project was dramatically different from other interventions. Advocates worked directly in family homes and neighborhoods rather than offices, focusing on development of youth and family capabilities to achieve long-term change.

The success of this approach resulted in YAP's expansion to its current international service area. YAP today works with over 8,000 families annually, providing family support services for families with abused, neglected or emotionally needy children, as well as prolific young offenders. YAP has programs in ten of the United States. Additionally, YAP/Ireland and YAP/UK are following the YAP model, as are 'sister agencies' in Hawaii, Belfast in Northern Ireland, Guatemala, Sierra Leone and Leicester and Sunderland in England. YAP works in major metropolitan areas including New York City, London, Dublin, Houston, Washington DC, Phoenix, Akron, Dallas, Fort Worth, and

Tampa as well as dozens of other urban, suburban and rural communities. YAP's model is proving effective in interventions with youth gangs in Fort Worth, Texas; members of the travelling community in the West of Ireland; families living in poverty in rural South Carolina; newly arrived immigrants living in inner-city London; families with substance abuse issues in North Dublin; young people returning from institutions to their communities in New York City; and street children in Guatemala.

YAP's Family Support Program follows an innovative wraparound/ advocacy model. Wraparound is an intensive, integrated and community-based intervention, pioneered in the United States by John VanDenBerg, who managed the Alaska [Wraparound] Youth Initiative in 1985. The Family Support model blends YAP's unique community advocacy approach and wraparound elements such as family teams introduced by Dr VanDenBerg. In YAP's context, advocacy encompasses an array of individualized services provided by trained, supportive adults, who live in or near the same communities as the families they serve.

Supportive evidence for YAP's approach is continuing to emerge. Eric J. Bruns, a leading services researcher, acknowledges that 'because there are so many variations of wraparound and so many ways in which this value-based process may be administered from community to community, the question: 'Does wraparound work?' has been difficult to answer' (Bruns 2004). Bruns concludes that 'what we have learned about wraparound so far is highly encouraging, and tells we are on the right track'. Bruns also notes that 'wraparound is not a simple phenomenon' but instead has been 'an evolving and grassroots movement' (ibid.).

For almost 30 years, YAP's model has also been evolving, influenced by practitioners, trainers and writers in the strength-based and individualized planning field. The work of John McKnight, Jerome Miller, Edgar Cahn, John VanDenBerg and others is reflected in YAP's model. A comprehensive discussion of supportive evidence is beyond the scope of this chapter; however, resources and reports are cited in the References.

Approaching 'difficult' families: tuning into the feelings of all involved

'Tuning into' and validating the feelings of both family members and the worker who is trying to help are critical elements of YAP's Family Support approach. As practitioners, we have all encountered persons who agree to service plans but seldom follow through and who seem to sabotage and undermine our treatment plans. YAP has worked with many young people who have been placed in institutions unnecessarily because human service systems and youth justice systems were unable to partner with clients and provide support necessary to keep the family together. Experience has shown that if we forget the labels and take time and energy to examine what the family members are feeling, we will often find that their behavior may be quite understandable – even 'normal'.

Families in crisis may feel guilty, humiliated, judged, blamed, disrespected, pushed, defensive, isolated, hopeless, exhausted, overwhelmed, alienated, angry, depressed, failed, coerced, frustrated, pessimistic, disappointed and distrustful. When we acknowledge the feelings that families may bring to a helping relationship, we can understand why those families sometimes get defensive, undermine plans, vent their anger or simply disappear from service. At the same time, many workers may feel overworked, under-supported, frustrated, angry, blamed, distrustful, skeptical, confused, defensive and hopeless that any progress can be made. When workers and families with such unacknowledged feelings come together, behaviors can be misinterpreted and premature recommendations for out-of-home placements can be made.

Workers need to understand their own feelings and the judgments and values they may convey – in essence place themselves in the 'shoes' of the family. The ability to convey understanding and interest in the absence of blame is the foundation for building trust between the worker and the family. Mutual trust is the basis of an effective working partnership that results in successful outcomes. As discussed in this chapter, a trust relationship is essential to YAP's model of Family Support.

The four pillars of YAP's community-based care

While Family Support services are flexible and individualized, there are consistent underlying core elements. These four pillars are:

- community advocacy
- a needs-led approach
- a no reject, no eject policy
- the development of semi-formal and natural supports.

Community advocacy: trust relationships with young people and families

Caring, trained and supportive adult role models (advocates) are matched with each young person and family. Working from a positive, strength-based perspective, advocates build trust relationships that are the basis for development of youth and family capabilities. The ability to build these relationships relates in part to the characteristics of the advocates themselves. Because they are recruited from the neighborhoods where the young person and family live, advocates are not viewed as 'outsiders'. Key qualifications for advocates are: knowledge of local culture and resources; availability; ability to relate well to troubled young people and their families; and a desire to help others and give back to the community. Also necessary are maturity and stability, self-aware-ness, ability to take a non-judgmental approach, willingness to learn new skills and a personal sense of optimism. Advocates recruited over the years include: social workers, teachers, youth workers, accountants, fire fighters, police, housewives, unemployed persons, recovering addicts, ex-offenders, business owners, horse trainers, former gang members, relatives of referred families, office workers, athletes, laborers, mechanics, redundant coal miners and ship builders, university students and graduates of YAP programs. While their backgrounds are diverse, advocates share a commitment to community, a good sense of per-severance, resourcefulness and dedication.

Although there are no rigid credential or experience requirements for advocates, they receive extensive orientation training, weekly supervision by a skilled supervisor, and ongoing monthly training. Advocates work with small caseloads (typically two to three youth at any given time), spending an average of 15 hours per week with the youth and family. Three or more weekly face-to-face contacts are made. Service levels can be increased or decreased according to youth and family needs. Staff are accessible to families at all times. Advocates support the family, broker for services, mediate conflict, teach life skills, provide crisis intervention, and help families and community team members implement individualized service plans. In some situations, a family may be assigned more than one advocate with each playing a different supportive role.

Needs-led approach

Rather than fitting family needs into narrow diagnostic categories, YAP takes a broader view, examining the interrelationships of various needs and the impact of unmet needs on youth and family functioning. Services are tailored to the unique needs and circumstances of each youth and family. While services are youth and family centered, they also provide for adequate supervision to insure the safety of both clients and communities. To develop resources and commu-nity linkages appropriate for each family, staff think creatively, going beyond the kinds of assistance or problems that are typically addressed. Through a strength-based team process, youth and families address the underlying causes of immediate problems and learn to prepare for the future.

Very often, it is necessary to address concrete as well as emotional needs to support the family in maintaining their children at home. Two extracts from YAP case histories demonstrate this point.

> Sam was a chronic offender who lived with his mother and sister. The family was on the verge of becoming homeless due to an eviction notice from their landlord. A YAP worker invited a real estate agent, some

neighbors and a local church pastor to a family team meeting. The real estate agent worked pro bono to help find an affordable apartment for the family. The neighbors agreed to mobilize and to help the family move their things. The church pastor offered to pay for the first month's utilities. In the midst of the meeting, Sam's mother turned to him and said that, with all of these people helping, 'if we can't make it now, we'll never be able to'. The meeting ended with Sam and his mother laughing, and sharing that this was the first time they had laughed and felt hope in a long time.

Brian was also a young man with a long history of system involvement. His parents were deceased, and he had been in care for most of his life. He was being released from placement in a residential facility, but had nowhere to go. His only known supports were his grandparents, who were residing in a welfare motel with no room for him. YAP was asked to plan for Brian's transition. A family team meeting included Brian, his grandparents, his juvenile probation officer (JPO), his child-welfare worker, and YAP staff. The primary needs were space for the entire family, access to public transportation, and air conditioning for the grandfather's emphysema. Through discussion, it was learned that the grandfather and JPO were both war veterans. The JPO helped the grandfather access a veterans' program for home-buyers. The family was able to buy a home for the first time. A lawyer was recruited to work pro bono with the family to help with the closing of the house, and a local church agreed to help the family with the cost of setting up their utilities.

While there were other problems to be addressed with these families, housing was clearly a priority need. Mobilization of informal supports not only solved an immediate problem, but also connected the families with community resources having potential to help address other issues. These are but two examples of how the needs-led approach provides meaningful family support.

'No reject, no eject' policy and commitment to unconditional care

In order to reach youth and families at highest risk, YAP operates under an inclusive intake policy. Youth and families are accepted regardless of their case histories, 'labels' they carry, or complexity of needs. Acceptance into a YAP program carries with it a commitment to unconditional care. YAP does not unilaterally terminate any youth or family due to case management difficulties, resistance, non-compliance or similar difficulties. When progress falls short of expectations, staff work with the family to revise strategies and try again.

Development of semi-formal and natural supports

A primary goal is to help youth and families build a network of supports that will help sustain them in the long term. The family team described later in the chapter represents one strategy used to develop natural supports. Other informal supports are very often neighborhood resources such as: a group run by a small neighborhood church; an informal special interest group such as a chess club or music group; or a local carpenter who is willing to teach woodworking skills to youth. Although they are easily overlooked they are often valuable in promoting behavioral change.

Michael, for example, was a gang-member at risk of detention for multiple offenses, primarily for stealing bikes and cars. He was initially very resistant at opening up to YAP staff but finally admitted that he was good at 'fixing things.' YAP worked with the local police department and arranged for them to donate unclaimed stolen bikes to Michael. He repaired the bikes and donated them to a local group home as part of his community service. He was also linked with a job at a bicycle shop, and his employer became a positive role model and mentor in his life.

Community linkages can also help high-risk young people learn to care about others and become helpers themselves. Like Michael, LaVar was also a gang-member with a long history of involvement in the juvenile justice system, including gun possession. The local judge allowed YAP to meet with LaVar at the detention facility to create an individual service plan for him. Although they were divorced, both of his parents also attended the meeting with the YAP team. Initially LaVar was very resistant, and neither he nor his family could identify any of his strengths. After many attempts to connect with him in the interview, it was discovered that he liked math. From that one strength, a plan was developed for LaVar to tutor younger children in math and receive a stipend. His mother was helped to organize a support group for mothers of children in gangs, and his father became more involved in LaVar's life. The local probation department tracked LaVar over the years and reported that he has not surfaced in the juvenile or adult systems at any point since the intervention.

Another of YAP's innovative linkages is its Supported Work program. The program is designed for young people and family members whose plan calls for a job or training program. Those persons who lack marketable skills and work experience are hired by YAP as an employee and placed in a local private sector work site. In return, the employer pledges to provide support, training and a beginning job experience. Supported Work is particularly effective for young offenders who need positive work experiences and income to replace their offending behavior. With the guidance of an advocate, the effort helps to link the young person with positive community persons in a normalized setting.

Guiding principles of the YAP model

The following core principles of service delivery comprise the framework for YAP's Family Support model. These principles are emphasized in staff training and are inherent in all Family Support interventions.

Principle: Focus on strengths

Interventions emphasize strengths of the family, not the pathology, weakness and deficits. A spirit of partnership is established with the families so that their capabilities can be developed in the context of discovered strengths.

Great effort is made very early in the helping relationship to identify the capacities, talents and competencies of each family member. Taking a strength-based approach early on helps to decrease defensiveness and begin development of a respectful, helping relationship. The worker relates to the person as a whole human being with an array of behaviors and characteristics. Family members are helped to feel that they are persons worthy of respect, not just 'problem people'.

Principle: Individualized service planning

Interventions are tailored to specific child and family needs and include a blend of formal and informal services and supports.

The principle of individualized service planning challenges the worker to seek ways to partner with the family and other community persons to fashion a way of support tailored to specific family circumstances and needs. Because needs change over time, it must be assumed that the plan will also need to change to remain meaningful to the family. Individualized service planning takes time, partnership, creativity, imagination and the ability to identify and link with both formal and informal supports in the community. For families who have been unsuccessful with traditional human service systems, crafting an individualized plan is not only worth the effort, but may in fact be the *only* way to achieve positive outcomes.

YAP's process for developing an Individual Service Plan (ISP) includes two components: the *strength-based assessment* and the *family team planning* meeting. Underlying each component are three basic questions:

1. What do you need?

2. How can we help?

3. How do we work together as equal partners?

It is interesting to note that many families who have been deeply entrenched in the system for years often comment that no one has ever asked them these questions. Strength-based assessments are essentially a means of gathering information on the capabilities, assets, needs and interests of the young person and family. The four tools YAP uses to gather this information are outlined below.

Strength-based assessment

1. *The life domain bubble chart.*

   The life domains illustrated on the chart reflect areas of each human being's life that can impact functioning at any given time. The chart is used to learn from the family:

   - what they identify as their *needs* in each life domain area

   - what *resources or supports* they have in their life at that time to address or help in each of those needs

   - their *priority order* of the needs they have identified.

   The bubble chart can be a very non-threatening way to involve the family. It can be written in multiple languages, pictures can be used to represent a particular life domain area, and families can actively participate.

2. *Strengths inventory.*

   The strengths inventory is used to *identify what skills and capacities the young person and family already have.* Oftentimes the youth or family may have difficulty identifying their strengths and may tell only the 'bad things' about themselves. The worker's role is to help them to see strengths by breaking them down into the simplest of components if necessary (i.e. if a young person has a history of not showing up for school or meetings, the worker can comment that his/her presence at the meeting is a strength indicating that they do care and want to try). Workers learn the strength of the young person by observing, interviewing and asking direct questions and asking others that young person knows.

3. *Community linkages/interests.*

   While the strengths inventory identifies past/current experience or expertise, the interest inventory helps to elicit *what the youth or family might be interested in becoming involved with,* regardless of whether they have had the opportunity to do so. The most effective interest survey is one that is developed within the local community based on the resources that exist within that area. The more resources listed on the survey, the greater chance of the youth and family identifying at least one activity that may be of interest to them. (One of the many benefits of hiring advocates from the local communities is their knowledge of such resources.)

4. *Strength-based planning tool.*
   The final tool is called the strength-based planning tool. It is used
   after completing the first three assessments with the family and is
   essentially a summary and template from which a family team is built.
   A list identifies supportive persons and associations who can help get
   a need met, a strength developed or an interest nurtured.

Family Team meeting and development of the individual service plan

The Family Team meeting is a critical part of the planning process. Organizational tasks include: working with the family to identify or recruit potential family team members; cultivating relationships with potential team members and identifying potential resources within the community. The family is the most important part of the team. Additionally a team may include many different people, both formal (or professional) and informal. Cultural sensitivity is particularly important with Family Teams. When case planning conferences include only professionals, the team members are not necessarily sensitive to the family's culture. YAP has found that families become active team players when they have the power to invite persons to the planning meeting. The persons they invite are often of the same culture as the family or persons familiar with and sensitive to the culture of the family. Some examples of potential family team members include:

- family
- juvenile probation officer
- teacher/guidance counselor
- coach
- pastor
- scout leader

- child welfare worker
- tutor
- employer
- neighbor
- local mechanic
- best friend.

If a family member is incarcerated or otherwise not available, workers must think creatively. The most important task for the worker is to make sure that all team members feel included in the process and that their role is valued by the group. After the team is organized, members meet to help link the needs, strengths and interests of the family with actual interventions, resources and people. The ISP is the final part of the planning process. Information gathered from the assessments and during the team meeting is compiled in a written plan that is shared with all team members. Roles and responsibilities are defined and agreed upon. The ISP is fluid, dynamic and frequently reviewed and amended by the family team as appropriate. The community advocate or advocates are then assigned to the family to provide support and to help to implement the plan.

Principle: True partnerships with parents

Families are co-designers of their own services.

A true partnership with parents or guardians is grounded in equality. Equality means that workers must share their power with the family in the development of an individualized service plan. This may be very difficult for professional workers to consider. Workers with years of education and experience may be reluctant to cede power to a parent or guardian who may have been abusive, neglectful or drug addicted. The reality is that the parent or guardian is the expert on their own family. They know their own children better than most and they typically want what is best for their children and family. Very often, YAP finds that young people do better when their service plan is developed with parent involvement rather than by strangers. Moreover, many parents will react defensively if they are simply told what to do by well-meaning professionals. They tend to take ownership and react with hopefulness and enthusiasm when they have a voice at the table, are treated with respect and can participate in a meaningful way. The resulting plan is much more realistic and effective when the family's needs and ideas are driving the work.

Principle: Neighborhood-based recruitment of staff

Staff respect, appreciate and understand different cultures and values. Staff recruitment policies help ensure that staff reflect, to the fullest extent possible, the ethnic and cultural backgrounds of the families they serve.

Not only are there many and varied formal cultures but we also find that each family has its own culture that requires attention. ISPs must include strategies and people sensitive to the subtleties of the family's culture to support those strategies. YAP's policy is to hire workers who live in the same neighborhood or community as the family. This type of 'postal code' or 'zip code' staff recruitment practice has been shown to help the family lessen its defenses and feel less intimated by 'outsiders'. When the worker is of the same culture, understands the neighborhood, and speaks the same language, the family is more willing to engage the worker and feels more comfortable with the helping process.

Principle: Family-focused intervention

The unit of the intervention is the family, not just the young person.

In many youth justice programs, the identified client is the young person and most or all of the work is done with the young offender. The principle of family focus redirects the work from the referred young person to the entire family. Needs of the young person as well as the family are assessed. The resulting individualized service plan addresses the needs of the whole family and is more meaningful than addressing only the needs of the offender. YAP's experience is that unless the needs of all the significant family members are addressed, our work with the young person often has only temporary benefits. Young persons are often more amenable to intervention when they know that the needs of their family are also being considered. Family support such as helping a parent find a job, supporting a family member with substance abuse issues, or helping the family find adequate housing greatly improves the chances of long-term, positive change and long-term success.

Principle: Unconditional care

Operating under a 'no reject, no eject' policy, referrals are accepted regardless of case histories or complexity of needs. YAP does not unilaterally terminate families due to case management problems, non-compliance, or similar difficulties.

The attitude and actions of the worker in the beginning stages of work with families is critical in establishing a respectful, hopeful and productive working relationship. Blaming families for their past failures or current circumstances is counterproductive to a trust relationship. Instead, workers must convey their recognition of the family's hardships. Families must know that they are respected as survivors and understood as people who have made good and bad decisions, have had successes and failures, triumphs and tragedies. The focus must be on the present: here we are now; what is the situation? and how do we all work as partners to make positive changes? Families are often particularly responsive to this approach because it is unique and positive, especially for those who have had long-term system involvement. Persistence, commitment, sincerity, resourcefulness and energy of the worker combined with a 'never give up approach' are contagious and help bring out the best in families.

Principle: Optimism

Staff training and development emphasizes the importance of maintaining an optimistic, hopeful attitude with youth and their families.

'Optimism of the worker' is perhaps the most important principle. Working with families of prolific young offenders who have been in the system a long time with no change and little remaining hope requires that workers possess an optimistic and hopeful attitude. If family members are feeling hopeless, helpless and overwhelmed, the worker's first task is to listen to their circumstances, demonstrate empathy and instill a sense of optimism and hope. One of the most effective messages workers can give to families is that they are 'not alone' and that, by working together, slowly and surely, the situation will improve. Workers may be very skilled and experienced yet still communicate covert messages that things are indeed hopeless and change is unlikely. On the other hand, a worker with less experience, but an optimistic attitude, can tap into the positive energy, strengths, resources and hopefulness still present in a family. More than degrees, credentials, experience or intervention modality, optimism of the worker may be the key to attaining positive change.

Evaluations and outcomes of YAP's Family Support programs

YAP's experience has been that its programming is most effective when it is developed with the involvement of all stakeholders such as youth justice, child welfare and education officials, judges, consumer advocates, and other community providers. As an example, funders such as the Northern Area Health Board and Western Health Board in Ireland organized stakeholder groups that helped to develop the model, monitored the programs, provided needed support and evaluated the programs. In this manner, the program model is 'owned' by the community it serves and the effectiveness is far greater than if the program existed in isolation or was not as connected to the consumers, funders and community partners. Given the breadth of YAP's service area, only selected outcome evaluations can be discussed here. The following are representative of success achieved with the Family Support model.

Program evaluations: England and Ireland

In 2003, the National University of Ireland, Galway and the Eastern Regional Health Authority (ERHA) conducted evaluations of YAP's Galway and Dublin programs respectively. Quantitative outcomes of the ERHA study included the fact that 62 per cent of the referrals deemed at serious risk of going into residential care have been maintained in the community. Two young people in secure care were enabled to step down to open residential care. Qualitative results included statements by parents in which YAP was cited as a primary source of support for dealing with their difficulties. In all interviews with families the practical support provided by the advocates was frequently cited. Families perceived that this support enabled them to become more organized and progress. Common themes for parents were availability of advocates, sense of reassurance that needs were being met, and that the young person was in safe hands.

PA Consulting conducted an evaluation of the YAP Thames Programme in London. The programme worked with prolific young offenders who had been arrested for at least five serious offenses before being referred to the programme. The evaluation found several strengths of the model: positive, committed advocates; individualized matching of young people and advocates; targeting activities to young persons' needs and goals; good working relationships with the courts; good access to education and training provision and a number of programme completions which exceeded the national average.

Juvenile justice programming in the United States: the Texas Youth Advocate programs

Based in Fort Worth, the Tarrant County Advocate Program (TCAP) is a highly successful long-term application of the YAP model and exemplifies partnerships with community stakeholders. YAP has been providing services for prolific young offenders and gang members (including the infamous Bloods and Crips) since 1992. Based on success of YAP's juvenile justice programs in Philadelphia, the Executive Director of Tarrant County Juvenile Services, Carey Cockerell, invited YAP to initiate services in Fort Worth's highest juvenile crime area. In this area, the percentage of youth being sent to state correctional institutions was the highest in the state. After the first year, commitments to state correctional facilities were reduced by 44 per cent (statistics compiled by Tarrant County Juvenile Services). In 2002, YAP served 500 young people and their families. Only 2 per cent were sent to the state correctional facility during their time in the program and only 6 per cent were sent to the state correctional facility after they completed the program. The American Youth Policy Forum has cited TCAP's success in its report *Less Cost, More Safety: Lights for Reform in Juvenile Justice* (Mendel 2001). The program has also been cited as a promising approach by the Annie E. Casey Foundation in its report *Barriers and Promising Approaches to Workforce and Youth Development for Young Offenders, Program Profiles* (Brown *et al.* 2002).

Elsewhere in Texas, statistics reported by referring agencies reflect similar success. In Austin, the juvenile probation department studied outcomes for youth who graduated the YAP program in 2002. Ninety-two percent of youth served were not committed to the state correctional facilities. In 2003, the Harris County Juvenile Probation Department (Houston) engaged an independent evaluation of the YAP Program. The report concluded that:

> Based on analysis of the closed cases, YAP is realizing successful outcomes for approximately 80% of the clients enrolled in their program. In other words, public protection is maintained at reasonable cost compared to secure confinement and placement in residential programs. Youth and families are generally satisfied with the services they receive.
>
> (Rea, Prior and Davis 2003)

Summary

Jerome Miller, a member of YAP's board of directors and a lifelong advocate of community-based alternatives to institutional placement has said that 'to label is to libel'. The Family Support model is grounded in basic values of respect, appreciation of diversity, and belief in the potential of youth and families regardless of the labels they carry. Staff sensitivity to the needs and perceptions of families is essential to the establishment of a trust relationship which forms the basis for service delivery. Family Support is distinguished from more traditional interventions in that services are provided directly in family home and neighborhoods. Staff are accessible 24 hours per day, seven days per week. Advocates, hired from the communities they serve, work in concert with families and a family team that is not limited to professionals but includes the family and members of the community. Incorporating elements of wraparound intervention, YAP's Family Support program addresses immediate presenting issues while empowering families with skills and resources that will help them function positively and independently in the future. Program evaluations to date indicate that the Family Support approach is a cost-effective alternative to out-of-home placement as well as a meaningful investment in family and community. The stories of families served by YAP can teach us a great deal, not the least of which is how much we as human service practitioners can learn from them.

References

Brown, D., Maxwell, S., DeJesus, E. and Schiraldi, V. (2002) *Barriers and Promising Approaches to Workforce and Youth Development for Young Offenders, Program Profiles.* Baltimore: The Annie E. Casey Foundation.

Bruns, E.J. (2004) *The Evidence Base and Wraparound.* Maryland: University of Maryland School of Medicine, Division of Child and Adolescent Psychiatry.

Mendel, R. (2001) 'Building a Community-based Continuum, Tarrant County Texas Juvenile Services Department', *Less Cost, More Safety: Guiding Light for Reform in Juvenile Justice.* Washington, DC: American Youth Policy Forum, 20–21, available at www.aypf.org

Selected evaluations of YAP programs

Rea, R., Prior, J. and Davis, P. (Rea and Associates, Inc., Houston, Texas) (June 2003) *Final Evaluation Report: Harris County Youth Advocate Program.* Independent evaluation commissioned by the Harris County [Texas] juvenile probation department.

Tarrant County Juvenile Services (2701 Kimbo Rd, Fort Worth, TX 76111, telephone (817) 838–4600) Various program evaluations, 1992–2004, including presentation at the Clara Pope Willoughby Symposium: Innovation in Criminal Justice, Texas Law Center, Austin, Texas.

Ireland programs

Youth Advocate Programme Ireland, in the Northern Area Health Board, 2002–2003. Interim Evaluation Report by the Northern Area Health Board.

Youth Advocate Programme Evaluation Presentation, 2002–2003. Child and Family Research and Policy Unit Health Service Executive National University of Ireland, Galway report (Galway Program).

Additional resources for the reflective practitioner

Bruns, E. J., Walker, J.S., VanDenBerg, J.D., Rast, J., Osher, T.W., Miles, P., Adams, J. and National Wraparound Initiative Advisory Group (2004) *Phases and Activities of the Wraparound Process.* Portland, OR: National Wraparound Initiative, Research and Training on Family Support and Children's Mental Health, Portland State University.

Burchard, J.D., Bruns, E.J. and Burchard, S.N. (2002) 'The Wraparound Approach.' In B.J. Burns and K. Hoagwood (eds) *Community Treatment for Youth: Evidence-based Interventions for Severe Emotional and Behavioral Disorders.* New York: Oxford University Press.

Cahn, E. (2004) *No More Throw-Away People, The Co-Production Imperative.* Washington, DC: Essential Books, see www.timedollar.org.

Kretzmann, J. and McKnight, J. (1993) *Building Communities from the Inside Out: A Path Toward Funding and Mobilizing a Community's Assets.* Illinois: Northwestern University Institute for Policy.

Miller, J. (1998) *Last One Over the Wall: The Massachusetts Experiment on Closing Reform Schools,* Ohio: Ohio State University Press.

Walker, J.S., Bruns, E.J., Adams, P., Miles, P., Osher, T.W., Rast, J., VanDenBerg, J.D. and National Wraparound Initiative Advisory Group (2004) *Ten Principles of the Wraparound Process.* Portland, OR: National Wraparound Initiative, Research and Training Center on Family Support and Children's Mental Health, Portland State University.

Youth Advocate Programs, Inc., website: www.yapinc.org

Chapter 9

Supporting Families with Disabled Children: A Case Study

Rosemary Kilpatrick

This chapter will illustrate how an innovative project and its evaluation can inform issues about policy and practice around support for families with disabled children. It will do this firstly by outlining the nature of support required by these families and then describing the implementation of an intervention programme offering a particular type of very practical support, namely a play and recreational facility for children and young people with moderate learning disabilities. The delivery of this programme and the outcomes for the parents and their children will then be described. This will be followed by reflection on the professional learning gained from the experience and how this learning might be used to enhance practice and support for families with disabled children in the future. Throughout the chapter the word 'parents' is used to refer to anyone who cares for a disabled child; it therefore includes adoptive parents, foster parents and carers working in residential care settings. Additionally, and after much deliberation, it was decided to use the phrases 'children with disabilities' and 'disabled children' interchangeably; this was because a review of the literature on this topic and discussion with professionals and parents did not come up with a consensus as to which was the preferred terminology.

Background

There are two main theoretical models which attempt to explain disability and thus inform the nature of any intervention plan. First, there is the medical model, which defines a person's disability in terms of his or her medical condition. This model would, for example, explain any stress experienced by the carers of disabled children as the inevitable reaction to having a disabled child. The model therefore focuses attention on the disability rather than the ability of the individual, and would suggest that any interventions or family support should focus on the disability. In contrast the social model argues that barriers imposed by society are disabling and that solutions can be found by removing those barriers. Within the framework of this model parental stress associated with having a disabled child would be explained by such factors as society's attitudes towards disability and the absence or inadequacies of appropriate services. Thus, this model proposes that family support and interventions should address social and environmental factors that result in failure to provide these families and their children with the support that they need.

Over the past two decades the growing emphasis on disability as an equality or fair treatment issue, accompanied by increased attention to human and children's rights, has been associated with a move away from the medical model towards the social model of disability. In the field of children's services, this is underpinned by the Government's formal commitment to the UN Convention on the Rights of the Child (UNCRC) which states that: 'parties recognise that a mentally or physically disabled child should enjoy a full and decent life in conditions which ensure dignity, promote self reliance and facilitate the child's active participation in the community' (Article 23) and that 'parties recognise the right of the child to rest and leisure, to engage in play and recreational activities appropriate to the age of the child and to participate freely in cultural life and the arts' (Article 31).

Additionally, there have been many changes in child care policies within health, education and social services across the UK, most recently *Every Child Matters* (Department for Education and Skills 2003a) in England and the forthcoming *Children's Strategy (Making it R Wrld 2)* (Office of the First Minister and Deputy First Minister 2004) in Northern Ireland. These have indicated commitment by government to move towards the inclusion of children with disabilities in mainstream social provision and towards ensuring that they have access to the facilities which should allow them to enjoy the 'full and decent life' referred to in the UNCRC. Such commitments have been reflected in the Children Act (1989) in England and Wales and the Children Order (NI) 1995 in Northern Ireland. In these statutes, children with disabilities are included in the category of 'children in need' which would seem to suggest that the underpinnings of any definition of disability in the context of child care are to be found in the social model. However, the definition of disability itself, as contained in the Children Order (NI) 1995, is much more focused on the individual differences among disabled children and between disabled and non-disabled children. It states that children who are disabled are: 'Blind, deaf or dumb or suffering from mental disorder of any kind or substantially and permanently handicapped by illness, injury or congenital deformity or such disability as may be prescribed' Article 2(2). It is somewhat surprising to find that the most recent legislation in this area uses such out-of-date language and labels which may provoke unhelpful generalising or stereotyping.

That families with disabled children have additional needs to those with non-disabled children is not disputed and the nature of these needs has been well documented (see for example, Dobson, Middleton and Beardsworth 2001; McConkey, Trewsdale and Conliffe 2004; Sloper 1999). On the basis of such evidence the Review of Mental Health and Learning Disability in Northern Ireland has argued that there are two types of family support which would benefit those who care for a child or children with disabilities, namely:

1. emotional support such as informal networks of support, mentoring, independent counselling and parent and sibling support groups

2. practical support such as early intervention and skills development work with the child; respite care; child care, play and supervised leisure facilities in out-of-school hours; transport to improve access to existing services, appropriate housing and aids to daily living.

Practical support also includes financial support such as the benefits system, which provides tailored packages of financial help designed to meet the greater cost of bringing up a disabled child.

While the Mental Health and Learning Disability Review group identified these different types of support it is important to note that these are closely interlinked and interdependent. Parents of learning disabled children can face major stress as a result of their experiences in dealing with the range of statutory bodies involved with their child, which can give rise to feelings of anger, powerlessness, frustration and low self-esteem. Informal networks of support and information sharing, particularly among other parents, can help alleviate stress but even where this type of support is available there will probably still be a need for some form of mentoring and accompanying practical support in all the areas mentioned above. Furthermore, it is important that the support is reviewed regularly to ensure that it caters for the changing needs of the family, which arise as a child becomes a young adult. There may also be a need for financial support to allow the purchase of additional or specialised equipment or services to help alleviate the situation.

Yet, despite the fact that there is evidence that these types of family support are available to at least some degree, and that the need for them to be better coordinated has been widely acknowledged, they still tend to be delivered, where available, on an ad hoc basis with little evidence of inter-agency and/or multi-disciplinary co-ordination (Audit Commission 2003; Kelly and Monteith 2003). For families with disabled children the situation is exacerbated by the fact that they tend to have lower income levels (Gordon, Parker and Loughran 1996), and struggle to meet the additional costs of supporting the disabled child (Dobson *et al.* 2001).

Practical family support: Play and leisure facilities

For most children and adolescents play and leisure activities take place in school and the local community, with the children and young people themselves frequently seeking out the activities they prefer and wish to engage in. For disabled children however, the situation is not quite so straighforward and in these cases trying to ensure access to such activities may place great stress on the child's parents and can lead to isolation of the entire family (Beresford 1995; Sloper 1999). Additionally, parents, and mothers in particular, appreciate the opportunity to have a break from providing childcare particularly after school and at weekends (McConkey and Adams 2000). Working mothers who face the double stress of ensuring that their child or young person is cared for during working hours and also has appropriate, enjoyable leisure opportunities are especially appreciative of such provision.

In the absence of any formal support group for them a group of parents of children with moderate learning disabilities came together to form a small voluntary organisation called Abacus. This group had first-hand experience of the difficulties in identifying appropriate recreational facilities for their learning disabled children and had encountered both acceptance and rejection of their children in various community groups and activities. However, even when their children were able to attend mainstream activies such as the local youth club there were many difficulties, regardless of how willing club leaders were to involve them, or as one parent put it:

> It highlighted how different he was and no matter how good people were, how kind they were and wanted to involved him, he just was not able to do that sort of mixing that would enable him to enjoy the activities.

Furthermore, while some of the parents felt that their social workers had supported them to the best of their ability others described frustration at the lack of involvement of the social worker in assisting in identifying such facilities.

> Well, she used to just phone every now and then to check that things were OK but I never really got any sense that she was there to help – it was like a courtesy call – she certainly didn't seem to understand the difficulties I encountered, or perhaps she didn't want to know; either way I just felt I had to try to solve the problems myself.

As a result the Abacus parents set up a steering group which sought funds to establish a pilot project, designed to provide play and recreational facilities for children with moderate learning disabilities who were all attending the same special school in West Belfast. With hard won funding from the Childhood Fund and Early Years Development Fund 'Is it Saturday?' was born. The project ran once a week on Saturday mornings for ten weeks between September and December 1998 and was attended by 11 children aged 8–12 years with moderate learning disabilities. The following summary of the project describes the establishment and management of 'Is it Saturday?', the barriers encountered and the outcomes of the programme.[1]

Establishing the project

The original proposal for the project had envisaged a part-time project manager who would have responsibility for developing and managing the project and a part-time researcher who would conduct an evaluation of the project but the restrictive budget meant that this was not possible. After many false starts and much negotiation, a consultant was identified within the university sector and this then allowed for a base for the project and the appointment of a project manager. The initial plan was that the project manager would be involved in a voluntary capacity but it quickly became apparent that the requirements of the work were too demanding for this and it was agreed that the project manager would be paid on an hourly basis on the research assistant salary scale.

A team of 12 volunteers was then appointed through a variety of means including advertising through voluntary agencies. Of this team there were nine who regularly participated in the weekly activities on a rota basis. All of the volunteers (plus the project manager) were screened through the DHSS Pre-Employment Consultancy Service (PECS) procedure and trained in working with children and young people with disabilities.

Following on from the identification of the volunteers it was necessary to determine the most suitable model for delivering the project and identify an appropriate programme of activities. Two alternative models for delivering the programme were considered. The first model – an inclusive model – was one where the 'Is it Saturday?' children would participate in already existing activities and thus allow for these young people to be fully integrated in community activities. The second model considered was a more segregated one where a programme of activities was designed specifically to meet the needs of the 'Is it Saturday?' group, and professionals were invited to contribute to the programme.

Contacts were made with a range of community groups, voluntary agencies, arts centres and leisure centres to identify the types and ranges of facilities which they provided. However, it quickly became apparent that the first model would not be a viable option. Many of the agencies contacted expressed an interest in the project but very few would have been able to accommodate children with learning disabilities since they did not have trained

---

1   The full report of the project may be found in: R. Kilpatrick and J. McClinton (2004) *Abacus: Is it Saturday? A play and recreational programme for children and young people with moderate learning difficulties.* Belfast: ICCR, QUB.

staff and were reluctant to take more than one or two such young people into their group. Given this, the second model (whereby a programme of activities is delivered specifically to the 'Is it Saturday?' group) was selected.

In order to ensure that activities identified met the needs and preferences of the young people concerned, focus groups were organised with the pupils in their school to talk about the types of activities they enjoyed doing. At the same time, the children were given cards with pictures of various activities on them (these activities being those which had been identified by the project manager as being available), and asked to sort these into piles according to whether they liked doing this activity 'a lot', 'a little' or 'not at all'.

On the basis of this information a programme of desired activities was drawn up and the project manager constructed a possible timetable for the project. Various agencies and therapists who had already indicated that they would be willing to participate in the project were contacted and the programme finalised. This consisted of a wide range of activities, and included therapeutic music-making, art activities (e.g. mask making), swimming, football, a visit to a folk museum.[2]

Finally, a location for the project had to be identified and after much discussion with representatives from the steering group and having visited several possibilities, it was eventually decided to base the project in a local community centre. Several factors contributed to this decision but particularly the fact that this centre was in close proximity to the school that the children attended. This meant that regardless of where in the city they were from, they would all be able to recognise certain landmarks such as the school. Furthermore, an appropriate room was found which was available on the Saturday mornings when the project was to operate. The centre was able to provide insurance cover for the group.

Unfortunately, the decision to hold the project in a community centre close to the school also created a difficulty – how best to transport the children to and from the centre. Originally it was planned to use taxis but this proved both expensive and difficult. With the permission of the principal of the special school, and the agreement of the bus driver to work on Saturdays, it was decided that the school bus was a much more sensible option. The final arrangements were that the children living in the immediate catchment area of the school would be transported in the school bus with a taxi (mini-bus size) being used for the remaining children and volunteers.[3]

---

2   All of those specialist agencies which provided input expressed great interest in the work of Abacus and on this occasion all gave their time free of charge.

3   Additional funding for the cost of transport was provided by the Health and Social Services Trust in which the school was located.

Outcomes

At the end of the project the parents of the children, their form teachers and those who worked on the project (i.e. the project manager and volunteers) were asked what they saw as its benefits and problems.

Benefits for the children

Overall, those involved described the project as highly successful. Parents reported being 'more than happy with the whole thing' and indicated that their child enjoyed all or most of the sessions with the main perceived benefit being that the children were able to get out and engage in different activities.

> Him getting out, cos he never goes out you see…he so looked forward to Saturday morning, to a few hours getting out. There's a wee club at the corner but there's too much fighting and all at it.

> He was just a different child and he loved going to his wee club – Friday night you had to get his juice and stuff in. It was something for him to look forward to, the social meeting of all his friends. He keeps asking when are we going back to it.

The form teachers also thought the programme was a valuable experience though they suggested there were some pupils who benefited more than others.

> He was very confident anyway but he wouldn't have done things on his own – he wouldn't have gone to the toilet or tuck shop by himself but he does now.

> He had difficulty relating to people – but he seems to find it easier to make friends now especially with those he went to Abacus with.

> She is really just the same – but I think there's a lot going on in that family – no matter what you do with her she's always the same.

Benefits for parents

All the parents saw the benefit of the programme for themselves, i.e. the respite from their children and having time to themselves on a Saturday morning. It was also important to parents that they could be sure of their child's whereabouts and that he or she was being cared for and receiving stimulating play.

> Just that break, having time all on my own where I didn't have to worry about him, I knew where he was.

> The element of choice for me was heaven. Knowing that you had two-and-a-half hours, you could afford to plan something.

> The satisfaction of being able to turn over in bed if I wanted, knowing that I had peace of mind about his whereabouts.

Unforeseen outcomes

'Is it Saturday?' was designed to provide practical family support in the form of out-of-school play and leisure facilities but its success also depended on it being linked into emotional and financial support. Some of the quotes above demonstrate the emotional support that was available to parents, if only in the form of having time for themselves at the weekend, without having to worry about their child. Furthermore, there was no financial cost associated with the project for the parents since all aspects were covered by the project itself.

A further unforeseen outcome of the project to which attention should be drawn was the issue of raised expectations. Many of the parents referred to the fact that their child had really enjoyed and benefited from 'Is it Saturday?', but that this then presented them with problems in that it was difficult for them to explain to their child why the project was no longer running.

> Maybe it's just him but I'm not sure if it's done him more harm or good. He expects that it should go on and on. It's left to mothers to do all the explanations as to why it's over. Children like him do not understand.

The issue of raised expectations is closely linked to the funding difficulty. As has been emphasised, 'Is it Saturday?' operated on an extremely restricted budget which meant that the project was not only time-limited but also very dependent on the goodwill of all those involved in it. However, this was particularly true of the project manager who worked many long hours, some of them on an entirely voluntary basis.

Reflections

It is of little surprise that 'Is it Saturday?' proved to be highly successful. There is little doubt that a well-organised and carefully planned scheme, whereby children with learning disabilities attend a programme every Saturday morning, is going to be enjoyable for the young people themselves and that the parents will benefit. It might therefore well be asked 'So what has been learnt from this project?' On reflection, a great deal was learned about the lives of these parents and their children. In addition, more was learned about the barriers they have encountered and the battles they have had to engage in to gain access to provisions which the vast majority of parents take for granted such as appropriate supervised out-of-school activities for their children. It has given us, as professionals working in this area, some insight into the attitudes and values of the statutory agencies who are tasked with supporting these parents, the ad hoc nature of play and leisure provision for children and young people with learning disabilities and an increased understanding of the policy and legislation in this area.

The approach to reflection on which this section of the chapter is based is that of Moon (1994, 1996, 2000) who, drawing on the work of Schon (1983,

1987, 1992) and Kolb (1984), suggests a sequence of guided phases for the facilitation of what she refers to as reflective activities. These phases are:

Phase 1:   Develop awareness of the nature of current practice.

Phase 2:   Clarify the new learning and how it relates to current understanding.

Phase 3:   Integrate new learning and current practice.

Phase 4:   Anticipate or imagine the nature of improved practice.

Phase 1: Develop awareness of the nature of current practice

While certain summer schemes were identified (mainly provided by education and library boards for children with severe learning disabilities), there was little evidence that any similar 'out-of-school' provision during term-time was being provided by the statutory agencies. Where such provision was identified this was usually driven by someone with a specific commitment regarding disability and not by policy or strategy. Frequently, we were told that children with disabilities were welcome in the leisure or community centre, or youth clubs or other organised activities but that there were no staff trained to work with this group. There was little sense that the agencies approached were talking to each other about provision for children with learning disabilities. This was despite the fact that a policy of ' inclusion' was often alluded to in organisational policy documents. In fact, the practice appeared to be far removed from this. This was also reflected in a comment made to a parent when she enquired about provision for her son with Down syndrome:

> He's not deaf is he by any chance? No? That's a pity otherwise he could have attended our...project.

Contact with the voluntary organisations working with disability also revealed little out-of-school provision for children with learning disabilities, though there was some provision in terms of training, awareness raising and resources from this sector which proved invaluable for the project.

Phase 2: Clarify new learning and how it relates to current understanding

The barriers that we encountered in setting up the project were numerous. These barriers included a lack of adequate funding, difficulty in finding appropriate provision and sourcing details as to what was available, problems in understanding the roles and responsibilities of the various agencies and identifying and accessing appropriate training. Having encountered these barriers ourselves, we were able to gain much better insight into the frustrations that the parents unquestionably meet due to the attitudes of some of the statutory agencies to them. If for example, you are continually told (as we were): 'oh we don't do that, why don't you try…' or 'that's not our responsibility, I think it is most probably…' then it becomes easier to understand why parents sometimes feel defeated and/or believe that the system works against them rather than with them. Working closely with the parents also allowed us to understand the frequently combative nature of their relationship with the statutory agencies. It also gave insight into their dilemmas regarding whether inclusive or segregated activities were the better option for their child.

Having said this, parents generally wanted their children to participate in mainstream activitiy but expressed anxiety as to how their child would cope in such situations:

> I have great trepidation about putting my child in any new situation – watching your kid not hacking it in a new integrated situation, yet they want to be involved.

Therefore, though they were keen that their children would be involved in mainstream activities where appropriate, there was a general consensus of opinion that the main social group that they identified was within the school setting.

> She wants to be with the only social group that she interacts well with, which is her school.

> School is a very secure place for my son.

A five-year follow-up of the young people and their parents in 2003 revealed that in the intervening period their situation in respect of leisure and recreational opportunities had become worse rather than better, that the young people were now even more socially isolated, that they had fewer social contacts and that they were more dependent on their families for social activities. As they grew older the difference between their social skills and those of their same-aged non-disabled peers became more noticeable. Thus, when they did attend mainstream provision they were often even more isolated than before and if involved at all played with much younger peers or were on the periphery of activities. This increased insight into the difficulties that these young people encounter when placed in mainstream situations must surely make us question whether the ever increasing drive towards inclusion is necessarily the most appropriate approach in all situations.

The ad hoc nature of the provision described above led us to examine existing policy and it quickly became apparent that there is no overarching policy with regard to play and leisure facilities, and little clarity around who is responsible for such provision in the case of children with disabilities. According to the Children (NI) Order 1995[4] and various public sector policy documents, this provision is the responsibility of the Health and Social Services Boards and should be of an inter-agency nature. However, when 'Is it Saturday?' was established in 1998 and at the time of the follow-up in 2003, there was still little evidence of any greater co-ordination and planning in terms of leisure and recreational activities for children with moderate learning disabilities. Indeed, it was often difficult to identify instances of this type of provision being linked into Health and Social Services Boards, District Councils or the Youth Service at all.

The preliminary discussions for the project highlighted a scarcity of practitioners with adequate understanding of, and training in, the needs of children with learning disablties in mainstream leisure and play provision. The importance of training, not just in working with children with disabilities, but also in relation to administration and management of intervention projects also emerged as an extremely important issue during 'Is it Saturday?' and is supported by the work of Thompson, Taylor and McConkey (2000) and McConkey (1999). It would seem that to provide successful schemes, either segregated or inclusive, for children with learning disabilities, priority must be given to preparation, planning and training of all those involved. Within this context, however, attention must be paid to the issue of raised expectations of the service users and the importance of balancing this against the benefits of a programme which has no potential funding for its continutation. Here, on reflection, there is a need to consider the inclusion of some form of exit strategy in initial proposals for projects.

Phase 3: Integrate new learning and current practice

The purpose of Phase 3 of the reflective process is to attempt to identify how the learning from Phase 2 might be translated into current practice in order to improve the situation. Four main areas of learning have emerged from Phase 2:

1. the frustrations that parents and children face

2. the tensions surrounding inclusive and segregated provision and the need for choice

3. lack of inter-agency collaboration or overarching policy

4. need for an appropriately trained and aware workforce.

---

4   Part IV 'Support for Children and their Families'; 'Children in need and their families'.

1. The success of any strategy or programme of provision is underpinned by the frontline staff who deliver it. From our experiences of developing and delivering 'Is it Saturday?' it is clear that the professionals engaged in working within the field of support for families with children who are disabled need to understand the range of support required and be sensitive to the stresses that these families experience to enable them to work in a respectful partnership. It is vitally important that they value the parents' expertise, views and opinions, otherwise there is a very real danger that they will alienate and distress further those very people whom they are supposed to be supporting.

2. At professional policy level there appears to be a general consensus that provision for children and young people with any form of disability should be inclusive. However, the Abacus parents argued very strongly that mainstream play and recreational facilities are not necessarily the best option for their children. There is a serious need to have regard to parental and children's wishes here and to plan for provision of both specialist and mainstream services to meet customer choice. Additionally, services need to be designed to take account of the child or young person's stage of development so that they do not become more socially isolated with increased age.

3. Academics and policy makers have time and time again called for greater inter-agency working, collaboration, coordination and partnership with parents and moves to promote this have included initiatives such as the Children's Services Plans. Thought is rarely devoted, however, to considering how the challenges of such inter-agency work might be addressed. It would seem that action on two levels is needed. At a *strategic level*, a cross-agency policy and strategy for provision of leisure and play facilities for children with learning disabilities is needed. At a *practice level* the true meaning of inter-agency work needs to be examined and, if we are to go beyond token gestures, a proper programme needs to be devised to allow inter-agency working to be developed in a meaningful and productive manner. This should lead to changes in practice, affecting those who are expected to engage in this type of work.

4. These changes cannot be successfully introduced in isolation so attention will need to be paid to providing support and training for staff to allow them to feel confident about going beyond their familiar routines and comfort zones.

Phase 4: Anticipate/imagine new improved practice

Within the context of play and leisure facilities for children and young people with learning disabilities a new and improved practice can readily be anticipated by drawing on the learning from the 'Is it Saturday?' project as well as other similar schemes, activities and related reports which have been identified through this study. Improved practice would have to be based on a clear strategy for addressing the needs identified in the above reflections. The strategy should be drawn up by statutory and voluntary agencies with responsibility in this area, supported by a strong, clear government commitment to its implementation and backed by the provision of adequate resources. To facilitate this a forum of parents and representatives from each relevant department, agency and voluntary sector organisation in the area would have to be established. This forum should answer to a lead department; develop a three-year rolling strategy with annual action plans containing time-bound targets and publish an annual report to the responsible minister.

The performance of the forum should be reviewed at least every four years. Such a strategy would allow for the development of coordinated service delivery which would recognise the inter-connectedness of all aspects of family and community life. This service delivery would be family-driven and directed and resourced accordingly. There would be a requirement to develop individual family support plans, coordinated by an identified family keyworker who would also act as a clear point of reference for the family as proposed in *Together from the Start* (Department for Education and Skills 2003) and the Review of Mental Health and Learning Disability (Northern Ireland) (2004). All frontline staff would be trained and supported to understand the individual needs of service users and skilled in inter-agency work.

Although the reflections above have focused on the provision of leisure and play facilities for children and young people with learning disabilities, this learning and vision for effective practice could easily be applied to the area of family support for carers of disabled children in general.

Summary

This chapter has attempted to illustrate how an evaluation of an innovatory project for children with learning disabilities can be used in a reflective manner to influence practice. It may appear that few advances can be made without the involvement of strategy and policy makers, but frontline staff can gain much insight by reflecting on certain aspects of the material. It is the frontline staff that families meet and work with; it is the frontline staff who need to have a flexible approach and the ability and confidence to adapt to the needs of individual families; it is the frontline staff who need to recognise the importance of the parents' expertise, perceptions, frustrations and difficulties; it is the frontline staff who can support parents in the way they want by listening to their needs and concerns and learning from these. For myself, writing this chapter has reminded me that much of what is highlighted in it has been identified previously by researchers on many occasions, but, disappointingly, has led to little change on the ground. As one parent put it:

> [We] are getting older and tireder, the children are getting older and lonelier, the pile of public sector strategies, plans, reviews and academic studies is getting higher and higher, meanwhile *plus ça change plus c'est la même chose*. There's an industry of officials and professionals out there, supposedly supporting our kids, but fellow stressed-out parents and the man who invented PlayStation have probably done more for my child than the lot of them put together. That makes me mad, and sad.

Such reflections might lead to despondency and despair. Alternatively they can lead to renewed determination and drive to find ways in which to ensure that the messages from the growing body of evidence-led practice no longer fall on deaf ears and that the families of children and young people with disabilities can truly be seen as fully participating members of society not only in policy but also in practice.

References

Audit Commission (2003) *Services for Disabled Children*. London: The Stationery Office.

Beresford, B. (1995) *Expert Opinions: A National Survey of Parents Caring for a Severely Disabled Child*. Bristol: Policy Press.

Department for Education and Skills (2003a) *Every Child Matters*. Norwich: The Stationery Office.

Department for Education and Skills (2003b) *Together from the Start – Practical Guidance for Professionals Working with Disabled Children (Birth to Third Birthday) and their Families*. Nottingham: DfES Publications.

Dobson, B., Middleton, S. and Beardsworth, A. (2001) *The Impact of Childhood Disability on Family Life*. Published for the Joseph Rowntree Association by YPS.

Gordon, D., Parker, R. and Loughran, F. (1996) *Children with Disabilities in Private Households: A Re-analysis of the OPCS Investigation*. Bristol: University of Bristol.

Kelly, B. and Monteith, M. (2003) *Supporting Disabled Children and their Families in Northern Ireland: A Research and Policy Review*. London: National Children's Bureau.

Kolb, B. (1984) *Experiential Learning as the Science of Learning and Development*. Englewood Cliffs, NJ: Prentice Hall.

McConkey, R. (1999) *Play and Leisure Activities for Children and Young People with Disabilities in the Eastern Health and Social Services Board Area: A Development Plan*. Belfast, Eastern Health and Social Services Board.

McConkey, R. and Adams, L. (2000) 'Matching Short Break Services for Children with Learning Disabilities to Family Needs and Preferences.' *Child: Care, Health and Development 26*, 5, 429–443.

McConkey, R., Trewsdale, M. and Conliffe, C. (2004) 'The Features of Short-break Residential Services Valued by Families who have Children with Multiple Disabilities.' *Journal of Social Work 4*, 1, 61–75.

Moon, J.A. (1994) *Advanced Training Skills Project*. Report on initial stages in the project. Birmingham: UK Professional Development Project/University of Central England.

Moon, J.A. (1996) 'What Can You Do in a Day? Advice on Developing Short Training Courses on Promoting Health.' *Journal of Institute of Health Education 34*, 1, 20–23.

Moon, J.A. (2000) *Reflection in Learning and Professional Development: Theory and Practice.* London, Kogan Page.

Office of the First Minister and Deputy First Minister (2004) *Making it R World 2.* Belfast: OFMDFM.

Review of Mental Health and Learning Disability (Northern Ireland) (2004) *Equal Lives: Review of Policy and Services for People with a Learning Disability in Northern Ireland* (draft). Website www.rmhldni.gov.uk/learning_disability.asp accessed 5 April 2005.

Schon, D. (1983) *The Reflective Practitioner.* San Francisco: Jossey-Bass.

Schon, D. (1987) *Educating the Reflective Practitioner.* San Francisco: Jossey-Bass.

Schon, D. (1992) 'The Crisis of Professional Knowledge and the Pursuit of an Epistemology of Practice.' *Journal of Interprofessional Care 6,* 1, 49–63.

Sloper, P. (1999) 'Models of Service Support for Parents of Disabled Children. What do We Know? What do We Need to Know?' *Child: Care, Health and Development 25,* 2, 85–99.

Thompson, B., Taylor, H. and McConkey, R. (2000) 'Promoting Inclusive Play and Lesiure Opportunities for Children with Disabilities.' *Child Care in Practice 6,* 2, 108–123.

Chapter 10

Enhancing Support for Young People in Need: Reflections on Informal and Formal Sources of Help

Pat Dolan and Brian McGrath

Introduction

Understanding and promoting social support for young people poses considerable rewards and challenges for practitioners. With this in mind, the principal concerns of this chapter are to:

- illustrate the nature and meaning of sources of support for young people
- outline how support is mobilised through such sources and identify some of the issues this raises for practitioners.

Using evidence from two recent studies in respect of community-based programmes in the west of Ireland, we document the workings of both informal and formal sources of support in practice settings and provide reflections on their usage for those working with youth. Two case studies – one quantitative and the other qualitative – are used to provide different, yet complementary, perspectives on the role and meaning of informal and formal sources of support in young people's lives. From these, we conclude with a number of key messages for reflective practice. Before exploring the substantive elements of the chapter, in the next section we provide an overview of current research literature concerning support for young people in adversity.

Sources of support for young people

Although social support can be accessed through a network combining a range of actors, in the literature there are two broad categories identified: one providing informal support and the other formal support (Cutrona and Cole 2000; Ghate and Hazel 2002). Informal support comes through networks of family, friends and neighbours ('natural helpers', as termed by Tracy *et al.* 1994), whereas formal support applies to help sourced from any person or service that is paid and who can provide assistance, for example, teachers, mental health professionals, youth workers ('paid helpers': ibid.).

Informal sources

The importance of informal support networks in young people's lives features prominently in the social support literature (Cutrona and Cole 2000; Ghate and Hazel 2002; Tracy *et al.* 1994). In general, informal networks of support are preferred by most people and are usually a first point of access to support in times of crisis. While informal support is delivered through family, friends and neighbours, a number of authors have found that family members constitute by far the largest proportion of supporters in respondents' networks (Canavan and Dolan 2003; Frydenberg 1997; Tracy *et al.* 1994). Nuclear and extended family members represent the most likely source of 'natural helpers', as well as the most durable and dependable source of support (Nic Gabhainn 2000), particularly as sources of psychological and practical support. On the other hand, families can also be the greatest source of stress within social network membership (Eckenrode and Hamilton 2000; Gardner 2003), and not all support offered by families can even be assumed as safe, given what is known about child abuse within families (Belsky 1997; Thompson 1995).

Friends provide a further source of network membership. For adolescents in particular, the peer group constitutes a key network source, in addition to parents and siblings (Cotterell 1996; Feldman and Elliot 1993). Youniss describes these network ties as occurring in an 'adolescent peer culture' (1999, p.20), while Coleman (1988), in his studies, found that the qualities that adults seek from other adult friends, such as loyalty and trust, are also present in teenage friendships. However, Bell and Bell (1993) suggest that adolescent friendships go somewhat further. Issues that may be deemed as taboo subjects are usually only talked about between adolescent friends. However, whereas adolescents seek information support from other adolescents, they are far more selective about choosing peers for emotional support (Cowie 1999). Where there are strong friendship ties, Cowie suggests that peers don't necessarily need to offer particular forms of support and simply having someone 'to hang out with' acts as a specific buffer to bullying in adolescence. As with all types of network relationships, it is important to recognise that not all peer relations are positive.

Formal sources

Workers in community and formal organisations (teachers, youth workers, counsellors) can provide support to young people in distinct ways. Several studies of youth transitions demonstrate the importance of such 'significant others' in how transitions are negotiated or where young people's system of social capital is generally weak (Raffo and Reeves 2000). Relationships with teachers, for instance, are critical in understanding young people's non-participation in school (Boldt 2000; Fagan 1995; Lynch and Lodge 2002; McGrath 2002).

For many young people attending family support services, their sense of connectedness to the professional can be a central factor. For example, when an adolescent is leaving care, where the young person feels that the help offered is provided out of genuine caring interest on the part of the professional, the likelihood of effective intervention is enhanced (Stein and Rees 2002). Similarly, for young people who have difficulty coping in schools, the quality of the relationship with his/her helper may be just as important as any positive outcomes for the young person (Dryfoos, Quinn and Barkin 2005).

In addition to the nature of the relationship with the formal helper, Cutrona (2000) highlights the importance of optimal matching of social support by professionals. This requires the professional to ensure that the type of support offered to the young person matches the type of help sought by him or her. Additionally, optimal matching requires help to be delivered in a timely way when the young person is most responsive to being supported by the service. Just as adolescence is a time of rapid change (Coleman and Hendry 1999), the nature of young people's perceived needs changes with their maturation and as a result of life events (Compas, Orosan and Grant 1993).

As institutional sources of support, one of the conclusions of Howard, Dryden and Johnson's (1999) review of resilience among young people indicates the importance of schools working not as sole agents but in unison with family and community, as part of a 'bank' of resources. This supportive function of schools was also found in an Irish study of schools as community agents in the lives of young people in north Mayo (Canavan 1998). In Ireland, there are other schemes that operate on the principle of enhancing human social capital for individuals through the use of building 'social support banks'. Schemes such as the Community Mothers Programme (Mullin, Proudfoot and Glanville 1990; O'Connor 1999) have operated similarly on the basis of paid supporters (mostly neighbours) offering help to young mothers under stress.

Mobilising support

It has been well established through research that mobilising support from informal sources is the preferred option (Cotterell 1996; Cutrona and Cole 2000; Ghate and Hazel 2002). Despite the importance of professional support in adverse contexts (Gardner 2003), there are three main reasons attaching to this preference for informal support:

1. its non-stigmatising nature

2. its availability outside normal working hours

3. the possibility to reciprocate support, thereby lessening feelings of being beholden to others.

This has important implications for professionals, who need to know when to supplement an existing network and when to intervene more directly (Dolan and Holt 2002; Tracy and Biegel 1994).

In addition to drawing from a professional pool to supplement the expertise within a network, professionals may be required to help optimise the value of the informal network. In essence, they need to know when to strengthen the network's capacity and how to do so (Gilligan 2001, 2003). For example, if a social worker is offering emotional support to a lone parent, there may be a sister, neighbour or parents' group who might be in a better position to help, who could be mobilised to offer such assistance through more informal support. Tracy and Biegel (1994) advocate that one of the key roles of mental health professionals lies in the task of knowing when to mobilise natural support for a client rather than offer direct intervention themselves. Cotterell (1996) concurs strongly with this approach, specifically in respect of working with adolescents and their social networks.

Case study 1: Neighbourhood Youth Project (NYP) study

The first case study explores the networks of social support of 172 young people attending three community-based day care programmes called Neighbourhood Youth Projects in Counties Mayo and Roscommon, Ireland. The first key objective was to identify and measure the sources, types and levels of perceived social support among all young people attending the programme over an initial nine-month period. Secondly, the study sought to compare changes in these factors among young people over the time period.

In this regard, two tools to measure social support were used, the Social Network Questionnaire (SNQ) (Cutrona and Russell 1990) and the young people version of the Social Provisions Scale (SPS) (Cutrona and Russell 1987; Dolan 2005). Both instruments were administered with respondents at time one (T1, n=172) and again nine months later at time two (T2, n = 149). In addition to the data accruing from use of both tools, the researcher gathered a set of field notes which provided additional qualitative data. While the SNQ establishes membership of young people's social networks and the perceived quality of relationships, the SPS measures perceived social support by type (concrete, emotional, esteem and advice support) and amount across four sources (parents, friends, siblings and other adults). The SPS is described elsewhere by Dolan in Chapter 13.

Neighbourhood Youth Projects (NYP) are community-based day care support programmes which offer individual and group work packages to young people in need of support, usually living at home and to varying extents still in school (Canavan and Dolan 2000). In this first case example, 172 young people participated in the study spread evenly across three NYP sites. There were slightly more girls than boys with one in five coming from an ethnic minority, most likely a traveller family. While just over one third of respondents were from one-parent families, over half of the respondents were referred to the projects primarily because of behavioural difficulties as identified by the referrer. Local primary and secondary schools were the highest source of referrals to the projects and the mean length of time for respondents attending the NYP at the commencement of the study was just over two years.

Key sources of support

A key finding in respect of the NYP study was that overall, respondents' perceived social networks were large, with the average social network containing 11 members, and 73 per cent of respondents nominating between 11 and the maximum allowable number of 14 members. The average number of network members living at home was four. More mothers than fathers were nominated in networks and while both were very frequently identified, just over 25 per cent did not nominate their father and 13 per cent did not nominate their mother. Siblings were frequently nominated and in about 80 per cent of cases respondents nominated between one and five siblings as part of their network. At least one extended family member was nominated in over two-thirds of cases with the average network containing two other relatives outside of the nuclear family. Nominations for friendships were less robust and whereas four out of five respondents could identify at least one close friend, 18 per cent of young people perceived themselves as not having a close friend. Similarly, almost half of the young people (49%) did not nominate a casual friend (friends other than close friends). Despite their involvement with services, including the NYP, young people tended not to include professionals in their network, with less than one in five respondents nominating a professional person.

Despite the fact that many young people were experiencing some difficulty in the home, school and/or community, overall relationships in networks were deemed to be positive with nearly all respondents identifying at least one network member with whom their interactions were good. Overall, respondents had a perception of accessing high levels of social support with most scoring support in the higher range. Parents were seen as consistently high supporters across all types of support and the greatest source of support.

Friends were also seen as supportive and almost as high a source of support as parents while 'other adults' were seen as better supporters than siblings but offered less support than parents. Siblings were perceived as providing least support amongst the four identified domains. In terms of forms of support, respondents' scores were consistently high in terms of concrete advice and emotional support. However, respondents scored esteem support as least available at T1.

The NYP study found informal supporters to be a very valuable resource and bank of help to young people. Parents are a key part of this 'arsenal of support' playing a crucial 'buffer to stress' role for the young people. Greater recognition and utilisation of this function of parenting is needed by professionals by using proactive models for working with parents as a way of supporting young people, even more so where the young person is experiencing problems (Herbert 2000). For example, Toumbourou and Gregg (2002) in their study on suicide among young people reinforce the importance of parenthood.

Continuity and change over time

The NYP study shows that while respondents nominated very few professionals as part of their networks, over time this tended to increase. This change may result purely from more contact between respondents and NYP staff and others such as social workers, or specialist teachers over the fieldwork period. However, it could also be argued that a low show for professionals in respondents' collective social networks is in fact positive. This could indicate that respondents were not becoming dependent on professionals for social support and that the potential of their natural network members such as family and friends was not being undermined (Tracy and Biegel 1994). Cutrona and Cole (2000) indicate that in the long term, dependency on professionals for social support can build up a false positive helping system, given that such relationships generally do not include reciprocity and closeness. Over time, this can have the negative effect of inadvertently undermining clients, both in terms of self-esteem and self-efficacy, in addition to lowering resiliency (Howard *et al.* 1999).

Given that in this present study the quality of the relationship in respect of those professionals who were nominated was generally rated as good by respondents (although some teachers received poorer scores), this indicates that service users were happy with those professionals whom they included in their networks. It may be that the young people in this present study were quite discerning about whom they chose from the set of professionals working with them, but generally, once chosen, these supporters were valued as positive. McKeown (2001) in his evaluation of the Springboard Family Support

Programme also found that parents and children perceived specific profession-als as important and supportive.

Similarly, two other evaluations of adolescent support projects found that the staff and the intervention on offer were seen as increasingly beneficial over time. Schofield and Brown (1999) found that the support from family centre workers was specifically related to an increase in social support among young girls, while more recently, the evaluation of the teen parenting support programme in Ireland had a similar finding (Riordan 2002). Riordan's research on teen parents, commissioned by the Department of Health and Children, found that supportive staff were a direct factor in helping young mothers to cope with parenting and influenced their ability to access more social network support. She also found that participants reported that their participation with the projects had made their lives better in 76 per cent of cases (2002, p.91).

Table 10.1: Percentage of respondents who gave optimal ratings of perceived support by type of support by source of support at T1 and T2

Support type	Parents	Friends	Other adults	Siblings
Concrete support T1	90	79	63	56
Concrete support T2	91	79	66	55
Esteem support T1	71	54	62	52
Esteem support T2	83	60	65	60
Emotional support T1	85	73	65	56
Emotional support T2	88	73	69	56
Advice support T1	82	75	64	55
Advice support T2	80	82	64	54

Forms of support

The NYP study found that concrete support was the preferred and the most accessed form of help. When rank ordered across sources of support at the top 'yes' rating, concrete support was perceived as the strongest type of available help at T1. Concrete support was found to be particularly high from parents and friends and less available from adults outside the nuclear family and from siblings (see Table 10.1). Although there was some change at T2, with a noticeable improvement in perceived esteem support, overall it was still the case that parents and friends were perceived as very strong suppliers of practical help. When one considers what parents offer their adolescent offspring in terms of financial and practical help the result may not seem surprising. However it does emphasise the ongoing need to offer adolescents tangible help and particularly so in this case where young people were experiencing difficulties to varying extents.

Case study 2: Youthreach study

The second case study concerns the Youthreach programme. The research findings are derived from a qualitative study undertaken with 15 young people between 2002 and 2004, based on repeated in-depth, semi-structured 'active' interviews (Holstein and Gubrium 1995, 1997). Interviews were also conducted with key members of staff. The purpose of the research was to examine the patterns of exclusion and inclusion within young people's school-to-work transitions. The young people at the centre of the research were all living in the west of Ireland and participating in a rural-based programme. Participants ranged in age from 15 to 25 years, with a mean age of 19 years. Seven males and eight females participated in the research.

The Youthreach programme is the principal interdepartmental policy measure in Ireland that has concerned itself with young people with no qualifications or who hold the 'Junior Certificate qualification only' (O'Shea and Williams 2001). Located in out-of-school settings, the programme offers unqualified young people, typically aged 15 to 18 years, an opportunity to pursue general education, vocational training and work experience. While originally starting out as vocational training in nature, which it still is, in more recent times it appears to have broadened its educational base to reflect a more flexible, needs-based and lifelong learning orientation and an overall concern for social inclusion (Ryan 2002, p.3). In this regard, the programme continues to evolve and now includes opportunities to pursue generalist educational credentials such as the Junior Certificate and the Leaving Certificate Applied Programmes.

Youthreach is organised around two distinct 'phases' of provision:

1. a Foundation phase which aims to enable a young person overcome learning difficulties, develop self-confidence and competencies required for further learning – typically in literacy and numeracy

2. a Progression phase which offers more skills development through a range of educational, training and work experience options – leading to different forms of certification.

Young people are provided an allowance, depending on age, as well as travel and meal allowances. Those who are lone parents continue to qualify for the One Parent Family Allowance while participating in the Programme. According to National Co-ordinator, Dermot Stokes (2001, p.3), the programme's key objectives are: independence rather than dependence; sustainability (in education, training, workplace and the home), active citizenship and lifelong learning. The ethos of the programme is its learner-centred and experiential approach. In this section, we focus specifically on the experiences of young mothers to illustrate the meaning of support derived from this formalised source. Specifically, results from the study are now presented regarding activating peer support, relationships with workers and practical support through formal sources.

Activating peer support

Peer support is evident in the Youthreach Study, specifically in relation to support for young mothers. This small group was set up in 2002 as a result of the programme's concerns about the social exclusion of young mothers in the locality. A specifically designed 'parenting skills course' was initiated, which combined certified 'taster' modules in personal development, maths, communication skills, childcare and computers. An additional module involved preparing young mothers to deal with some of the practical tasks associated with independent living, e.g. being able to change a car tyre, assemble shelves, change electrical plugs or operate electrical tools. Many of the young mothers were living alone with their child(ren) at the time of this initiative and, given the lack of support or experience in dealing with practical problems, were targeted for participation. One young mother, Emma, explains what can be termed the 'lateral connectivity' (Bloomer 2001, p.429) inherent within the programme; that is, where learning is linked to the reality of young people's lives outside of formal learning institutions:

> It was good, we used to come about 11 o'clock in the day, sit down and do a few different things. It was nothing like work, just more or less a get-together, to talk about things and work out budgets for yourself and manage your money. We talked about banks and loans. We also did some childcare.

While this young mother, who comes from a large family, says that she was aware of many of the issues covered in childcare, another participant, Patricia, valued some new insights about children's welfare and the possibilities of gaining support and validation outside her family:

> I know the childcare helped me a lot, because I hadn't coped with that area before... I had no idea about anything about kids at all, [unclear] the learning stages, the talking and all that kind of stuff. We used to sit down for about an hour and everyone would talk about their own experiences and I thought 'Oh

God, I am not the only one who has this problem' or I would be able to help someone else with their problem. Whereas before if I would ask my mother, she would say 'well, you shouldn't be doing that'. It's kind of hard to ask parents for advice too sometimes.

Group inclusion can be identified as an outcome of the emotional and practical engagement fostered among participants. Group inclusion comes from the everyday support that each participant can offer to the other, not just in terms of completing assignments. The participants felt they were supportive of one another and appreciated the opportunities to know more about each other's lives. As Ciara explains:

there is six of us and we all get on pretty well – we've been together for two years – and everybody knows each other's situation, so there is no shyness. Now we have drama and that goes on for six weeks, so every week we have to say something good that happened during the week and a bad thing that's happened during the week. And it's confidential as well, so that is great and I love the drama as well.

Additionally, both Ciara and Emma took turns in looking after each other's children and constituted important relational resources for one other as part of each other's social network. Emma also conveyed a strong sense of group solidarity with other members of the Leaving Cert Applied class: 'every couple of weeks we meet up... I think we will always stick together'.

Relationships with workers
The Youthreach study offers some insight as to how relationships with professionals can be most helpful. This was particularly evident in the context of a major event in the young people's lives, namely pregnancy. The experience of parenthood for young mothers exposes them to particular vulnerability, which comes in the form of potential social isolation and the significant constraints that limited practical and emotional supports have for aspirations and access to the labour market or education (see also Anderson *et al.* 2002). It can also come from the insecurities felt in the stigma of being a 'lone parent' (see Smith 2002). Support is required in an emotional as well as practical sense. A distinct point of departure from their school experiences was the renewed sense of trust and security that young people felt about the Youthreach learning environment. Such trust and security is a relational experience and the key figure mentioned in all participants' narratives was the coordinator, Anne. For several young women, Anne has come to occupy the place of a central 'significant other' within their lives and is described and valued as a 'mother' figure, providing practical advice, guidance and emotional support. Having a close adult figure with which to confide constitutes a crucial resource at critical moments. In the

following extract, a respondent describes the underlying sense of emotional connection and trust she feels exists within her relationship with Anne:

How well do you get on with Anne?

Pauline: Very well, Anne has helped me a lot. When I found out that I was pregnant first, Anne was the first person I told. When I first told Mum she didn't talk to me for a week. When I told Anne, it was all hugs, she was crying and everything. I love Anne to bits... If I was stuck for anything, I just go to Anne and she helps you out.

One particular mother, Ciara, was referred to Youthreach by social workers. Her story was one of considerable vulnerability, in terms of her upbringing and her poor social capital with which to negotiate her way in society. She expressed the firm belief that her situation could not have improved were it not for the unconditional support of the coordinator: 'Anne is like a second mother to me; I could tell her anything'.

Importantly, such relationships of trust and security activate key resilience resources on the part of the young mothers. In their narratives, we can detect for some a clear change in their belief system and self-identity. Depending on their initial experiential and social context, transformations can assume different degrees of meaning. For instance, Patricia felt freer from the potential 'trap' that motherhood might have been for her and without the support of Youthreach, her prospects would have been bleaker:

It gave me a more positive outlook I think, because I didn't think I would be able to go back out into the workforce so quick. Or even develop my skills more. It was a great opportunity.

In Emma's case, she moves towards a more positive sense of self in which she gains new levels of self-belief and security. Where once she risked 'burning' herself out at school in order to prove herself to others, she now is able to reappraise the potential open to her:

I am not shy any more, and I don't think everybody is better than me and I don't have to work around the clock to get what I want.

Practical support through formal sources

One substantive resource recently provided through Youthreach is the crèche facility, which has had significant implications for the participation of young mothers. All mothers agree that without the crèche being available to them, they could not participate either in further education or the labour market in a full-time capacity (see also Anderson *et al.* 2002). Without such vital support, the evidence suggests that 'early pregnancy very often means a blunted education' (Hudson and Ineichen 1991, p.83). Finding childcare arrangements with which mothers are happy constitutes a vital element of educational continuity (ibid., p.84). Importantly, the young mothers in the present research study differ in the availability of family support when it comes to practical arrangements, like childminding, which in turn affects their participation in the Programme. Three of the mothers in particular – Ciara, Cathy and Emma – experienced a greater level of constraint in their educational choices since they had few relational resources to draw on. Compensating for limited family support, the Youthreach crèche is thereby an obvious means towards participation.

Key messages for reflective practice

Three key themes have been distilled from the evidence across both case studies, each one constituting a reflection for working with young people in a family support context.

1. Both studies reinforce the importance of close friendships and peers as key sources of informal support, which can be better utilised by practitioners. In particular, attention should be given to working with young people on developing and maintaining close friends and positive interaction with peers through individual and group work methods (Weiss 2001). Additionally, practice programmes that build sibling and parental reciprocal support, particularly when relationships are tumultuous, would be most useful for young people. For example, closeness building and conflict resolution work, comprising methods whereby all parties are helped to reciprocate positive helpful support, need to be developed. In sum, findings from both studies suggest that informal sources of support comprising family, friends and peers are not just key players in young people's social networks, but a key resource in helping young people face difficulties in their lives.

2. Both studies acknowledge that professionals have an important role to play in terms of offering practical, emotional and advice support to young people. Whereas professionals need not take over the young person's network by displacing family or friends, they are still well placed to provide support once this is based on solid, authentic relationships. Without necessarily realising its full extent or significance, professionals can be assumed to be a critical source of meaningful support to a young person.

3. The centrality of practical support in the lives of respondents is underlined by both studies. Whereas the NYP study shows that concrete support was plentiful from all sources, equally, the

Youthreach study demonstrates exactly how such support needs to be mobilised in the particular contexts of young people's life events. A clear case can be made that, in the absence of pressing practical supports, other forms of help come close to being redundant despite the best intentions of practitioners.

Conclusion

This chapter has considered some key findings from two recent, concurrent but separate studies on young people living in the west of Ireland. Both pieces of research were concerned with understanding and promoting key forms of support for young people in adversity. Both studies offer different, yet related, insights to understanding the support needs of vulnerable youth and despite the difference in research orientation (one primarily quantitative, the other qualitative), similar policy conclusions can be derived. In the context of developing reflective practice in working with young people, the empirical evidence suggests three key points. To accentuate our argument, these interrelated messages are distilled and demonstrated in schematic form in Figure 10.1.

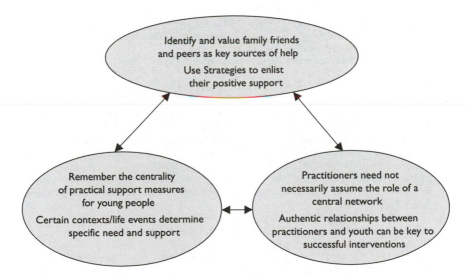

Figure 10.1 Working with adolescents and their social networks: Reflective practice messages

Finally, whereas these messages for reflective practice in working with young people and their networks are strongly promoted by the authors, they should not exclude a focus on other practice principles, for example as outlined in Chapter 1. Nor should they be seen as replacing basic human intuition or common sense on the part of any 'actively reflective' practitioner. Moreover, they highlight a set of common key messages from two comparative studies on adolescents in need which, it is hoped, will add to the ever-growing body of knowledge on how best to help young people cope.

References

Anderson, M., Bechhofer, F., Jamieson, L., McCrone, D., Li, Y. and Stewart, R. (2002) 'Confidence amid Uncertainty: Ambitions and Plans in a Sample of Young Adults.' *Sociological Research Online 6*, 4, www.socresonline.org.uk/6/4/anderson.html

Bell, N.J. and Bell, R.W. (1993) (eds) *Adolescent Risk Taking*, London: Sage.

Belsky, J. (1997) 'Determinants and Consequences of Parenting: Illustrative Findings and Basic Principles.' In W. Hellinckx, M. Colton and M. Williams (eds) *International Perspectives on Family Support*, Ashgate.

Boldt, S. (2000) *Powerful Hopes: An In-depth Study of the Potential of Young People from the Inner City of Dublin.* Dublin: Marino Institute of Education.

Bloomer, M. (2001) 'Young Lives, Learning and Transformation: Some Theoretical Considerations.' *Oxford Review of Education 27*, 3, 429–449.

Canavan, J. (1998) 'North Mayo Schools Project: A Blueprint For Supporting Young People in School.' Evaluation Report for Foroige by NUI, Galway.

Canavan, J. and Dolan, P. (2000) 'Refocusing Project Work with Adolescents towards a Family Support Paradigm.' In J. Canavan, P. Dolan and J. Pinkerton (eds) *Family Support: Direction From Diversity.* London: Jessica Kingsley Publishers.

Canavan, J. and Dolan, P. (2003) 'Policy Roots and Practice Growth: Evaluating Family Support on the West Coast of Ireland.' In I. Katz and J. Pinkerton (eds) *Evaluating Family Support: Thinking Internationally, Thinking Critically.* Chicester: Wiley.

Coleman, J.S. (1988) 'Social Capital in the Creation of Human Capital.' *American Journal of Sociology*, 94, S95–121.

Coleman, J.C. and Hendry, L. (1999) *The Nature of Adolescence, Adolescence and Society.* London: Routledge.

Compas, B.E., Orosan, P.G. and Grant, K.E. (1993) 'Adolescent Stress and Coping: Implications for Psychopathology during Adolescence.' *Journal of Adolescence 16*, 3, 331–349.

Cotterell, J. (1996) *Social Networks and Social Influences in Adolescence.* London: Routledge.

Cowie, H. (1999) 'Children in Need: The Role of Peer Support.' In M. Woodhead, D. Faulkner and K. Littleton (eds) *Making Sense of Social Development.* London: Routledge.

Cutrona, C.E. (2000) 'Social Support Principles for Strengthening Families: Messages from America.' In J. Canavan, P. Dolan and J. Pinkerton (eds) *Family Support: Direction From Diversity.* London: Jessica Kingsley Publishers.

Cutrona, C.E. and Cole, V. (2000) 'Optimizing Support in the Natural Network.' In S. Cohen, L.G. Underwood and B.H. Gottlieb (eds) *Social Support Measurement and Intervention: A Guide for Health and Social Scientists.* Oxford University Press.

Cutrona, C.E. and Russell, D. (1987) 'The Provisions of Social Relationships and Adaptation to Stress.' In W.H. Jones and D. Perlman (eds) *Advances in Personal Relationships* vol. 1, pp.37–67. Greenwich, CT: JAI Press.

Cutrona, C.E. and Russell, D. (1990) 'Type of Social Support and Specific Stress: Toward a Theory of Optimal Matching.' In I. Sarason, B. Sarason and G. Pierce (eds) *Social Support: an Interactional View.* New York: Wiley and Sons.

Dolan, P. (2005) 'Helping Young People at Risk through Social Support: NYP Youth Study Summary Report.' A Joint Foroige /Child and Family Research and Policy Unit publication.

Dolan, P. and Holt, S. (2002) 'What Families Want in Family Support: An Irish Case Study.' *Child Care in Practice 8*, 4, 239–250.

Dryfoos, J.G., Quinn, J. and Barkin, C. (2005) *Community Schools in Action: Lessons from a Decade of Practice.* Oxford: Oxford University Press.

Eckenrode, J. and Hamilton, S. (2000) 'One to One Support Interventions.' In S. Cohen, L.G. Underwood and B.H. Gottlieb (eds) *Social Support Measurement and Intervention: A Guide for Health and Social Scientists.* New York: Oxford University Press, Inc.

Fagan, G.H. (1995) *Culture, Politics and Irish School Dropouts – Constructing Political Identities.* Westport, CT and London: Bergin and Garvey.

Feldman G.R. and Elliot S.S. (1993) 'Capturing the Adolescent Experience.' In G.R. Feldman and S.S. Elliot (eds) *At the Threshold: The Developing Adolescent.* Harvard: Harvard University Press.

Frydenberg, E. (1997) *Adolescent Coping: Theoretical and Research Perspectives.* Adolescence and Society Series. London and New York: Routledge.

Gardner, R. (2003) *Supporting Families: Child Protection in the Community.* Chichester: NSPCC and Wiley.

Ghate, D. and Hazel, N. (2002) *Parenting in Poor Environments: Stress, Support and Coping.* London: Jessica Kingsley Publishers.

Gilligan, R. (2001) *Promoting Resilience: A Resource Guide on Working with Children in the Care System.* London: British Agencies of Adoption and Fostering.

Gilligan, R. (2003) 'The Value of Resilience as a Concept in Evaluation Family Support.' In I. Katz and J. Pinkerton (eds) *Evaluating Family Support: Thinking Internationally, Thinking Critically.* London: NSPCC and Wiley.

Herbert, M. (2000) 'Children in Control: Helping Parents to Restore the Balance.' In J. Canavan, P. Dolan and J. Pinkerton (eds) *Family Support: Direction From Diversity.* London: Jessica Kingsley Publishers.

Holstein, J.A. and Gubrium, J.F. (1995) *The Active Interview: Qualitative Research Methods,* vol. 37. Thousand Oaks, CA, London and New Delhi: Sage.

Holstein, J.A. and Gubrium, J.F. (1997) 'Active Interviewing.' In D. Silverman (ed) *Qualitative Research: Theory, Method and Practice.* London: Sage.

Howard, S., Dryden, J. and Johnson, B. (1999) 'Childhood Resilience: Review and Critique of Literature.' *Oxford Review of Education 25,* 3, 307–323.

Hudson, F. and Ineichen, B. (1991) *Taking it Lying Down: Sexuality and Teenage Motherhood.* Basingstoke: Macmillan.

Lynch, K. and Lodge, A. (2002) *Equality and Power in Schools: Redistribution, Recognition and Representation.* London and New York: RoutledgeFalmer.

McGrath, B. (2002) 'Towards the Enablement of Unqualified Rural Youth: A Structurationist Perspective on Socially Inclusive Policy Interventions.' *Journal of Youth Studies 5,* 3, 291–312.

McKeown, K. (2001) *Springboard Promoting Family Well-being through Family Support Services.* Final Evaluation Report of Springboard January 2000 to May 2001. Dublin: A Springboard Publication, Dept. of Health and Children, Stationery Office.

Mullin, E., Proudfoot, R. and Glanville, B. (1990) 'Group Parent Training in the Eastern Health Board: Programme Description and Evaluation.' *Irish Journal of Psychology 11,* 4, 342–353.

O'Connor, P. (1999) *Parents Supporting Parents.* Limerick: Mid-Western Health Board.

O'Shea, C. and Williams, J. (2001) *Issues in the Employment of Early School Leavers.* Dublin: The Economic and Social Research Institute.

Raffo, C. and Reeves, M. (2000) 'Youth Transitions and Social Exclusion: Developments in Social Capital Theory.' *Journal of Youth Studies 3,* 2, 147–166.

Riordan, S. (2002) *Final Evaluation Report of the Teen Parents Support Initiative.* Dublin: Dublin Institute of Technology for the Department of Health and Children, Stationery Office.

Ryan, S. (2002) *Youthreach 2000: A Consultative Process; A report on the outcomes: National Coordinators of Youthreach* Dublin: Youthreach. Available at www.youthreach.ie

Schofield, G. and Brown, K. (1999) 'Being There: A Family Centre Worker's Role as a Secure Base for Adolescent Girls in Crisis.' *Child and Family Social Work 4,* 21–31.

Smith, P. (2002) 'Pregnant with Meaning: Teen Mothers and the Politics of Inclusive Schooling, Extended Review.' *British Journal of Sociology of Education 23,* 2, 497–504.

Stein, M. and Rees, G. (2002) 'Young People Leaving Care and Young People Who Go Missing.' In J. Bradshaw (ed) *The Wellbeing of Children in the UK.* London: Save The Children.

Stokes, D. (2001) 'Developing a European Gateway for Youth Social Inclusion Programmes.' Paper given at European Partnership Conference, September 2001, Roehampton College, London. Available at: www.youthreach.ie

Thompson, R. (1995) *Preventing Child Maltreatment Through Social Support – A Critical Analysis.* London: Sage.

Toumbourou, J.W. and Gregg, E.M. (2002) 'Impact of an Empowerment-based Parent Education Program on the Reduction of Youth Suicide Risk Factors.' *Journal of Adolescent Health 31,* 277–285.

Tracy, E.M. and Biegel, D. (1994) 'Preparing Social Workers for Social Network Interventions in Mental Health Practice.' *Journal of Teaching in Social Work 10,* 1\2, 19–41.

Tracy, E.M., Whittaker, J.K., Pugh, A., Kapp, S. and Overstreet, E. (1994) 'Support Networks of Primary Caregivers Receiving Family Preservations Services: An Exploratory Study of Families in Society.' *The Journal of Contemporary Human Services,* 481–489.

Weiss, H.B. (2001) 'Reinventing Evaluation to Build High-Performance Child and Family Interventions in Perspectives on Crime and Justice: 1999–2000.' *Lecture Series, National Institute of Justice 4,* (March), 99–126.

Youniss, J. (1999) 'Children's Friendships and Peer Culture.' In M. Woodhead, D. Faulkner and K. Littleton (eds) *Making Sense of Social Development.* London: Routledge.

Chapter 11

Cultural Competence, Cultural Sensitivity and Family Support

Fatima Husain

Practice is an intersection where the meanings of the worker (theories), the client (stories and narratives) and culture (themes, myths and rituals) meet.

Saleebey 1994, p.351

In Britain, the 1950s signposted the beginning of an era marked by the arrival and subsequent settlement of large groups of minority ethnic individuals and families. These individuals and families were principally from the former British colonies in the Caribbean, South Asia and to a lesser extent from Africa. Britain's minority ethnic communities were and to a large extent are, marked by social, economic and political marginalization. This marginalization is based on the interplay of ethnicity, racial background, faith affiliation, class, level of literacy and access to resources.

To address the complex and interrelated issues and concerns faced by minority ethnic communities, families and individuals, structural changes have taken place marked by the adoption and acceptance of Britain as a multicultural society. While there have been many shifts in ideology, policy and practice, the situation of minority ethnic families in the UK continues to be marred by multiple deprivations. Family support initiatives often appear to lack the necessary tools to provide needs-based reflexive care. Contributing to the growing debate on needs-based reflexive care, and developing further the theoretical underpinnings of this debate, this article presents a conceptual framework based on the notion of cultural competence. This central framework provides a theoretical approach to working with and supporting minority ethnic families that can be used in developing specific policies, practice guidelines, tools and methods of enhancing support and care.

The theoretical framework presented below need not be specific to any national context, or any ethnic group for that matter. It is, however, presented here in the context of the histories and experiences of minority ethnic communities in Britain because it forms the conceptual base of a practitioners' toolkit developed by the National Family and Parenting Institute (Husain forthcoming 2005). In the context of multiracial, multicultural and multifaith Britain, it is important to briefly overview current anti-racist/anti-discriminatory legislation. Additionally significant for the theoretical framework of this toolkit are developments in social work theories and the resulting changes in social support practices and social care provision for Britain's black and minority ethnic communities.

Anti-discrimination legislation

The Race Relations Act 1976 as amended in 2000 makes it unlawful to discriminate against anyone on grounds of race, colour, nationality, or ethnic and national origin (Commission for Racial Equality 2004). This is echoed in a more recent European Union Race Directive. The Race Directive provided protection against discrimination on grounds of race or ethnicity irrespective of nationality (Commission for Racial Equality 2000). The Race Relations Amendment Act and the European Union's Race Directive, which was incorporated into British legislation in 2003, offer protection against direct and indirect discrimination across the public sector, including the provision of services. In contrast to the Race Relations Amendment Act, the EU Race Directive is slightly more inclusive in that it also protects against religious discrimination in employment but not in service delivery. Many organizations lobbying for comprehensive legislation protecting against religious discrimination, while disappointed with the current limited legislation, feel that there will nevertheless be an indirect effect of the religious discrimination legislation on service provision and delivery (Muir and Smith 2004).

The EU Race Directive encourages member states to take 'positive action to correct situations of inequality' and the Race Relations Amendment Act imposes general duties on public authorities to promote race equality (CRE 2004). Both the national act and the European directive make it a statutory duty for the public sector to incorporate a race equality agenda at both institutional and individual levels. Although under no legal obligation, the voluntary sector should move towards integrating the equality and diversity agenda as best practice.

Developments in social work theories

Since the 1960s there have been several developments in the theoretical approaches to working with black and minority ethnic families. These approaches range from the cultural deficiency model of the 1960s to the more recent anti-racism framework. Ely and Denney (1987) provide an excellent overview of these developments. The most recent framework, developed in the 1980s, is the anti-racism or the Black professional perspective. This perspective shifted the emphasis from preserving culture to the experiences of racism common to minority ethnic communities. This perspective was instrumental in the adoption of the term 'Black' to symbolize the political identity shared by all non-white minority groups that were subject to individual or institutional racism (Sachdev and Van Meeuwen 2002 p.9). Central to this perspective is the incorporation of the views of Black communities in policy and service develop-ment. Emphasis is also placed on identifying family strengths and constraints and demonstrating sensitivity towards cultural expectations throughout the assessment and intervention process (Ahmad 1993).

One of the principal criticisms of this perspective concerns the entrench-ment of colour or 'visibility' as a marker of difference, while other equally relevant ethnic and cultural factors are considered less significant components of identity (Modood and Beishon 1994). While racial discrimination remains a significant factor that negatively affects the lives of many black and minority ethnic individuals and families, the complex social world we all inhabit requires that the effects of factors such as age, gender, class, access to resources, cultural diversity, faith affiliation also became part of the assessment and intervention processes. It is the influence of the complex interplay of these social factors and their effects on family life that is not explicit in the anti-racism framework.

Research and practice

Despite this evolution in support frameworks, practice has tended to remain in a 'multi-cultural limbo' (Becher and Husain 2003). Although the importance of 'culture' is acknowledged, little detailed information is available on analyzing cultural information and relating it directly to a family's lived experiences. Additionally, practice which is labelled 'culturally sensitive' often fails to take into account the diverging biographies and distinct value systems of minority communities, and of families as distinct and organic units within their specific communities. Services labelled culturally sensitive have often depended on an essentialist notion of cultural values and practices, assuming that individuals passively receive and incorporate a fixed set of normative practices and 'culture' into their everyday life. This approach does not comprehensively examine the 'interplay of minority and majority structures (culture) and agency (selfhood)' (Rosaldo as quoted by Saleebey 1994). A more sensitive approach needs first to place individuals and families within their socio-economic context and, second, to understand that these individuals and families are active agents in the modification and negotiation of values and actions.

Generally, there is a tendency to view minority cultures and communities as fixed over space (changes due to migration and settlement as minorities) and time (developments after settlement in the UK) and removed in some way from majority structures. This has resulted in ineffective service delivery and often culturally inappropriate interventions. While there are pockets of good practice prompted by the desire to improve policies and adequately respond to the needs of diverse families, research points to a variety of issues in service development and delivery that continue to hinder the provision of effective and appropriate support (Bowes and Domokos 1996; Butt and Box 1998; O'Neale 2000; Pankaj 2000; Parsons, Macfarlane and Golding 1993; Qureshi *et al.* 2000). Two recent reviews of research studies of child welfare services for children of minority ethnic origin (Thoburn, Chand and Procter 2004) and of family support provision for South Asian families (Becher and Husain 2003) have highlighted a range of persistent barriers (for example, institutional discrimination, linguistic issues and client anxiety) that impede the provision of appropriate and needs-based support for British families from minoritised and racialised cultural backgrounds.

Cultural competence in Family Support

In order to address some of the persistent barriers that have been discussed in previous research and develop further the idea of cultural sensitivity and what it implies both at organisational and practice levels, a 'Communicative Family Support Model' was outlined in an earlier (National Family and Parenting Institute) report (Becher and Husain 2003). This model has been refined and modified here to accommodate the concept of cultural competence, which responds to the need to have an over-arching framework that incorporates cultural sensitivity for all ethnic groups. Theoretical and methodological models of 'cultural competence, in care' have been incorporated in many health care settings in the United States. There is a paucity of literature on the subject in the UK but the notion of cultural competence within health care settings is gaining currency (Burford 1997; Papadopoulos 2003).

The Culturally Competent Family Support Model presented here is essentially a combination of two interconnected theoretical models: cultural competence in care and intercultural communication competence. Embedded within both the cultural competence in care and the intercultural communication models is the notion of linguistic competence. In combining relevant aspects of these theories that are outlined below, and by producing corresponding guidelines, the model attempts to provide an inclusive framework that accommodates individual needs and places culturally and socially relevant issues at the heart of every intervention.

Cultural competence in care

The cultural competence model of care was developed and is used in the United State by professionals working with minority ethnic communities (Campinha-

Bacote 1994; Carballeira 1997; Cross et al. 1989; National Association of Social Workers 2004). While there is no universal definition of cultural competence, in the broadest terms it is the ability to respond to the unique needs of individuals and families by integrating cultural knowledge and awareness into interventions and thus support and sustain clients within their appropriate cultural context (McPhatter 1997).

Within the cultural competence model, culture is generally defined as 'the integrated pattern of human behaviour that includes thoughts, communications, actions, beliefs, customs, values, and institutions of a racial, ethnic, religious or social group' (Cross et al. 1989). If culture consists of patterns of behaviour then every practitioner–client encounter is essentially conceptualized as the meeting of two sets of 'culture'. Because learned cultural patterns influence how the behaviour of others is judged (Smith 1998), this interaction can either be one exemplified by conflict or it can be one where two sets of knowledge and behaviour patterns come together to reach a consensus. Critical to this definition of culture and the conceptualisation of 'cultural competence' is that culturally prescribed behaviour is situational rather than static and can be modified by individual characteristics as well as contextual social factors (Lynch and Hanson 2003).

Knowledge of culture, i.e. the gathering of information and learning about people from cultures other than one's own, does not necessarily translate into effective policies and practices, nor does it change practitioner behaviour (Smith 1998). Institutional culture and practitioner behaviour is modified through a process of skills development which can be defined as competence. Competence requires a certain level of ability and skills, 'the know how' to perform a task effectively to the demand of a particular situation (Smith 1998). In the context of family support, it can be defined as the capacity to function effectively as an individual or an organization by taking into account clients' lived experiences (Meadows 2000).

In light of these definitions, cultural competence can be conceptualised as a process by which practitioners combine their knowledge and understanding of culturally influenced behaviour with certain skills and abilities in a cross-cultural interaction. However cultural competence is not only about individual understanding of the complexities of cross-cultural interactions but also refers to the development and provision of systems of support and care. More precisely, cultural competence requires:

1. the development of an understanding of the specific cultural, linguistic, social and economic nuances of individuals, families and communities

2. the application of this understanding to all aspects of service development and delivery (National Association of Social Workers 2004).

The adoption of a cultural competence framework by an organization requires the development of 'a set of congruent behaviours, attitudes, and polices that come together in a system, agency or amongst professionals and enables that system, agency or those professionals to work effectively in cross-cultural situations (Cross *et al.* 1989). Literature in this field describes cultural competence as a process which comprises various components (Campinha-Bacote 1994; Carballeira 1997; Cross *et al.* 1989). Within the context of family support services in the UK, engaging in the process of becoming culturally competent necessitates working on three interrelated and interdependent components, which are:

- cultural knowledge
- cultural awareness
- cultural sensitivity.

Cultural knowledge

Organizations and practitioners seeking to enhance their ability to serve culturally diverse communities need to familiarise themselves with the background of the families and communities they will be serving. Cultural knowledge entails seeking information about culturally patterned behaviour, values, belief systems, history of communities and processes of migration and settlement. Cultural knowledge also includes knowledge and understanding of the dynamics inherent when cultures interact. Within the family support sector knowledge of the lived experiences of families and communities when seeking formal support (for example, the high rates of black children in care) should be incorporated into interventions. However, working solely on the basis of cultural knowledge without simultaneously developing cultural awareness and sensitivity carries the risk of stereotyping individuals and families, essentialising cultural practices. Service provision underpinned solely by factual knowledge of culture and culture-based practices will result in the provision of inappropriate services.

Cultural awareness

The second component of the cultural competence framework, cultural awareness, has to be developed alongside cultural knowledge to continuously challenge the notion of static cultures as well as that of viewing one's culture practices as better or superior. Within the family support context, organizations and practitioners need to use cultural knowledge in a constructive manner. A positive and open attitude enables service providers and practitioners to value diversity and respect difference. Critical to this openness is the ability to assess cultural assumptions and be aware of and analyse individual cultural backgrounds, at both the organisational and individual levels. Significant for developing and internalising cultural awareness is the notion of reflexivity.

REFLEXIVITY

Reflexivity is the ability to think critically about our own assumptions and monitor our own actions (Cunliffe and Jun 2002). By thinking and questioning our own assumptions, values and actions, reflexivity leads to an awareness and openness to other, alternative possibilities. Reflexivity in social care enables practitioners to recognize that we construct our social world and make sense of it as we interact with those around us (Schotter and Cunliffe 2002). Therefore what we know about ourselves and about other people and communities should not be viewed as objective fact but as constructed social reality, a social reality that can change. Reflexivity differs from reflection in that reflection is about understanding a situation based on the idea of objective reality (Woolgar 1988); it involves distancing oneself from a situation and analysing it as an 'outsider'. Reflexivity on the other hand is about being an 'active subject' within a situation or process and exploring how one's own social realities affect that particular situation or process.

At an organizational level reflexivity helps service providers to question their policies and practices and devise constructive ways to develop and modify existing organizational structures. Additionally, reflexivity in relation to diversity and cultural pluralism, that is, *cultural reflexivity*, anticipates cultural differences and attempts to understand and appreciate them (Kalantzis and Cope 1997). At the level of practitioner–client interaction reflexivity enables practitioners to question their own cultural backgrounds, values, beliefs and understanding of a particular situation and to explore how these might influence the intervention process and affect outcomes for clients.

In summary, cultural awareness refers to flexibility and openness on the part of practitioners. These attributes are considered essential for developing a sensibility to diversity and difference that questions ethnocentrism and results in a positive approach to cultural pluralism.

Cultural sensitivity

Cultural sensitivity in the cultural competence framework is the ability to change working practices and develop skills and strategies to work positively with cultural differences. At the organizational level it is about customising services in order to reflect diversity within and between cultures. Sensitivity in particular refers to a practitioner's attitude to each client's cultural uniqueness and his or her ability to relate to clients in a culturally relevant and appropriate way (Cummins 2003). Practitioners also need to demonstrate a willingness to let clients determine their own future in accordance with their values and beliefs (Day 2004). In the context of family support, a culturally sensitive practitioner demonstrates the ability to recognize issues affecting minority communities (such as poverty and discrimination) and transform interventions in response to a family's specific needs. Cultural sensitivity involves approaching a situation or encounter with an awareness of the complexity and contradictions inherent in people's lives and a determination not to assign judgemental values (good/bad; right/wrong) to cultural differences. To enhance their level of cultural sensitivity individuals have to rely on a range of interpersonal and communication skills (this is further elaborated in the section on intercultural communication competence).

Cultural competence as a system of care

Cultural competence as a system of care is a combination of knowledge, awareness and sensitivity that can be incorporated into all aspects of service development and delivery, including an organization's policy framework, service administration, and manager and practitioner training. Cultural competence in social care is the integration and transformation of knowledge about individuals and groups of people into specific standards, policies, practices and attitudes that are utilized in appropriate cross-cultural settings to increase the quality of services and produce better outcomes (Davis 1997).

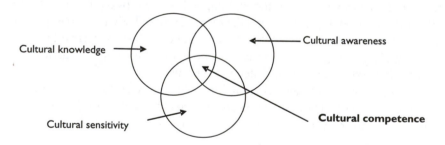

Figure 11.1 Cultural competence and its components

Organizations working to develop a culturally competent system of care need first to demonstrate that they value diversity by incorporating cultural knowledge into their equal access and non-discriminatory policies. Culture here refers not just to ethnic or national cultures of clients but also to the culture of social care, the culture of the majority/ dominant society, the culture of the practitioner and the dynamics and tensions inherent during encounters where any combination of these cultures interacts (Day 2004). Second, and crucially, at this organizational level resources need to be targeted to areas and services (such as interpretation/translation) that will assist practitioners in providing culturally competent interventions.

At the level of service development, providers need to understand the needs and help-seeking patterns of the communities they intend to serve. Additionally, information about informal support systems and the development of working partnerships with community groups will enable providers to target services according to community and family needs. Within the cultural competent framework, 'practice is driven in service delivery systems by client preferred choices, not by culturally blind or culturally free interventions' (National Centre for Cultural Competence 2004).

For practitioners, cultural competence requires organizational support, targeted resources and a commitment to staff recruitment that reflects the ethnic composition of the communities being served. However, ethnic matching of client to practitioner does not result in cultural competence. To enable the practitioner to work in a culturally competent way, ongoing training and skills development is required irrespective of similarities in ethnic or cultural background of practitioners and clients. Training is considered necessary because of potential differences in class, power and access to resources. In theoretical terms, cultural competence is perceived as a process in which 'the practitioner continuously strives to achieve the ability to effectively work within the cultural context of an individual family or community with a diverse cultural or ethnic background (Campinha-Bacote, Yahle and Langenkamp 1996).

Intercultural communication competence

While the cultural competence in care model requires organizations and practitioners to have a specific knowledge base, open-mindedness as well as a positive attitude towards cultural differences when working with culturally diverse clients, the intercultural communication model concentrates on the interaction that takes place between people in a cross-cultural setting. It is the detail about verbal and non-verbal communication that makes this model particularly significant for practitioner–client interactions.

There appears to be no consensus in defining communication competence or its components in discussions of intercultural communication theory (Chen and Starosta 1997; Clark 2004; Gudykunst and Kim 1995; Wiseman, Hammer and Nishida 1989). With our ultimate aim of improving the quality of family support provision and practice, intercultural communication competence proves useful in informing and enhancing the cultural competence in care framework. Intercultural communication competence can be particularly effective in conceptualising and guiding practitioner–client interactions. In the context of practitioner–client interactions, intercultural communication competence refers to the ability:

1. to understand the dynamics of a communication event in a cross-cultural encounter

2. to behave effectively and appropriately (Chen and Starosta 1997) thus minimizing misunderstandings and negative impressions (Wiseman *et al.* 1989).

Wiseman *et al.* (1989) define and analyse two components of intercultural communication competence: knowledge and attitude. Knowledge in this context is defined in a similar manner to the cultural competence care model and attitude refers, in effect, to openness and respect for cultural differences. Chen and Starosta (1997) also outline two components of communication competence: intercultural awareness and intercultural sensitivity. In Chen and Starosta's framework, intercultural awareness is the ability to understand cultural similarities and differences and 'is enhanced and buffered by inter-cultural sensitivity (p.15)', defined here as a positive attitude to cultural differences and a demonstration of flexibility in behaviour.

In summary, while there is some overlap in definitions and a need for further clarity, it is clear that crucial to a successful practitioner–client encounter are the notions of cultural knowledge, awareness and sensitivity. By focusing on specific intercultural encounters or situations, the communication competence framework provides tools for two important areas: knowledge of cultural differences in effective communication such as the importance of verbal and non-verbal behaviour and a possible framework for measuring the level of individual intercultural sensitivity (see the section on evaluation below).

Linguistic competence

A professional may successfully acquire some level of cultural competence by obtaining information about cultural and socio-economic facts of a particular minority ethnic community or family, and may also have developed the necessary attitudes, working ethos and an understanding of cross-cultural communication. However, this knowledge and these skills will be of little use if the organization providing the service has not dedicated resources to establish linguistic competence within its workforce. Goode and Jones (2004) define linguistic competence as:

> The capacity of an organization and its personnel to communicate effectively, and convey information in a manner that is easily understood by diverse audiences including persons of limited English proficiency, those who have low

literacy skills or are not literate (in English or their own language), and individuals with disabilities.

Linguistic competence is crucial if service providers and practitioners wish to understand the worldview of their clients because language is not just a means of communication but also a tool for constructing reality (Leigh 1998). As with all aspects of cultural competence, even if the practitioner and client are of the same cultural or ethnic background, linguistic competence may still be an issue. For example if a South Asian Muslim practitioner is matched with a South Asian Muslim family, the practitioner may have background cultural knowledge and may have the appropriate skills and strategies to communicate in a culturally sensitive manner, that is, the practitioner may be culturally competent, but if the linguistic competence of both practitioner and client have not been assessed, the intervention itself would not be culturally competent. This could happen in an instance where the professional speaks English and Punjabi and the family is of Gujarati origin and has no English proficiency and limited literacy skills in Gujarati.

Practitioner responsibilities and possible outcomes

It is apparent that in cross-cultural interactions there are two participants or groups of participants, both of whom will benefit from developing appropriate communication skills and positive attitudes to understanding each other's cultures. However, in the context of family support or social care in general, it is important to concentrate on the qualities of the practitioner and the attitudes they bring to the cross-cultural interaction rather than the client's. This is particularly salient in work with clients from minority ethnic, faith and racial backgrounds because practitioners are working in organisations structured according to the values and belief systems of the dominant ethnic group. As representatives of structures and practices embedded in the dominant ethnic culture, practitioners have considerable power in encounters with marginalised and minoritised families needing support. They need to be aware of the level of control they exercise during interventions and should recognise that 'communication does not take place in a vacuum isolated from the larger socio-political influences of society. It mirrors the state of inter-racial relationships in wider society' (Robinson 1997, p.16).

Practitioners occupy a position of power because they can dictate where, when and how each meeting will be conducted and have knowledge of and access to resources that a client might require. How this power is demonstrated and how knowledge is shared with clients depends on the practitioner's awareness of and attitude to his or her own position. Because of this power differential, practitioners working within the cultural competence framework should aim to work in partnership with families or act as 'co-facilitators in the deconstruction (to develop an understanding of lived experiences) and collaborate in the intervention process to reconstruct and transform the parts of client's lives which need readjustment' (Saleebey 1994, p.353).

It is important to note that whether services are generic or specialised, appropriate or inappropriate, support is dependent on the values, skills and attitudes the professionals brings to a specific interaction when working with a minority ethnic individual or family. Therefore even in an organization where 'one size fits all' is the underlying ethos 'the equitable approach is to honour diversity and seek to understand what culturally sensitive care means for each family being served. To meet such a goal, professionals have to establish close communication with families and work together with them towards positive outcomes' (Gonzalez-Mena 2001).

Smith (1998) indicates that for staff and practitioners a culturally competent system of care provides a supportive working environment where skills development is encouraged and minority ethnic practitioners do not feel marginalised or reduced to ethnic-matching interventions. For clients, the possible positive outcomes resulting from a culturally competent system of care are:

- increase in client satisfaction as a result of feeling respected and empowered

- decrease in client's anxiety concerning formal support systems

- increase in help-seeking from targeted communities (Smith 1998, p.6).

As mentioned above, research indicates that theoretical social care frameworks that have been used during the past decades have been unsuccessful at some level in providing support that adequately incorporates the socio-economic and cultural needs of Britain's black and minority ethnic individuals and families. The current model is proposed because it addresses key concerns and provides a structural framework and working ethos that will possibly move the discussion on appropriate support provision in a positive direction.

Evaluating cultural competence and cultural sensitivity

A key question that can be raised regarding cultural competence is how it can be measured in a coherent and systematic way. A range of indicators of cultural competence are available in the US where the cultural competence framework has been implemented in the health care sector. The federally funded Office of Minority Health (OMH) (1999) has developed standards for culturally competent services and the Center for Mental Health Services (CMHS) (1998) has produced standards and implementation guidelines. Both of these comprise checklists and guidelines to assess organizational capacity, intervention processes and outcomes. Measures are provided for a range of topic areas including self-assessment survey of organizational policies and procedures (Weiss and Minsky 1994); agency cultural competence (Dana, Behn and Gonwa 1992); staff hiring (OMH 1999); linguistic competence (CMHS 1998); communication styles (Goode 2000a); patient satisfaction (Tirado 1996); cultural knowledge/knowledge of community needs (CMHS 1998; Mason 1995); community/client participation (Weiss and Minsky 1994; Maternal and Child Health Bureau 1995); cultural sensitivity (Massachusetts Chronic Disease Improvement Network 1999) and respect and appreciation of different cultures (Goode 2000b).

In a social care setting, cultural sensitivity as demonstrated by a practitioner's acceptance and respect for and ability to work with another person's cultural uniqueness is crucial. To measure cultural sensitivity at the level of individual attitude the concept of intercultural communication competence is particularly relevant because it offers the possibility of calculating whether an individual has the ability to be culturally sensitive in encounters with people from other cultures.

To measure cultural sensitivity, Chen and Starosta (2000) have developed a scale with six measurable elements that can be calculated to establish the level of cultural sensitivity of an individual. The characteristics that Chen and Starosta consider essential and that can be measured are: self-esteem, self-monitoring, open-mindedness, empathy, interaction involvement and non-judgement. This is a relatively new measure and has been developed and validated in the context of intercultural communication and has not been tested in social care settings.

In the context of measuring sensitivity in social support, Ho (1991) presents an Ethnic-Sensitive Inventory (ESI) consisting of 24 items covering the range of 'process stages of client-worker interaction' (p.59). The reliability of this measure has been tested on social work students; however, the ESI has not been used as an assessment tool in evaluating interventions developed and structured according to the cultural competence in care framework.

Because the development of a cultural competence framework is at a fledgling stage in Britain, there are no suitable assessment instruments available at the present time. If the cultural competence in family support model is found to be a useful theoretical framework for working with Britain's minority ethnic and faith families, the development of measures to assess cultural competence as a comprehensive and effective system of care would be the necessary next stage in enabling organizations and practitioners to continue enhancing their skills, practices and attitudes (Smith 1998).

Concluding comments

The central cultural competence framework presented in this article places the emphasis on providing appropriate support squarely on the shoulders of practitioners. While many practitioners may be skilled in providing a level of care to their minority ethnic clients that incorporates the three components of cultural competence, the emphasis of this model of support is not on the idea of 'becoming culturally competent' but on viewing cultural competence as a continuous journey.

Salient to the cultural competence framework is the notion of culture as a flexible and transformative process that mutates as societies, communities, families and individuals interact. In addition, it is important for practitioners to understand this transformative nature of culture and to work in a constant state of reflexivity, thereby assuring that each family is treated within their cultural context as a unique group of individuals attempting to find a unique formula to enhance their life circumstances.

Finally, the cultural competence framework presented above need not be specific to any national context or any ethnic or racial group for that matter. However, its development and implementation into policies and practices will be influenced by national, regional and local policy and practice debates and service provision requirements.

References

Ahmad, B. (1993) *Black Perspectives in Social Work*. Birmingham: Venture Press.

Becher, H. and Husain, F. (2003) *South Asian Hindus and Muslims in Britain: Developments in Family Support*. London: NFPI.

Bowes, A.M. and Domokos, T.M. (1996) 'Pakistani Women and Maternity Care: Raising Muted Voices.' *Sociology of Health and Illness 18*, 1, 45–65.

Burford, B. (1997) 'Cultural Competence: Myth, Useful Concept or Unattainable Goal?' Unpublished dissertation, Durham University.

Butt, J. and Box, L. (1998) *Family Centred: A Study of the Use of Family Centres by Black Families*. London: REU.

Campinha-Bacote, J. (1994) *The Process of Cultural Competence in Health Care: A Culturally Competent Model of Care*. Wyoming, OH: Perfect Printing Press.

Campinha-Bacote, J., Yahle, T. and Langenkamp, M. (1996) 'The Challenges of Cultural Diversity for Nurse Educators.' *Journal of Continuing Education for Nurses 27*, 5, 59–64.

Carballeira, N. (1997) 'The Live & Learn Model for Culturally Competent Family Services.' *Continuum 17*, 1, 7–12.

Center for Mental Health Services (1998) *Cultural Competence in Managed Care*. Washington DC: The Center for Mental Health Services.

Chen, G.M. and Starosta, W.J. (1997) 'A Review of the Concept of Intercultural Sensitivity.' *Human Communication 1*, 1, 1–16.

Chen, G.M. and Starosta, W.J. (2000) 'The Development and Validation of the Intercultural Communication Sensitivity Scale.' *Human Communication 3*, 1–35.

Clark, J. (2004) 'Beyond Empathy: An Ethnographic Approach to Cross-cultural Social Work Practice.' Available at www.mun.ca/cassw-ar/papers2/ clark.pdf (downloaded 2004).

Commission for Racial Equality (2000) *Article 13: Proposals from the European Commission for Combating Discrimination*. London: CRE. Available at www.cre.gov.uk/legaladv.art13.html.

Commission for Racial Equality (2004) *Race Relations Act*. Available at www.cre.gov.uk/legaladv/rra.html (downloaded 2004).

Cross, T., Bazron, B., Dennis, K., and Isaacs, M. (1989) *Towards a Culturally Competent System of Care*. Washington DC: Georgetown University Child Development Center.

Cummins, L. (2003) *Multicultural Competence in Social Work Practice*. Toronto: Allyn and Bacon.

Cunliffe, A. and Jun, J. (2002) 'Reflexivity as Intellectual and Social Practice'. Paper presented at the Public Administration Theory Network, Cleveland, Ohio.

Dana, R.H., Behn, J.D., and Gonwa, T. (1992) 'A checklist for the examination of cultural competence in social service agencies.' *Research on Social Work Practice 2*, 2, 220–233.

Davis, K. (1997) *Exploring the Intersection between Cultural Competency and Managed Behavioral Health Care Policy: Implications for State and County Mental Health Agencies.* Alexandria, VA: National Technical Assistance Center for State Mental Health Planning.

Day, P.A. (2004) 'Cultural Competence Materials for MSW Students, Staff, Faculty and the Community.' Available at www.d.umn.edu/sw/culcomp.html (downloaded 2004).

Ely, P. and Denney, D. (1987) *Social Work in a Multi-racial Society.* Aldershot: Gower Publishing Co.

Goode. T. (2000b) *Checklist on Values and Attitudes.* Washington DC: Georgetown University Child Development Center.

Goode, T. and Jones, W. (2004) *A Definition of Linguistic Competence.* Available at gucdc.georgetown.edu/nccc (downloaded 2004).

Gonzalez-Mena, J. (2001) 'Cross-cultural Infant Care and Issues of Equity and Social Justice.' *Contemporary Issues in Early Childhood 2*, 3, 368–371.

Gudykunst, W. and Kim Young Yun (1995) 'Communicating with Strangers: An Approach to Intercultural Communication.' In J. Stewart (ed) *Bridges Not Walls.* Columbus, OH: M'Graw-Hill

Ho, M.K. (1991) 'The Use of the Ethnic-Sensitive Inventory (ESI) to Enhance Practitioner Skills with Minorities.' *Journal of Multi-Cultural Social Work 1*, 57–67.

Husain, F. (forthcoming 2005) *Culturally Competent Family Support: A Toolkit for Supporting Minority Ethnic Families.* London: NFPI.

Kalantzis, M. and Cope, B. (1997) 'Why Cultures Will Win Out Over Markets.' *Crossings: Bulletin of the Australian Studies Association 2*, 1, 1–2.

Leigh, J.W. (1998) *Communicating for Cultural Competence.* Toronto: Allyn and Bacon.

Lynch, E.W. and Hanson, M.J. (2003) *Developing Cross-Cultural Competence: A Guide for Working with Children and Their Families.* Baltimore, MD: Paul Brookes Publishing.

Massachusetts Chronic Disease Improvement Network (1999) 'A Model for Cultural Competence in Health Care.' *Progress Notes: A Newsletter of the MCDIN 3*, 3.

Maternal and Child Health Bureau (1995) *System Indicator: Development of Community Performance Measures: A Preliminary Assessment.* Washington DC: Maternal and Child Health Bureau.

McPhatter, A.R. (1997) 'Cultural Competence in Child Welfare: What is it? How do we achieve it? What happens without it?' *Child Welfare 76*, 1, 255–278.

Meadows, M. (2000) 'Moving Towards a Consensus on Cultural Competency in Health Care.' *Closing the Gap: A Newsletter of the Office of Minority Health, US Department of Health and Human Resources.* Available at www.omhrc.gov.

Modood, T. and Beishon, S. (1994) *Changing Ethnic Identities.* London: PSI.

Muir, H. and Smith, L. (2004) *Islamophobia: Issues, Challenges and Actions.* Stoke on Trent: Trentham Books.

National Association of of Social Workers (2004) *NASW Standards for Cultural Competence in Social Work Practice.* Available at www.socialworkers.org/sections/credentials/cultural_comp.asp (downloaded 2004).

National Centre for Cultural Competence (2004) *Conceptual Frameworks/Models, Guiding Values and Principles.* Available at www.gucchd.georgetown.edu//nccc/ framework.html (downloaded 2004).

Office of Minority Health (1999) *Assuring Cultural Competence in Health Care.* Washington DC: Office of Minority Health.

O'Neale, V. (2000) *Excellence not Excuses: Inspection of Services for Ethnic Minority Children and Families.* London: Department of Health.

Pankaj, V. (2000) *Family Mediation Services for Minority Ethnic Families in Scotland.* Edinburgh: The Scottish Executive Central Research Unit.

Papadopoulos, R. (2003) 'The Papadopoulos, Tilki and Taylor Model for the Development of Cultural Competence in Nursing.' *Journal of Health, Social and Environmental Issues 4*, 1. Available at www.mdx.ac.uk/www/rctsh/modelc.htm.

Parsons, L., Macfarlane, A. and Golding, J. (1993) 'Pregnancy, Birth and Maternity Care.' In W.U.I. Ahmad (ed) 'Race' and Health in Contemporary Britain. Buckingham: Open University Press.

Qureshi, T., Berridge, D. and Wenman, H. (2000) Where to Turn? Family Support for South Asian Communities – A Case Study. London: National Children's Bureau and Joseph Rowntree Foundation.

Robinson, L. (1997) 'Inter-racial Communication and Social Work Practice: Some Issues and Guidelines for Social Work Trainers and Practitioners.' Issues in Social Work 16, 2, 15–25.

Sachdev, D. and Van Meeuwen, A. (eds) (2002) Are We Listening Yet? Working with Minority Ethnic Communities – Some Models of Practice. London: Barnardos.

Saleebey, D. (1994) 'Culture, Theory and Narrative: the Intersection of Meanings in Practice.' Social Work 39, 4, 351–359.

Schotter, J. and Cunliffe, A. (2002) 'Managers as Practical Authors: Everyday Conversations for Action.' In D. Holman and R. Thorpe (eds) Management and Language: The Manager as Practical Author. London: Sage.

Smith, L. (1998) 'Concept Analysis: Cultural Competence.' Journal of Cultural Diversity 5, 1, 4–10.

Thoburn, J., Chand, A. and Procter, J. (2004) Review of Research on Child Welfare Services for Children of Minority Ethnic Origin and Their Families. London: Jessica Kingsley Publishers.

Tirado, M. (1996) Tools for Monitoring Cultural Competence in Health Care. San Francisco, CA: Latino Coalition for a Healthy California.

Weiss, C. and Minsky, S. (1994) Program Self-assessment Survey for Cultural Competence: A Manual. New Jersey: New Jersey Division of Mental Health and Hospitals.

Wiseman, R., Hammer, M. and Nishida, H. (1989) 'Predictors of Intercultural Communication Competence.' International Journal of Intercultural Relations 13, 349–370.

Woolgar, S. (ed) (1988) Knowledge and Reflexivity: New Frontiers in the Sociology of Knowledge. London: Sage.

Chapter 12

Reframing Practice as Family Support: Leaving Care

John Pinkerton

Introduction

Family support continues to be an attractive overarching child welfare policy direction for the state in its relationship to the family as a key institution within civil society. It promotes reciprocity based on recognition of the strengths and the weaknesses on both sides of the relationship. The state commands authority and resources with which to promote and protect the well-being of its citizens, but it is the intimate exchanges of family life that provide the stable attachments and positive reinforcement on which personal well-being depends. Worry over the capacity of the family to cope successfully with the pressures, complexity and uncertainty of present day life is matched by concern over high-cost, low-quality, intrusive state intervention. So it seems that mutual support through a range of state provided or funded services for family life and the informal networks of social care that surround it is the way to generate the optimum balance between state intervention and family autonomy. Both the state and the family provide and receive support from each other in the struggle to ensure social well-being in times of change.

However, despite the appeal of family support as a policy direction it continues to pose a considerable challenge at the operational level. There is a real danger that an inability to spell out the detail of what committing to family support means in practice will undermine it as a policy goal. Family support may still become just one more historical twist in the difficult relationship between state and family. If that is not to happen there is a particular onus on operational managers and front line workers to consolidate and develop what they understand to be family support and how to give it expression in practice. That is not a matter of practitioners embracing a new way of working but rather critically reflecting on the work they are already engaged in. The development of family support cannot be achieved by policy dictated from above. It depends on learning from below about what needs to change in practice to make family support a reality.

This chapter will argue that front line workers and operational managers who want to contribute to the development of family support need to engage in a process of reframing their practice. This requires describing the basic characteristics of their existing work, locating that within a view of the wider child welfare system, considering the extent to which their services are delivered in a manner consistent with family support principles, planning what needs to be done to strengthen that alignment and then acting accordingly. As an aid to that process of reflection this chapter offers a number of conceptual frameworks and checklists. For operational purposes family support is best thought of as an integrated service system within which a broad range of provision is brought together. Accordingly the first framework to be presented will be a four-level model of the child welfare system. It allows for a full range of needs and interventions to be considered as family support. That 'whole system' framework is then linked to a checklist of eight criteria for evaluating family support service delivery.

Much of the activity around family support is focused on prevention and early intervention goals for children. Here however the focus will be on adolescents leaving out-of-home care. Two conceptual frameworks from that area of practice, the care continuum and the coping wheel, will be related to the family support four-level framework and to the eight evaluation criteria checklist. Making those connections not only reframes leaving care in accordance with the overarching policy goal of family support but also reinforces what is now recognised as the major goal for these young people – not independence but interdependence. A checklist outline for a group work programme to prepare young people for leaving care will be used as illustration. In this way the chapter aims to demonstrate and promote the importance and usefulness of taking a family support perspective at all levels of need and intervention within a child welfare system.

Location in the system

It is increasingly recognised that what goes on in any particular part of the child welfare system can only be fully understood if it is seen in the context of the system as a whole (Coles 2000; Hardiker, Exton and Barker 1991; Hill and Aldgate 1996; Pinkerton, Dolan and Percy 2003). This has been promoted under the slogan of 'joined up' thinking. Despite that, there continues to be a tendency to think in practice of the child welfare system as being made up of three very distinct systems – child protection, out-of-home care (residential care and foster care) and family support. To date most of the operational debate about family support has not been concerned with how to put the policy into practice on a whole-system basis. Instead family support is seen to be restricted to a set of low-status, community-based, early years provision. The systemic question becomes not whole-system integration but how to relate narrowly defined family support to the high-priority child protection services and the high-cost substitute care that is linked to it. From this perspective family support can only be validated by its capacity to prevent child abuse or entry into substitute care. As a result it becomes a desirable but not essential adjunct to the child protection and substitute care systems. This is particularly clear in terms of resource allocation.

The appeal of this way of thinking for operational managers and front-line workers is that it appears to reflect the daily reality of their existing work. However, as a review of government sponsored research in England pointed out, this splitting has been shown to be unhelpful to children:

> The studies suggest that, by separating the two systems [child protection and family support], some children have missed the value of early intervention to prevent more intrusive and intensive activity at a later stage. Conversely, some children, who need safeguarding because of neglect are slipping through the net of family support services because these services fail to address the importance of safeguarding children's welfare.

(Department of Health 2001, p.144)

One of the gains from having family support as an overarching goal for child welfare is that it encourages whole-system thinking in place of split thinking. All provision has to be seen as combining to express the desired relationship between the state, intermediary organisations in the voluntary and community sectors and family life. However if operational managers and front-line workers are to embrace this joined-up thinking they still need to be able to locate the particulars of their existing daily practice within the system as a whole. The starting point of any reflective practice must be description of the work the practitioner is primarily involved with. This requires being clear about the characteristics of that work. Asking the five questions set out in the checklist in Table 12.1 can help with this.

Once a practitioner has described the work she or he is involved in as clearly as possible, the next step is to locate it within the child welfare system as a whole. This requires a conceptual framework which can encompass a full range of needs and services and consider them all to be contributing to family support. This can be achieved, as outlined in Figure 12.1, by thinking of the child welfare system as a set of separate but interconnected levels of need and matched services (Hardiker *et al.* 1991). Each successive level represents a deeper engagement with formal state-provided or funded and sanctioned services. Level One provides open access support to families such as pre- or after-school provision. Similar services are also likely to be available on a purely commercial basis. Although take-up of these services in the state sector may be

Table 12.1 Checklist 1: Basic description of provision

Aspects of provision	Questions to ask yourself	Examples of answers
Target client group	Who is the central target service user group for my work?	Parents, toddlers, teenagers, children with a disability
Major activities	What activities am I primarily involved in delivering or managing?	Home visits, play school, youth group, parenting course, counselling sessions, family therapy, residential care
Skills and methods	What skills and methods am I using?	Information giving, empathy, advocacy, counselling, group work, community development
Work force	Who is it that I work with as colleagues?	Social worker, family centre worker, psychologist, community mother, youth and community worker
Purpose	What is the purpose of my work?	Community development, child protection, social inclusion of marginalised youth, promotion of child development, alternative care

limited by availability and cost, the support provided is in principle there for parents as they themselves judge they need it. Thus these services strengthen the functioning of families on their own terms. However, it also needs to be recognised that by using a service of any type a family is entering into a relationship which compromises its autonomy. Support always carries with it a degree of control.

By contrast Level Two support, whilst still provided to families at their request, is targeted by assessment of need. Need has to be assessed as beyond the coping capacity of the family and so additional support is required and mandated by the state as part of its responsibility towards supporting family life. For example a home support worker might be allocated by statutory social services for a prescribed period to help a stressed single parent with domestic management and child care. It is also possible that a Level One service, such as a

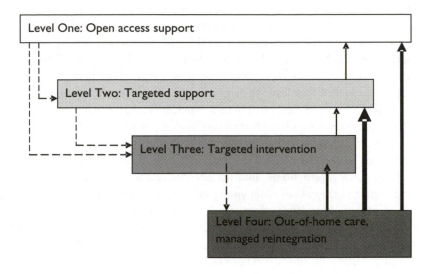

Figure 12.1 Levels of support for families (adapted from Hardiker et al. 1991)

play group, is included in the package of support provided at Level Two. Through being combined with Level Two services, the Level One service shifts its position to the deeper level. While the extent of need and the type of service is different at these two levels, the goal of family support is common to both. Provision at Level Two will always be working to lower need and/or raise coping capacity so that family functioning can be achieved at Level One. It is also a concern at Level Two to ensure that need does not increase and/or coping capacity lessen to a point where Level Three intervention is required.

At Level Three support is termed intervention to indicate that the voluntary element is gone because severe and established difficulties placing children at risk have been assessed and work with the family is mandated by the courts. This targeted intervention combines support and monitoring through a package of care. This might include home visiting, parenting training, treatment for alcohol abuse and periods of respite out-of-home care. As already noted, a combination of care and control is a feature of all support but at this level the tension between the two becomes a central feature to be managed. It is also possible that services used at Levels One and Two can be included in the intervention at Level Three. Through being used at this deeper level they shift position. Although the need and service at Level Three can be differentiated from the two lower levels and state power is being used to back up the intervention, the goal still continues to be support of family life. Work at this level will always aspire to reducing need and/or improving coping capacity so that it can be met at a shallower level in the system. Provision at Level Three is also concerned to ensure that need does not increase and/or coping capacity lessen to a point where Level Four intervention is required.

At Level Four the need within a family is so acute or the coping capacity so inadequate that children and young people have to be placed in medium- or long-term out-of-home care. The aim at this level is that children and young people experience and leave their placements in a way that minimises the ill effects resulting from their birth family experience, their separation from home or their involvement with the formal care system, or a combination of the three. Intervention at this level aims to minimise the length of time a child or young person has to spend in an out-of-home placement. This is achieved through working for a return home, finding alternative family permanence through adoption or, in the case of older young people, supporting them in their transition to adult independence from family of origin. It should be noted that the latter is an important function in any family. Again the thrust of the work is about supporting family life – though no longer necessarily through shoring up a birth family. Work at Level Four is about lowering the level of need and/or improving coping so that re-engagement with services at the shallower levels become sufficient.

The reflective practitioner grappling with family support as front-line worker or operational manager needs to be clear about location in this integrated four-level system to provide understanding of the systemic context of their work. Explaining the position of those delivering and receiving services at any one level requires reference to the other levels and acknowledgement of movement between levels. That movement and its implications for defining practice becomes particularly clear when staff consider how children and their parents have come to be known to them at their level and to which level they may be moving next. For example, work with a stressed single parent at Level Two who has moved from Level One and is at risk of moving deeper into the system requires different handling from work at that level with a similar parent who has been at level Three and Four and is now progressing back out of the system.

In most cases a service will be primarily located at one particular level – for example: community play group at Level One, family centre at Level Two, family and child care team at Level Three and after-care team at Level Four. That said, in locating their practice using the four-level framework, operational managers and front-line workers may well find that they move across a number of levels in their work with a family or work at different levels with different families. It is important to acknowledge this and explore the positive and negative implications. For example, if there seems to be a lot of movement across levels, is this due to the flexibility of the service or is it because the service lacks focus? Conceptual modelling must not artificially tidy up the messiness that is part of everyday practice but rather make it explicit in order to aid reflective practice.

Application to practice

Taking the example of a residential worker, it is possible to locate the service she and her unit provide to different young people at a number of levels. An admission aiming to provide a brief period of respite for the parent of a young person with challenging behaviour is at Level Two. It is part of a service that is aiming to get a family over a difficult period so that they can move back down to Level One support and to prevent them from needing to be moved deeper into the system to Level Three. Providing a short-term placement in the unit for a young person on a care order as part of an intervention package sits at Level Three. The aim of the package is to meet the needs of the young person and family and boost their coping capacity sufficiently to move them back to Level Two or One – or if that proves unachievable to move to Level Four. Preparing a young person aging out of a care order to live on his or her own is work at Level Four.

From these examples it is apparent that the work of a residential worker and her unit could be located at a number of levels for the same young person at different stages in a single care career. For any one receiving services at Level Three or Four it is helpful to think of the levels as stages in a care career, in addition to them being parts of a system. It is possible to superimpose the care continuum model which presents the care career of a child or young person as movement from Pre-care to In-care to After-care over the four levels. As can be seen from Figure 12.2 Level One and Level Two provide for Pre-care, Level Three for In-care and Level Four is concerned with the leaving care transition from In-care to After-care, where engagement at Levels One and Two may once again become appropriate.

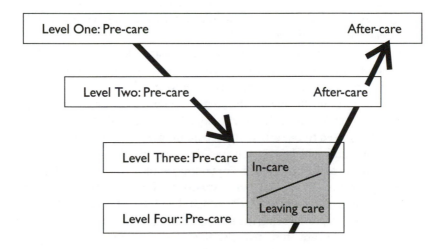

Figure 12.2 Linking a care career to levels of support

Delivering leaving care as a family support service

Once the characteristics of the provision have been described and located within the four levels of the system, the front-line worker or operational manager trying to make sense of what he or she is doing in terms of family support needs to consider the manner in which services are delivered. This builds on the description of the work provided by the five questions suggested earlier (Checklist 1, Table 12.1) which sought to clarify target group, major activities, skills and methods, occupations of work force and purpose of provision. The eight service criteria set out in the first two columns of Checklist 2 in Table 12.2 can help focus on this further description in a way that links it to family support. (The third and fourth column in the figure will be discussed later.)

The criteria are taken from one section of a set of 23 criteria developed for evaluating family support as part of a regional study undertaken in Northern Ireland (Pinkerton, Higgins and Devine 2000). The criteria were based on a combination of what was required by child welfare legislation and messages from empirical research on the characteristics of preventive services. In applying the criteria to work underway the reflective practitioner is moving from description to evaluation.

Returning to the example of a residential care worker wishing to orientate her work towards family support, she would start by describing the roles and tasks she presently undertakes. It is increasingly being recognised that a core task of residential care is preparation of young people for leaving care and this is likely to be part of how all residential workers describe their role. Having identified this aspect of her role and its associated tasks, the second step for our family support residential worker is to locate her work in the four-level model. The preparation for leaving care aspect of her work is located at Level Four. Through preparation the residential worker is trying to help young people in her unit move back up the system.

As is now well established by practice and research, leaving care challenges young people in every aspect of their lives (Wheal 2002). They have to find ways of meeting their material needs: maintaining good health, finding accommodation, getting an income, continuing or entering education, training or employment. They also have the psycho-social needs typical of their age group to be met. They need to be sufficiently secure in their own identity to have the self-confidence and social competence to deal with the day-to-day aspects of their lives outside of the care system. For young people to meet these challenges requires support from their peers and trustworthy adults. This range of complex and demanding needs, and the way in which they interact both positively and negatively, can be captured using the idea of a coping wheel (see Figure 12.3).

Six areas of need are presented as spokes of a wheel, held in place by a rim of 'rights and responsibilities' reinforced by an outer rim of 'expectations and

Table 12.2 Checklist 2: Eight services delivery criteria

Criteria		Achieved Yes/No	Planned improvements
1	Services are delivered through a clearly planned and managed but flexible process	YES	Closer attention to agency policy and procedure
2	Services are delivered using an explicit set of methods, techniques and skills which promote engagement and creativity	NO	Develop and run group work programme
3	Services are delivered in a manner that effectively draws on the expertise of other service providers	NO	Involve other agencies in developing, running and contributing to the programme
4	Services are delivered in a manner that effectively draws on the contribution of relatives, friends and neighbours	NO	Involve members of the young people's informal networks in contributing to the programme
5	Services are delivered in a manner that is responsive to the opinions, wishes and feelings of both children/young people and parents/carers who use them	YES	Involve young people and their families in planning the programme – see plans for Sessions 1, 2, 8 and 9
6	Services are delivered in a manner that expresses understanding and respect for issues of race and culture in the lives of the children/young people and parents/carers who use them	NO	Involve young people and their families in planning the programme – see plans for Sessions 1, 2, 8 and 9
7	Services are delivered in a manner that incorporates concern for child protection	YES	Include risk as an underlying theme for the programme – see plan for Session 3
8	Services are delivered in a manner that minimises as far as possible the effect of children's disabilities	NO	Identify those young people with special needs and plan accordingly

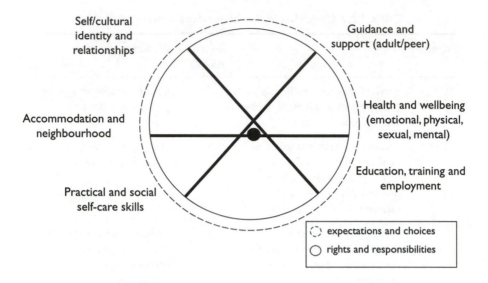

Figure 12.3 Leaving care coping wheel

choices'. Each of the spokes and both rims need to be in place, strong and secure if the wheel is to cope with the bumpy ride up through the system from Level Four to Level One. Preparation for leaving care aims to ensure that is the case.

To help a young person make the journey from deep in the system at Level Four back up to Level One is a challenging area of practice. However, if it is viewed from a family support perspective it is possible to identify the major aspects of that challenge and plan to meet them. Using the family support services criteria from Checklist 2 (Table 12.2) as a prompt, there are seven characteristics that emerge for working in this area:

1. Acceptance of social services' lead role (Criterion 1)

2. Active participation of young people preparing to leave care (Criterion 5)

3. Attention to process (Criterion 1)

4. Attention to method (Criterion 2)

5. Engagement of a range of formal services (Criterion 3)

6. Engagement of informal supports (Criteria 4 and 5)

7. Focusing on rights and needs common to all young people (Criteria 6, 7 and 8).

The first two characteristics establish the relationship between residential worker and the young person leaving care which must be at the core of the work. The third and fourth characteristics make it clear that even this deep into the system the state has not substituted itself for the family. The residential worker is involved in managing a process of matching needs and services which requires the adoption and development of particular methods. She is part of a formal system and her involvement is justified by her professional competence. At the same time this support work needs to draw on a wider range of help than the residential worker alone can provide and this is recognised in the fifth and sixth characteristic. They promote the engagement of both formal services and informal supports. The final characteristic makes it clear that the issues requiring attention set care leavers alongside their peers, not apart from them. Social inclusion is the goal of this work as with all family support.

Planning a group work programme

If the residential worker being used as an example applied Checklist 2 (Table 12.2) to her leaving care work, and assuming she is only involved in one-to-one preparation work, the contents of the third column show how she might evaluate what she is doing. From the five 'No' responses it is clear there are improvements she needs to make to more closely align her work with the family support criteria. One way to do this is to use a group work approach to her work (Brown 1992; McCrea and Pinkerton 2005; Ward 1998). Group work is a frequently used but under-discussed method within family support. It is also an important medium for engaging young people who are leaving care. The improvements the residential worker would plan for her practice using a group work approach are set out in the fourth column. Checklist 3 (Table 12.3) provides an outline for a preparation for leaving care group which addresses the improvements planned. From this family support perspective preparation for leaving care is about ensuring young people can access support at the shallower levels of the system. It provides a 'reality check' for the young people about what is involved in coping with life when they are no longer deep in the system; what the challenges will be for them and what support, formal and informal, is available to them at the shallower levels. This needs to be done in a way that is both challenging and reassuring. Care leavers need the opportunity to think realistically about the challenges they have to face and the capacity they have to cope – the spokes and rims of the coping wheel. A group provides an ideal milieu for empowering young people through identifying and exploring their expectations, strengths and weaknesses, rights and responsibilities, and the choices that lie ahead for them.

A key goal for a leaving care preparation group is to provide information about formal support services that will be available to young people on leaving care. It needs to provide up-to-date local information about the help young

Table 12.3 Checklist 3: Outline of a preparation for leaving group within a family support framework (adapted from McCrea and Pinkerton 2005)

Group membership	Nine young people, mixed sex 16–18 years old, mixed placement, preparation for leaving care phase of care continuum / Level Four Family Support
	Three facilitators – social services and youth services staff plus a care-experienced young person.

Session no.	Content	Those involved
1	Introductory session: • choices, hopes and fears around leaving care • self-evaluation • purpose of the programme	Young people Facilitators
2	Review of Session 1 Planning and agreeing the detail of the remaining sessions	Young people Facilitators
3	Coping with leaving and aftercare: • personal knowledge and skills • sources of information and support	Young people Facilitators Youth counsellor
4	Looking after myself: • physical • emotional • mental health and well-being	Young people Facilitators Health promotion peer educator
5	Money matters: • benefits • pay • budgeting	Young people Facilitators Social security officer
6	Keeping a roof over my head: • accommodation • neighbours	Young people Facilitators Housing officer
7	Taking my opportunities: • education • careers • employment	Young people Facilitator Training and employment adviser
8	Planning session for residential weekend	Young people Facilitators
9	Residential weekend: • programme evaluation • self-evaluation • next-step planning	Young people Facilitators

people could look for in health matters, accommodation, leisure services, income support, further education and training. Other agencies can be called upon to use their particular expertise to plan and lead single sessions and provide co-facilitators for them – see Checklist 3 (Table 12.3): youth counsellor in Session 3; health promotion peer educator in Session 4; social security officer in Session 5; housing officer in Session 6; training and employment adviser in Session 7. In addition informal sources of support such as families and friends should be tapped (Marsh and Peel 1999). The older sister of a group member who has already left care and is coping well might be recruited as a facilitator. The friend of a group member's family who retrained after being made redundant and is now self-employed could be invited to contribute to Session 7.

Keeping the numbers involved in the group small and using speakers from the local offices of the various agencies, can ensure that the information is very much tailored to the particular circumstances of the young people in terms of matching their needs with local services. Guest speakers can put a human face to an organisation, making it less impersonal. The speaker may be the person the young person will be dealing with when involved with that service. This helps to break down barriers and encourage the young people to be more confident in making appointments to find out more about services as they need them. Where possible, information giving should be backed up by activities, such as visiting the type of accommodation likely to be available to them or by going to see what is on offer at the local youth club.

The young people will derive benefit not only from being involved in active learning but also from learning as part of a peer group. The group has to be more than just a series of information sessions. It needs to be participatory and fun for the young people as well as informative and challenging. There needs to be a social side to the group meetings as well as the 'business' side. The importance of the social side of the group is something that cannot be overstated. A residential weekend away at the end of a programme can provide not only a good opportunity for self-evaluation and next-step planning but also a memorable fun social occasion.

The group facilitators also need to deal with the group process and interpersonal dynamics. This is not an easy task. Combining information giving from outside speakers with successful management of group process is difficult to achieve and sustain. A group must be flexible enough to respond to the special emotional and intellectual needs that some care leavers will have. Sufficient numbers of appropriately skilled facilitators are needed. In Checklist 3 (Table 12.3) the outline suggests partnering a social services staff member, the residential worker, with a youth worker. The involvement of a care-experienced young person as facilitator, as suggested in the outline, is likely to greatly increase the receptiveness of the young people. This is both because they feel more comfortable discussing the issues with others like themselves and because they have greater respect for people who have actually been through the experience. Managing group dynamics can be challenging for both facilitators and group members, but it also makes for a very stimulating and engaging context in which to learn about and explore shared issues relating to leaving care. When working well, the group approach can offer a sense of sharing to the members, reducing feelings of isolation and the fear of not being able to cope with life after care.

Conclusion

If family support is to be the overarching policy goal for child welfare by which the state and family provide and receive support from each other to promote social well-being, it is essential that a shared approach to practice is developed and located within an integrated service delivery system. The necessary practice can only be developed by reflecting on the experience of front line workers and operational managers. This chapter has argued that this reflection can be achieved through a process of reframing and building on existing practice. A number of conceptual frameworks and checklists were offered to help focus the process:

- Describe present practice (Checklist 1 Table 12.1, Figure 12.3).
- Locate it within the system as a whole (Figures 12.1 and 12.2).
- Evaluate against family support practice criteria (Checklist 2 Table 12.2).
- Set a personal agenda for improvement (Checklists 2 and 3 Tables 12.2 and 12.3).

Front-line workers and operational managers who want to contribute to the development of family support must engage in a process of reframing their practice. The aim of this is not to take a practitioner away from his or her practice to broad generalities but rather to promote clearer engagement with the detail of what they are presently engaged in. Reflection through reframing requires describing the basic characteristics of existing work, locating that within a view of the wider child welfare system, considering the extent to which services are delivered in a manner consistent with family support, planning what needs to be done to strengthen that alignment and acting on it. The new work that results can then be the starting point for repeating the reframing process. With every repetition a deeper understanding of family support and a more effective practice will be achieved.

References

Brown, A. (1992) *Groupwork*. 3rd edn, Aldershot: Ashgate.

Coles, B. (2000) *Joined-up Youth Research, Policy and Practice: A New Agenda for Change*. London: UCL Press.

Department of Health (2001) *Children Act Now: Messages from Research*. London: Stationery Office.

Hardiker, P., Exton, K. and Barker, M. (1991) *Policies and Practices in Preventative Child Care*. Aldershot: Avebury.

Hill, M. and Aldgate, J. (1996) 'The Children Act 1989 and Recent Developments in Research in England and Wales.' In M. Hill and J. Aldgate (eds) *Child Welfare Services*. London: Jessica Kingsley Publishers.

Marsh, P. and Peel, M. (1999) *Leaving Care in Partnership: Family Involvement with Care Leavers*. London: Stationery Office.

McCrea, R. and Pinkerton, J. (2005) '"Preparation for Adulthood" A Group Work Programme for Young People Leaving Care – From Board Prototype to Trust Implementation.' Unpublished evaluation for the Southern Health and Social Services Board, Northern Ireland.

Pinkerton, J., Higgins, K. and Devine, P. (2000) *Family Support – Linking Project Evaluation to Policy Analysis*. Aldershot: Ashgate.

Pinkerton, J., Dolan, P. and Percy, A. (2003) 'Family Support in Ireland: Developing Strategic Implementation.' *Child Care in Practice 9*, 4, 309–321.

Ward, D. (1998) 'Groupwork.' In R. Adams, L. Dominelli and M. Payne (eds) *Social Work: Themes, Issues and Critical Debates*. London: Macmillan.

Wheal, A. (ed) (2002) *The RHP Companion to Leaving Care*. Dorset: Russell House Publishing.

Chapter 13

Assessment, Intervention and Self-appraisal Tools for Family Support

Pat Dolan

Introduction

Within the process of supporting families in need there are two essential sets of skills which underpin any individual professional's practice. First, the knowledge-based skills which the worker uses in order to understand and meet the needs of service users. Second, there are the interpersonal skills that the worker uses to connect with and work alongside families. In this chapter, three practice tools are presented which can help maintain and develop these essential skills. In each case the background and context, description and administration, and the potential limitations of the tool will be considered and an example given. The aim is to inform reflective practice while clearly focusing on the 'how to' of working with children and families on a one-to-one, micro level. As the task of providing family support is everyone's business, regardless of discipline or service, the tools presented have multi-professional and multi-agency currency.

The three specific tools for practice which will be described and assessed along with an example in each case are: the Social Provisions Scale (SPS) for assessment; the Intervention Matrix Model (IMM) for planning; and the Self-Appraisal Model (SAM) for promoting a reflective style of working. All three directly address key aspects of family support. The SPS as a child-friendly practice tool for the identification of a young person's perceived sources, levels, types and qualities of social support assesses the potential for the enhancement of responsive social networks as a key factor in family support. The IMM is primarily concerned with finding ways of building resiliency whilst working with families on meeting their needs. The focus on SAM as a means for monitoring reflective practice through self-appraisal underlines the importance of front line workers and their styles of work being compatible with family support. All three tools have been used recently in family support service contexts in the west of Ireland and are subject to ongoing review and development.

It must be stressed that this chapter does not purport to cover the wide range of available methods and tools for assessment, intervention and evaluation of family support practice. Rather, the aim is to show some examples of such tools to encourage practitioners to seek out tools appropriate to supporting them in developing their practice and self-evaluation. Notwithstanding the very limited number of tools presented, some connection is drawn between the set of tools chosen and core elements in the wider agenda for reflective practice in family support.

The Social Provisions Scale (SPS)

Background and context

Providing social support to service users is a key and common task for all professionals working with children and families experiencing adversity. The presence of social support involves enlisting help from social networks comprising informal, semi-formal and formal sources (Ghate and Hazel 2002). Furthermore the perceived presence of a responsive support network is central to enhancing children's and parents' resiliency and mental health (Brugha 1995; Gilligan 2001; Rutter, Giller and Hegel 1998). Having the right types of support available when needed in crisis ongoing living contexts helps abate the need for professional intervention (Gottlieb 2000; Tracy *et al.* 1994). Generally, most people receive abundant concrete emotional advice and esteem support from natural sources and primarily from informal sources comprising family and friends (Canavan and Dolan 2000; DePanfilis 1996). Apart from these benefits the case for 'social support building' as a way of working with children and families is particularly strong given that it is one of the few proven successful areas of social science (Brugha 1995; Gottlieb 2000; Hill 2002). However, it should be noted that whereas, in general, natural sources of social support are preferred, sometimes family can be the cause of most stress in the network and there are contexts in which professionals are the only viable source of social support (Gardner 2003). Similarly, there may be factors in a person's affect that not only isolate that person, but makes him or her difficult to support (Cutrona 2000). Ghate and Hazel (2002) suggest that the key task for professionals may be to change not only a person's network to make it provide more support but also to help a service user become more supportable.

Description

The Social Provisions Scale (SPS) is a multidisciplinary social support assessment tool that comes in two versions (general and source-specific versions), which measure perceived availability of social support by type and quantity of support. The SPS can be described as primarily quantitative in that it establishes an overall score per person in respect of perceived social support (Cutrona and Russell 1990). It measures support across types and sources of support. The SPS can be used repeatedly over time with the same respondent leading to a measure for patterns of social support. Unlike most other social support assessment tools, the SPS can provide not only quantitative data on social support by a scoring mechanism but also qualitative data on the specific nature of support available across Weiss's well-recognised categories of support (Weiss 1974). Thus the SPS establishes the extent to which ample support is perceived to be available across specific areas, e.g. advice support, tangible support, esteem and emotional support. In 2002, the author in collaboration with one of the creators of the tool, Professor Carolyn Cutrona of Iowa State University, co-devised a 'child/adolescent-friendly' version of the instrument (Figure 13.1), for use in a repeated measures-tracking study of adolescents in the west of Ireland (Dolan 2005).

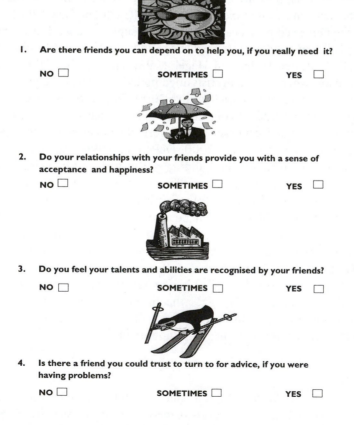

Figure 13.1: Social Provision Scale (child/adolescent version)

Administration

The SPS establishes a young person's perception of the presence of four forms and sources of support: tangible support, emotional support, esteem support and advice support. Additionally the tool focuses on four sources of support: friends, parents/carers, siblings and other adults. In order to support the child/adolescent's understanding and comprehension of the questions a series of repeated 'picture prompts' are used. Respondents complete the SPS by giving each source grouping a rating against each question which relates to a form of support. The questionnaire takes on average no more than ten minutes to complete. The SPS is scored separately in terms of sources and forms with an overall total score per respondent for perceived support. In respect of scoring across sources, all groupings are given the same value. This means that, on the basis that there are four sources containing four questions each, the range of possible total scores go from a minimum 16 (i.e. where in all cases the response is 'no') to a maximum possible score of 48 (where in all cases the response is 'yes'). However, in cases where a respondent does not have a sibling, this naturally reduces the minimum and maximum potential scores.

Potential limitations

Although the SPS is a well-recognised reliable and validated research tool in the US, it was being used for the first time with Irish adolescents. So whereas administration of the tool worked well in accessing the required information, its applicability is still something new and to an extent an unknown, certainly within a non-American context. In addition, despite the author introducing child-friendly picture props, one-to-one support during administration and a full pilot study, there remains the risk that some young people may have either not understood certain questions, or as a result of not knowing the researcher particularly well, decided to give false information. However, although one can never be totally certain, generally, over a series of repeated use of the SPS, the young people remained consistent in their response and usage of the questionnaire, which in itself reduces the likelihood of false reporting or poor understanding on their part.

Case example: the Social Provisions Scale

Margaret, a 12-year-old girl attending a community-based youth project in a rural town in the west of Ireland, was doing very poorly in school and had behaviour difficulties which brought her to the attention of services. Through completion of the Social Provision Scale, she identified her need for more emotional support from her parents, particularly around school issues and a need for better esteem support from her friends, whom she described as always 'putting me down'. By working with her case worker over a six-month period on both of these problems (post-SPS assessment,) Margaret began to regularly discuss her problems regarding school, particularly with her father. In addition, she was supported by the programme in developing friendships through a model of 'social support banking' or increasing support exchanges with friends. The combative effect of these interventions led to her being more settled and content in school and her perception of doing better in her attention to school work. At her follow-up assessment (nine months later) when she again completed the SPS, she reported higher scores for support from parents and friends alike. This gave added evidence of Margaret's improvement.

The Intervention Matrix Model (IMM)
Background and context

It is now generally accepted that the best way of helping families experiencing difficulty lies within a needs-led approach both in child protection and welfare services (Gardner 2003; Parton 1997). This focus suggests that families who have specific needs can be helped to overcome their difficulties and progress. This has been strongly established and advocated within the literature in Ireland (Dolan and Holt 2002; McKeown 2000; Pinkerton, Dolan and Percy 2003) the United Kingdom (Jack 2001; Little and Mount 1999) and in the USA (Belsky 1997; Dryfoos, Quinn and Barkin 2005; Weiss 2001). Whereas there are some mixed results (McAuley 1999) many studies on family support programmes have evidenced that a 'needs-led' focus is worthwhile (Munford and Saunders 2003). Certainly within community-based Family Support in Ireland, the Springboard Initiative (McKeown 2001); the Youth Advocacy Programme (O'Brien, Canavan and Curtin 2004); Neighbourhood Youth Projects (Canavan and Dolan 2003; Gavigan 2002) and the Teen Parenting Programme (Riordan 2002) have all provided some evidence of the worthiness of such an approach.

However, it could be argued that whereas needs-led practice is useful, there is less evidence that families who successfully had their needs met are in any way more capacious in terms of their ability to deal with repeated stressors or repeated negative events (Hains 1992). In the USA, Compas, Orosan and Grant (1993) have suggested that intervention is not just about meeting the expressed or assumed needs of families but should also involve the provision of a battery of skills and responses to self-help in order to cope with negative minor and major life events. The promotion of resiliency building as a way of enabling children and families to be more robust in terms of coping with adversity is certainly not a new concept (Gilligan 2001; Howard, Dryden and Johnson 1999; Rutter *et al.* 1998). However, few tools have matched the notion of meeting need and targeting resiliency building at the same time. Just as one simultaneously takes paracetemol and vitamin C when suffering with a head cold, thereby dealing with the immediate illness, but also working on building a defence force against reoccurrence, a needs-led approach or plan in supporting a child or parent in trouble can include resiliency building as part of the longer-term intervention.

Description and administration

The Intervention Matrix Model (IMM) comes in the form of a three-page spreadsheet plan (see Figure 13.2 below) and using it entails following five simple steps:

1. List a set of needs, perceived by the service user as real and important and which he or she wants help with.

2. Divide the 'need list' into a set of smaller sub-issues in order to make goals more achievable.

3. Agree a set of interventions (practical) steps in order to match each sub-issue with a clear time-frame for action, delegated actor and stated outcome/output to know when either things are improving or reasonable effort is being put in place for improvement to occur.

4. Simultaneously target for the child or adult at least one of the eight matched resiliency building factors with some measurement for the respective factor(s) as part of the intervention process.

5. Review progress.

Need	Intervention by specific tasks	Time-frame	Indicator	Lead person
List here	Insert Step 1 Insert Step 2 etc.	By when?	Output or outcome	By whom?
List here	Insert Step 1 Insert Step 2 etc.	By when?	Output or outcome	By whom?
List here	Insert Step 1 Insert Step 2 etc.	By when?	Output or outcome	By whom?
List here	Insert Step 1 Insert Step 2 etc.	By when?	Output or outcome	By whom?

Figure 13.2: Matrix of need for child, family or community matched with time-frame and lead person – short summary version

Need	Intervention	Targeted resiliency factor	Indicator
Matched to main needs list	Summarised	Those that reduce sensitivity to risk	Outcome of improvement, no change or deterioration
		Reduction of risk impact	
		Reduction of negative chain reactions	
		Increase positive chain reaction	
		Promote self-esteem and self-efficacy	
		Neutralising or compensatory positive experiences	
		Opening-up of positive opportunities	
		Positive cognitive processing of negative experiences	

Figure 13.3: Matrix of need (for child matched with resiliency building – short summary version)

The IMM is completed jointly by the worker and the service user and requires that the worker has positively engaged with the young person or adult. The spreadsheet takes about 30 minutes to complete. Having talked through the spreadsheet and identified existing need, the worker then helps the child or adult to divide the needs into a smaller list which is then sub-divided further into an action plan set. The worker and service user then 'arrow' one or more of the eight factors for resiliency building which they agree match the need for help. Tasks are agreed that the worker will do alone, or with the service user or that the service user will do alone or for others. Finally, a time-frame and expected outputs ('how will we know we have done what we set out to do') or outcomes ('how will we know things have improved') are listed. These can then be summarised as a one-page agreement with any barriers to achieving the task acknowledged and ways of overcoming the obstacles listed. A joint review or 'remapping' of the IMM takes place regularly to assess progress and ensure all parties are fulfilling their obligations.

Potential limitations

According to Neuman (2000) any social research or practice instruments like any other tools have limitations. The IMM has limitations which include the following:

- It requires the service user to be motivated and willing to engage with it.
- The service user needs to have competence in understanding the emergent plan.
- It assumes engagement between the worker and child or adult.
- It requires close attention and commitment by professionals who need to remain focused on its implementation despite other ongoing work demands.
- It is new and needs to be tested out and possibly amended over time.

Case example: Intervention Matrix Model

John, a 10-year-old boy, has problems in school attendance and presents with challenging behaviour (fights continually with classmates). From his initial assessment John states that he sees no chance of things changing for the better. The worker successfully uses the IMM as a way of targeting both the child's negative self-esteem (through one-to-one work and friendship building) and negative cognitive processes (working on specific behaviour methods for avoiding fights or dealing with confrontation in a more controlled way). Over time and through repeated use of the IMM as part of a one-to-one direct work programme, John's behaviour improves and he begins to be more positive about himself with an increased sense of hopefulness.

Reflective practice – Self Appraisal Model (SAM)

Background and context

Style of working and personal presentation are key factors in the delivery of effective family support and are subject to huge variation by professional and agency culture (Reder, Duncan and Gray 1993). At a basic level, this suggests that two workers of similar training, ability and skills can be differentiated by how they do their job and where they work. One worker can come across as committed, caring and responsive, giving the service user time and really 'being there' for that person. Conversely, the other worker for whatever reason or pressure can appear as non-caring and uninterested, basically just about 'doing the job'. Whereas one might argue that difference of work practice styles is just part of human nature, for people in urgent need of support and/or in a state of distress, the difference in approaches is crucial to their well-being (McKeown 2000). The worker's approach is also likely to affect the success of the intervention by the worker (Gardner 2003; McKeown 2001). Thus there should be an expectation that all workers regardless of discipline or position within an agency should treat all those they engage with respect and understanding (Clarke 1999).

Such reflexivity on the part of staff cannot be assumed as ever-present by agency management (Sinclair and Gibbs 1998). Certainly in Ireland and the UK child and family care services, we know that this is not always the case. Much has been written about poor and dangerous culture and individualised practice in respect of residential care (Reder *et al.* 1993). When an agency culture in a service is reflective, child-centred and supportive of staff, workers in turn are astute in relation to their practice with the needs of young people paramount. Not only are young people safer, positive outcomes as a result of their placement are more likely to accrue. However, despite the crucial relationship between the worker and service user, it could be generally argued that attention to in-service training of professionals within child care services does not focus on basic reflective learning (see Chapter 7).

In order to bring focus on the need for such reflective practice within family support services, the author in collaboration with a local health trust's community-based family support services and the Irish National Social Services Inspectorate initiated, implemented and evaluated a one-year pilot programme to model positive practice maintenance and development. The programme incorporated a triad of measures:

1. the development of a set of written multi-disciplinary family support standards for community-based project staff

2. a comprehensive work practice manual to assist staff in meeting each standard

3. a year-long self-appraisal programme to gauge practice goal achievement.

The programme was underpinned by an assumed supportive agency culture and desire by staff to attain best practice. The key elements of the programme are presented in Figure 13.4 as a 'growing tree'.

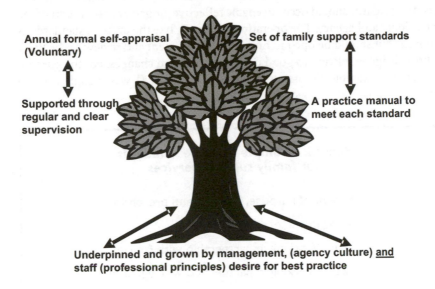

Annual formal self-appraisal
(Voluntary)

Set of family support standards

Supported through
regular and clear
supervision

A practice manual to
meet each standard

Underpinned and grown by management, (agency culture) and
staff (professional principles) desire for best practice

Figure 13.4: Key elements of the self-appraisal model

Administration

Implementation of the scheme occurs in three steps and across two points in time as follows.

STEP 1

The agency project or centre, management staff and service users agree to formalise a set of agency-specific 'practice' standards. Each standard is a declared intent or requirement against which practitioners are expected to measure themselves. In the case of the pilot programme, 21 key practice areas were identified with a specific standard for each one (see Box 13.1). Whereas this list is not exhaustive it does act as a template or guide to the nature of standards required by practitioners.

STEP 2

The manager and staff in collaboration with other stakeholders simultaneously develop a work practice manual which offers assistance to the worker in meeting the practice standards. The manual should cover everything from mundane matters such as agency induction policies and annual leave requirements, right through to programme intervention description and tools such as those described here. Where possible, the matching of the manual items to specific standards should occur to enable reflective judgement on the part of the practitioner and agency. The operational manual, like the practice standards, is not static but should be open to ongoing development and review as the body of knowledge in relation to good practice grows and changes. For the purpose of this case example the itemised list (see Table 13.1) was included in the practice manual.

Box: 13.1: Sample Practice standards for family support services

1. Statement of purpose, function and prevention.

2. Working in partnership

    2.1 Working in partnership with families

    2.2 Working in partnership with agencies

3. Referral procedure

4. Programme planning and review

    4.1 Family support plans

    4.2 Review of needs plan

    4.3 Family involvement

5. Staff recruitment and support

    5.1 Recruitment

    5.2 Staff support

6. Children's rights

    6.1 Consultation

    6.2 Complaints procedures

6.3 Confidentiality

7. Child protection and safeguarding issues

8. Behaviour policy

9. Quality of services

10. Life skills

11. Psychological and emotional development

12. Discharge procedure

13. Physical aspects of the family support services

14. Respect for young people's privacy, dignity and individuality

15. Education support

16. Health care

17. Administration

    17.1 Fire precautions

    17.2 Insurance

    17.3 Young people's/parents' records

    17.4 Administrative records

    17.5 Register

    17.6 Supervision of young people and service user safety

18. Management

    18.1 Project management

18.2 Management support

19. Reward

20. Family support service development

21. Research and evaluation

STEP 3

Once the written standards and supporting practice manual have been 'signed-off' by all stakeholders, the agency is then ready to commence actual appraisal with staff. This involves each worker meeting with his or her appraiser (which ideally should not be the line manager) and self-measuring against each of the standards through a facilitated reflective process. Thus the worker at the time of first appraisal sets a practice target for himself or herself, and having done so, uses regular supervision to devise a plan to attain the practice goal(s) set. Obviously, good supervision is key to success of the programme which apart from engaging in the ongoing organisational educative and emotional needs of the worker, needs to include a monitoring process in respect of the appraisal target(s).

At an agreed date (for example one year later) the worker again meets with the appraiser to review progress in respect of reflective practice goal(s) and to reset his or her target(s). The specific nature of the issues which the worker may wish to improve on can vary from matters as wide as administrative skills such as better record keeping right through to specific practice skills like engaging with fathers or personal coping in respect of managing difficult behaviours among children.

Table 13.1: Sample practice manual for family support services to accompany practice standards contents

Heading – Item	Materials
Mission statement	Insert here
Induction package	
Charter of rights of service users	
Supervision v Self-appraisal	
Support supervision model	
Managing people	
Disciplinary and complaints procedure	
Time management for staff	
Client record keeping system	
Health and safety	
(including safety of service user/staff)	
Work practices – Assessment models/tools	
Work practices – Intervention models/tools	
Work practices – Evaluation models/tools	
Job descriptions	
Referrals	
Needs assessment	
Involvement of project	
Discharge	
Reviews of progress in casework	
Miscellaneous	

Potential limitations

The programme assumes ongoing and consistent trust between the agency and the practitioner. This may be difficult to maintain and may place limitations on implementing a self-appraisal reflective practice programme. These could include:

- the worker setting unrealistic practice goals which are not relevant to the areas he or she needs most to work and reflect on

- the agency not engaging or complying with the support needs of the worker

- the risk of the agency using the self-acknowledged weaknesses on the part of the worker against him or her

- the programme not being followed when the workload becomes excessive which is when workers actually need to reflect most.

Case example: Self-appraisal model

John, a project worker, had some difficulty in giving parents time to discuss their strains of parenting; he preferred to 'get on' with working directly with the young people whom he saw as the main customers of the adolescent service. Through the reflective practice programme, John began to appreciate the importance of the role of parents, especially those who were having serious difficulties in dealing effectively with their offspring. He also learned to value the importance of not working with young people at risk in isolation from their parents. Thus as a result of utilising the self-appraisal programme (standards and manual) he engaged in more parenting work, ensuring (on his part), a greater facilitation of the needs of parents of adolescents attending the programme.

Some further considerations

It is reasonable to suggest that there is a growing consensus among academics, policy makers, social service managers and practitioners that working with troubled children and families involves a focus on meeting need through a model of accurate assessment matched by a distinct intervention (Jack 2001). Despite some questioning as to the exact validity of this approach by certain practitioners (Little and Mount 1999), from a policy and practice perspective it is now generally seen as the way forward. Furthermore, family support work has moved on from being some vague activity based on a worker visiting a service user with only a vague notion of why exactly he or she is doing so (Pinkerton et al. 2003; Whittaker 1999). Supporting families has now become a much more specific form of helping (Canavan and Dolan 2003; Tracy et al. 1994). In order to advance this approach the core message contained in this chapter advocates reflexivity on the part of the worker. Meeting need through family support should occur in a clearly specific way, which does not deflect from the ongoing need for caring and empathy and warmth on the part of the professional towards the person or people he or she supports, and which can be monitored through self-reflexivity.

Increasingly, having an effective set of tools and models for intervention will be key to family support professionals being successful and central to their 'confidence in practice'. Many workers from a wide hue of disciplines wish to enhance the positive impact of their intervention with families and rightly see the acquisition of new skills as central to this aim (Brady, Dolan and Canavan 2004). Similarly, agency managers want to ensure the best possible service to people and recognise that having staff who are well skilled and well motivated is the key to achieving this aim. The tools demonstrated in this chapter are samples of how this can be promoted in any family support agency setting.

However, it could be argued that such a simple perception of reflective practice in family support is naive and ignores the wider issue of professional context. For example, it could be suggested that 'workers do not live on tools alone' and the well-enthused worker who engages with this approach through reflective practice and willingly learns to use new tools is paid the same as the worker who is not so willing and continues to do the 'bare basics'. Despite the fact that differences in such practice approaches by workers is crucial for families, it may be that service managers do not give enough attention to appraisal of staff either by themselves, or via peer, line manager or, most importantly, service user feedback (Dolan and Holt 2002; Tehrani 2001).

On the basis that workers are by far the most important asset in any agency, there remains a dilemma regarding how best to ensure best practice is applied. Apart from the need to have robust programmes and models of practice for workers, in the interest of children and families in need, it is incumbent on all stakeholders to ensure the best quality of services, which means optimum performance from staff through a quality assured 'reflective' professional system.

It should also be noted that apart from assessment and intervention tools for practice, there also now exists a growing range of diverse service models (Brady et al. 2004; Dryfoos et al. 2005; Weiss 2001). For example, one-to-one child mentoring has international programmes of varying intensity, such as the Youth Advocacy Programme (see Chapter 8) and Big Brothers Big Sisters International (Tierney, Grossman and Resch 1995). Nevertheless, as with tools in family support, the lack of standardised uniformity in use of programmes at present limits the addition to our body of knowledge and capacity for reflectivity in family support.

Conclusion

This chapter has highlighted the importance of assessing the potential of social network interventions. It has shown how resiliency can be a key goal of planned interventions, and the importance of a reflective working style in helping families. An associated matching set of non-discipline specific tools has been described in respect of these three key family support factors. The three tools illustrated were the Social Provisions Scale, a method for assessing perceived sources types and levels of social support; the Intervention Matrix Model, a pathway to match 'help to need' with a further focus on resiliency building and the Self-appraisal Model, a mechanism for self-monitoring practice competence. These represent just a sample of what is available to enhance work with families. They are an invitation for family support practitioners to find and develop the tools necessary to their jobs.

If the emergent focus on prevention and family support is to advance, it has to be matched and supported by standardisation of the tools used for assessment, intervention and evaluation, locally, nationally and internationally. For it to become clearer what 'works best' for which children and families there must be trials and assessments of a range of tools. Having the right tools will provide not only the means to better skilled professionals, but also the most important goal of better meeting the needs of children and families.

References

Belsky, J. (1997) 'Determinants and Consequences of Parenting: Illustrative Findings and Basic Principles.' In W. Hellinckx, M. Colton and M. Williams (eds) *International Perspectives on Family Support*. Aldershot: Ashgate Publishing.

Brady, B., Dolan, P. and Canavan, J. (2004) *Exploring Good Practice in Child and Family Services, Research Report*. Department of Health and Children, WHB/National University of Ireland, Galway, Child and Family Research and Policy Unit Publication.

Brugha, T.S. (1995) 'Social Support and Psychiatric Disorder: Recommendations for Clinical Practice and Research.' In T.S. Brugha (ed) *Social Support and Psychiatric Disorder, Research Findings and Guidelines for Clinical Practice*. New York: Cambridge University Press.

Canavan, J. and Dolan, P. (2000) 'Refocusing Project Work with Adolescents towards a Family Support Paradigm.' In J. Canavan, P. Dolan and J. Pinkerton (eds) *Family Support: Direction From Diversity*. London: Jessica Kingsley Publishers.

Canavan, J. and Dolan, P. (2003) 'Policy Roots and Practice Growth: Evaluating Family Support on the West Coast of Ireland.' In I. Katz and J. Pinkerton (eds) *Evaluating Family Support: Thinking Internationally, Thinking Critically*. Chichester: Wiley.

Clarke, M. (1999) *Lives in Care: Issues for Policy and Practice in Children's Homes*. Dublin: Mercy Congregation and the Children's Research Centre, TCD.

Compas, B.E., Orosan, P.G. and Grant, K.E. (1993) 'Adolescent Stress and Coping: Implications for Psychopathology during Adolescence.' *Journal of Adolescence 16*, 3, 331–349.

Cutrona, C.E. (2000) 'Social Support Principles for Strengthening Families: Messages from America.' In J. Canavan, P. Dolan and J. Pinkerton (eds) *Family Support: Direction From Diversity*. London: Jessica Kingsley Publishers.

Cutrona, C.E. and Russell, D. (1990) 'Type of Social Support and Specific Stress: Toward a Theory of Optimal Matching.' In I. Sarason, B. Sarason and G. Pierce (eds) *Social Support: An Interactional View*. New York: Wiley and Sons.

DePanfilis, S. (1996) 'Social Isolation of Neglectful Families: A Review of Social Support Assessment and Intervention Models.' *Child Maltreatment 1*, 35–72.

Dolan, P. (2005) *Helping Young People at Risk through Social Support: NYP Youth Study Summary Report.* A Joint Foroige /Child and Family Research and Policy Unit Publication, Dublin: Foroige Publications.

Dolan, P. and Holt, S. (2002) 'What Families Want in Family Support: An Irish Case Study.' *Child Care in Practice 8*, 4, 239–250.

Dryfoos, J.G., Quinn, J. and Barkin, C. (2005) *Community Schools in Action: Lessons from a Decade of Practice.* New York: Oxford University Press.

Ghate, D. and Hazel, N. (2002) *Parenting in Poor Environments: Stress, Support and Coping.* London: Jessica Kingsley Publishers.

Gavigan, C. (2002) 'A Follow Up Study of Perception of Service Users Who are Experiencing Adversity and Attending NYPs of the Service they Receive.' Unpublished BA thesis, Athlone Institute of Technology, Co. Westmeath.

Gardner, R. (2003) *Supporting Families: Child Protection in the Community.* Chichester: NSPCC and Wiley.

Gottlieb, B.H. (2000) 'Selecting and Planning Support Interventions.' In S. Cohen, L.G. Underwood and B.H. Gottlieb (eds) *Social Support Measurement and Intervention: A Guide for Health and Social Scientists.* New York: Oxford University Press.

Gilligan, R. (2001) *Promoting Resilience: A Resource Guide on Working with Children in the Care System.* London: British Agencies of Adoption and Fostering.

Hains, A.A. (1992) 'A Stress Inoculation Training Program for Adolescents in a High School Setting: A Multiple Baseline Approach.' *Journal of Adolescence 15*, 2, 163–176.

Hill, M, (2002) 'Network Assessments and Diagrams: A Flexible Friend for Social Work Practice and Education.' *Journal of Social Work 2*, 2, 233–254.

Howard, S., Dryden, J. and Johnson, B. (1999) 'Childhood Resilience: Review and Critique of Literature.' *Oxford Review of Education 25*, 3, 307–323.

Jack, G. (2001) 'Ecological Perspectives in Assessing Children and Families.' In J. Horworth (ed) *The Child's World: Assessing Children in Need.* London: Jessica Kingsley Publishers.

Little, M. and Mount, K. (1999) *Prevention and Early Intervention with Children in Need.* Aldershot: Ashgate.

McAuley, C. (1999) *The Family Support Outcomes Study.* Northern Ireland: Northern Health and Social Services Board.

McKeown, K. (2000) *A Guide to What Works in Family Support Services for Vulnerable Families: Springboard Programme.* Dublin: Government Publications, Ireland.

McKeown, K. (2001) *Springboard Promoting Family Well-being through Family Support Services.* Final Evaluation Report of Springboard January 2000 to May 2001. Dublin: A Springboard Publication, Dept. of Health and Children, Stationery Office.

Munford, R. and Saunders, J. (2003) *Making a Difference in Families: Research That Creates Change.* Sydney, NSW: Allen and Unwin Pty Ltd.

Neuman, W. (2000) *Social Research Methods: Qualitative and Quantitative Approaches.* Boston: Allyn and Bacon.

O'Brien, M., Canavan, J. and Curtin, C. (2004) *Youth Advocacy Programme: Evaluation Report.* Galway: WHB/NUI, Galway Child and Family Research and Policy Unit Publication.

Parton, N. (1997) 'Child Protection and Family Support: Current Debates and Future Prospects.' In N. Parton (ed) *Child Protection and Family Support: Tensions, Contradictions and Possibilities.* London: Routledge.

Pinkerton, J., Dolan, P. and Percy, A. (2003) 'Family Support in Ireland: Developing Strategic Implementation.' *Child Care in Practice 9*, 4, 309–321.

Reder, P., Duncan, S. and Gray, M. (1993) *Beyond Blame: Child Abuse Tragedies Revisited.* London: Routledge.

Riordan, S. (2002) *Final Evaluation Report of the Teen Parents Support Initiative.* Dublin: Dublin Institute of Technology for the Department of Health and Children, Stationery Office.

Rutter, M., Giller, H. and Hegel, A. (1998) *Antisocial Behavior by Young People.* Cambridge: Cambridge University Press.

Sinclair, I. and Gibbs, I. (1998) *Children's Homes: A Study in Diversity.* Chichester: Wiley.

Tehrani, N. (2001) *Building a Culture of Respect: Managing Bullying at Work.* London and New York: Taylor and Francis.

Tierney, J., Grossman, J. and Resch, N. (1995) *Making a Difference: An Impact Study of Big Brothers Big Sisters of America.* Philadelphia: Public Private Ventures.

Tracy, E.M., Whittaker, J.K., Pugh, A., Kapp, S. and Overstreet, E. (1994) 'Support Networks of Primary Caregivers Receiving Family Preservations Services: an Exploratory Study of Families in Society.' *Journal of Contemporary Human Services,* 481–489.

Weiss, R. (1974) 'The Provision of Social Relations.' In Z. Rubin (ed) *Doing Unto Others.* Englewood Cliffs, NJ: Prentice Hall.

Weiss, H.B. (2001) 'Reinventing Evaluation to Build High-Performance Child and Family Interventions in Perspectives on Crime and Justice: 1999–2000.' *Lecture Series, National Institute of Justice 4,* 99–126.

Whittaker, J.K. (1999) 'Intensive Family Preservation Work with High-risk Families: Critical Challenges for Research, Clinical Intervention and Policy.' In W. Hellinckx, M. Colton and M. Williams (eds) *International Perspectives on Family Support.* Aldershot: Ashgate Publishing.

Chapter 14

Culturally Appropriate Family Support Practice: Working with Asian Populations

Monit Cheung and Patrick Leung

This chapter focuses on culturally competent practice in family support with Asian and Pacific Islander (API) clients and proposes a single system design practice strategy. Single system design is an evidence-based method that tests service effectiveness. Its evidence-focused design becomes a practice strategy with Asian clients because it is both process and outcome oriented. Based on a cultural competency framework, two case examples will be used to illustrate the six steps involved in this process.

Family support services: A cultural competency perspective

Similar to involving clients in a community-based needs assessment project, single systems research aims at evaluating clients' needs from an individual and/or family perspective with client participation. Although there are several types of practice evaluation methods, the discussion here primarily focuses on single systems research because of its applicability to working with culturally diverse populations and its emphasis on an individualized planning process and concrete outcome analysis. In social work, Corcoran (1993) reports that practice evaluations have not been incorporated into the service routine because of their image of complexity. He recommends that simple design with observations and graphing be used for achieving efficiency.

Uniqueness of evaluating services with API clients

The unique aspects of evaluating service effectiveness with API clients and their families are:

1. It is considered important to engage the clients in defining their outcomes.

2. Client participation in defining the target variables in concrete terms is essential.

3. Repeated measures are helpful especially for those who usually do not verbalize their concerns without encouragement.

4. Mind-body connections are considered a process, not an end product.

Single system design is an appropriate procedure in evaluating practice with API Americans because it is both process and outcome oriented. It requires quantitative repeated measures, qualitative data analyses and a mutual commitment to data collection and data analysis (Bloom, Fischer and Orme 2006).

> When clients are participants in the evaluation process, the measures being used for evaluation may be perceived as a part of the intervention. The Empowering Education Theory proposed by Wallerstein and Bernstein (1988) validated that client participation can enhance self-perceived control over the situation. Through these measures, clients define their outcome, learn about the progress, become more aware of their effort, and eventually move toward helping themselves. API American clients are receptive to ideas that will help them help themselves.

Steps and procedures

Two questions are central to single systems design evaluation:

1. How do clients know that their target behavior of concern has changed?

2. How do helping professionals know that their intervention has caused the change?

In an individual counseling process, repeated measures provide a visual effect to the client and facilitate further discussions about the client's progress. However, in a family counseling process, API American clients are reluctant to engage with their family members in discussion about family members' mental functioning. Anonymous responses seem to be more acceptable than open discussions. By means of a single system design, each of the family members can anonymously answer the clinician's questions on an individualized measure. Collective data may be shared with each of the individuals or in a family meeting. By means of collective data, family members feel more comfortable disclosing their feelings after finding out whether there is any significant change or if a specific pattern occurs after commencement of the intervention.

When working with API clients and families, helping professionals must realize that concreteness is the key to engaging clients in evaluations. In addition, repeated measures are invaluable when addressing clients' needs and concerns.

The first step in the evaluation process is to define the service target (i.e. the perceived problem) in measurable terms (Fang and Wark 1998). Five subsequent steps are then required:

1. setting goals and objectives

2. identifying constraints/resources

3. measuring the target and monitoring actions

4. analyzing data

5. reporting results and making recommendations.

STEP 1: DEFINING THE SERVICE TARGET

Specifying targets for change is a major step in practice evaluation. Most API clients view their problems as family targets, rather than individually based targets. This does not mean that they do not have individual problems, but that they will seek mental health services only when the problem affects family functioning. Taking into consideration their family-focus philosophy, many API Americans have expressed that their mental health issues include cultural adjustment, school performance, school behaviors, caregiver stress, peer pressure and parent–child relationships (Dinh, Sarason and Sarason 1994; Kim 1997).

According to Watson and Tharp (1997), the worker must focus first, on the target behavior for modification and second, on the specific situation in which the behavior occurs. They suggest seven tactics that can provide concrete definitions for these behavior-in-situation targets:

1. Provide concrete examples, such as a child's bed-wetting behavior, or not communicating with parents for a number of days

2. Describe the problem specifically, such as coexisting conditions, when it occurs and the people involved

3. Assign the client as an observer, either of him- or herself or of the relevant family member

4. Try to increase desired behaviors, such as encouraging the family member to think positively, rather than to reduce undesirable behaviors, such as crying

5. Set achievable targets, such as identifying actions linked to the increase of desirable behavior

6. Notice what is working for other people in comparable circumstances

7. Remain open to alternative ways in which to facilitate desirable changes.

Professionals must be aware when helping that encouragement is an important ingredient to success. Based on a study by Wong *et al.* (1999), self-reinforcement is a predictor of depression among API Americans. This finding supports the use of positive thinking to reduce mental health symptoms. Many API clients show low levels of self-esteem when seeking help and their negative self-concept can be an obstacle. They need nurturing and support and are eager to hear professional advice and reassurance. During this step, professionals must obtain input from the clients to accurately identify the service target because a professional's definition of the problem can vary from the client's perspective.

STEP 2: SETTING GOALS AND OBJECTIVES

Self-directed projects are appropriate for certain clients. Most API clients continue seeking help only because their goals in locating sufficient resources to support the family growth have not been reached, not because they believe they have a problem. Because concrete services are considered important, both short-term and long-term life goals should be included. API clients share a common philosophy that when problems dissipate, their body and their family will grow harmoniously with positive energy. Therefore, it is important to set short-term goals to achieve this 'problem-free' perception before long-term goals can be independently achieved by the clients. Kline and Huff (1999) suggest that Asian beliefs and practices are shared by their cultures and determine 'what is important in one's life' (p.387). This life perspective is congruent with the social work mission of helping clients to enhance quality of life. With minimal help API clients usually are able to find a connection between short-term achievement and long-term growth.

Suggested evaluative areas in this step include:

• rationale for setting up short-term goals

• motivating factors for the clients to get involved

• specific steps in the self-contracting process

• the matching between the service target and the life goals of each individual in the family.

STEP 3: IDENTIFYING CONSTRAINTS AND RESOURCES

Formal and informal resources are critical in practice. In evaluations, API clients must identify constraints that might interfere with their success. These blockages generally arise from the immediate environment due to cultural changes and acculturation factors. In order to evaluate the effectiveness of an intervention, the professional must involve the clients in determining how cultural differences might contribute to this process. The professional can also help them identify language difficulties, express thoughts and ideas, and understand communication constraints due to the various degrees of cultural adjustment within a family.

Lack of emotional support is another constraint and reason for API clients to seek social services when they find no support within their family. Since the family is the most important resource for many Asian individuals, helping professionals often find it difficult to empower clients whose family values are strong but family resources weak. Fong (1994) suggests that empowerment and shared responsibility must be emphasized in order to minimize shameful feelings attached to locating resources outside of the family. However, this dilemma of 'family vs. family' may be utilized as a strategy if locating family resources is considered a task, rather than an intervention, for evaluation purposes. It becomes a means to encourage family involvement, rather than a solution to the stated problem.

STEP 4: MEASURING THE TARGET AND MONITORING ACTIONS

Since API clients are interested in monitoring their progress, targeting a measurable outcome is an appropriate means for practice evaluation. Watson and Tharp (1997) suggest five elements for a good evaluation plan:

1. rules to define change

2. goals and sub-goals

3. feedback from self-observations

4. comparisons between feedback and goals

5. plan adjustments.

When working with API clients, it is culturally appropriate to empower them to hear their own feedback since communication is often a major issue in most families (Yu 1999). The feedback comparisons will provide clients with a means to enhance communication skills. Within many API families, the lack of communication skills is further complicated by multiple social and cultural adjustment issues within the family, cross-cultural learning difficulties in the school or work environment, and difficulties in expressing concerns to others while seeking help. Therefore, when helping professionals measure and evaluate service effectiveness with input from their API clients, they must encourage the clients to express themselves by showing an understanding of cultural differences and a respect for self-analyses and self-observations.

API clients will benefit from experiencing and witnessing the change of a measurable target over a trend analysis. As Rubin (1998) states, it is important to study human development from a cultural perspective that includes individual's responses, interactional factors and relationship observations. Observations throughout all intervention phases provide important data to measure the effect of an intervention. API clients will gain insight through data related to individual responses and interactions with others. During the course of monitoring progress and evaluating family involvement, the professional would help the individual client realize the importance of collecting relevant data consistently over time.

STEP 5: ANALYZING DATA

As previously stated, data collection is a means to evaluate practice effectiveness. In evaluating services for API families, the purpose of data collection is twofold:

1. Identify what is important to the family.

2. Assess the outcome of the intervention related to the family.

In single system studies, these two purposes help the professional answer the questions related to the change of target behavior and the cause of such change. Individual-focused measures are used, but the emphasis is related to how the family receives or perceives the benefits of treatment.

While data collection increases clients' awareness of their problem-solving ability, the significance of data analysis is to bring the clients closer to their goal. In reference to API clients, the effect of service is the demonstrable power of their ability and achievement, which moves them one step closer to self-appreciation. Many standardized tests may not be applicable to API clients because their responses are based on negative moods or behaviors (Feldman 1993). Through a self-designed and self-anchored scale, most issues such as self-esteem, assertiveness, parent–child conflict and marital power imbalance can be resolved by achieving a self-appreciated state (see suggestions in Welzler 1989). It is important that the measure of this achievement is concrete and straightforward. When data are analyzed with the clients, the professional may use graphic presentations of a self-anchored scale to measure the client's feelings (e.g. from 1 to 9 with client's own definitions of the low, mid and high points; see Boxes 14.1 and 14.2 for examples), frequency observations (number of times) and duration (time, days) of target behaviors (such as positive self-talks, parent–child mini-conferences). Clients themselves draw a conclusion, with their worker's input, based on these observable data.

In a clinical setting, an average of the change over the last evaluation period in terms of number and percentage helps the client understand how much progress is being made.

Box 14.1 Defining problem indicators

Name:	Mrs Shen
Major complaint:	Loss of sleep (sleeps only 2–3 hours at night)
Target goal:	Increase sleep to reach at least 5 hours a night without disturbances
Body discomfort:	Legs
Definition of stress:	Feeling anxious and not able to sleep

Indicators that may define each level of stress:

Low   1 – No symptoms; sleep at least eight hours without waking up

2 – Sleep at least six hours without waking up

3 – OK

4 – Still OK

Mid   5 – Not able to concentrate

6 – Bad appetite

7 – Feeling unable to take care of myself

8 – Unable to take care of others; leg pain

High   9 – Unable to sleep; wake up many times at night and cannot fall asleep again

---

STEP 6: REPORTING RESULTS AND MAKING RECOMMENDATIONS

When a self-observation instrument is used for data collection, the step of reporting results is a two-way assessment process. Both the client and the professional play key roles in collecting data, sharing perceptions via data analysis, and analyzing outcomes by means of concrete measures. Once the client clarifies the perception and listens to various views of the problem, the client will be able to draw a conclusion based on observations. Recommendations will therefore come from a mutual assessment of the target problem.

Box 14.2 Record keeping

Instructions

Please use the scale developed by you and your practitioner to collect data daily.

A.   Circle your *feeling of stress today*, then write down the date and time when recording this stress level.

Low 1——2——3——4——5——6——7——8——9 High

Date: _____

     Time: _____a.m./p.m.

B.   Put three words below to describe your current feelings.

    _____

    _____

C.   Record your sleep patterns last night:

    Total hours slept last night: _____hours

    Record number of disturbances during your sleep:

    Waking up ____times

    Using the bathroom ____times

    Nightmares: ____yes ____no

    Feeling thirsty: ___yes ___no

Case examples[1]

Two examples are described to illustrate the use of the six steps of practice evaluation with API individuals and families. After each step, hints and implications to practice evaluation are included. To repeat, these six steps are:

---

1   All identifiers of clients reported in this chapter have been changed or disguised to protect confidentiality. Clients have signed consent forms in relation to their participation in this research.

1. defining the service target

2. setting goals and objectives

3. identifying constraints and resources

4. measuring the target and monitoring actions

5. analyzing data

6. reporting results and making recommendations.

The first case is a situation of an individual trying to resolve her problem through her participation in a community project. The second case demonstrates the importance of hearing the problem definition from family members and involving the family in the data collection process.

Working with an individual within the family system

STEP 1: DEFINING THE SERVICE TARGET

Mrs Shen's (50 years old) major complaint is insomnia. She has been having repeated sleep–wake patterns during the night for six months. She only slept two to three hours each night and could not concentrate on work during the day. Her physician could not find any organic reasons for the problem. Mrs Shen tried different herbal remedies. Searching for effective herbal medicine, Mrs Shen was introduced to a social worker. She did not come forward as a client. Instead, she wanted to participate in the project being conducted by the social worker as a research subject on stress reduction. She indicated that she was not sick, because doctors had already ruled out all physical possibilities. She defined her problem as 'something Asian' and therefore Western medicine was not right for her. The professional explained to the client what would happen to her body without sleep. Mrs Shen would only agree to use 'non-Western' remedies. Sleeping without disturbances would be her goal and using an Asian massage technique to reduce stress would help her relax and reexamine reasons associated with insomnia.

Hint 1

Help the client reframe the problem and focus on culturally acceptable interventions.

Implications 1

Many API clients do not realize the need for mental health services. Even though their problem may not be physiologically based, they may still look for health care alternatives, rather than admitting that they suffer mental health problems. The 'sick and crazy' label associated with mental health is too negative. Approaching clients with familiar alternatives that fit their framework seems to be more effective than pushing them to accept the fact that they may have psychological problems, emotional distress or social issues to deal with. Evaluation will focus on the combined effort of applying more than one intervention if so desired, rather than strictly relying on one type of intervention with which the professional is familiar.

STEP 2: SETTING GOALS AND OBJECTIVES

Mrs Shen would act as a helper in the process of demonstrating whether massage therapy would help her reduce insomnia. The first step was to assess her willingness to talk about her problem and she was not reluctant at all. Once the problem was verbalized, she wanted to help the practitioner because she perceived her role as a helper. 'Medical attention' is being reframed as 'talking therapy', with massage therapy included. Her goal was to increase hours of sleep. She would monitor the hours and report the daily sleeping patterns to the social worker once a week for the following two months.

Hint 2

Help the client understand her helping role in goal setting and design records that can be kept in a concrete way.

Implications 2

Seeking help is not considered desirable, but offering help seems to be more acceptable. API American clients like to offer help. Respect for their input and asking them what they can offer are two major keys to open the door to intervention. Once the door is opened, they will accept their role as clients. Evaluation will focus on the type and frequency of concretely measured variables that have significant meanings to the clients.

STEP 3: IDENTIFYING CONSTRAINTS AND RESOURCES

Mrs Shen identified major constraints in her life. She felt that immigration to this country had been the biggest burden on her. She could not find jobs that fitted her interests and skills. She lost her appetite and did not feel happy. Her resources, on the other hand, included her supportive husband, her willingness to look for jobs and her family in China. The social worker helped Mrs Shen to focus on her accomplishments within her family and what is important to her. Mrs Shen found that she regained her energy when talking about her family support system. She would continue monitoring her thoughts into positive aspects of life.

Hint 3

Involve the client in analyzing cause and effect with a strengths-based perspective.

Implications 3

Many API Americans are intellectually capable of solving problems and therefore they will feel inferior when asking for help. The professional's role is to identify what the clients' strengths are, rather than focusing on what they have not done to resolve their conflicts or issues. By focusing on even a small indicator of success, the professional will redirect the clients' energy to overcome current barriers. Evaluation will focus on utilization patterns of available resources.

STEP 4: MEASURING THE TARGET AND MONITORING ACTIONS

Mrs Shen continued recording her sleeping patterns. With the intervention focused on connecting body and mind, Mrs Shen assessed her stress level based on her own definition of stress as it was related to sleep on an individualized scale from 1 to 9. She liked the massage therapy and it helped her to relax. She continued the massage treatment and talked about her feelings immediately after. She found that her extended family issues were more distant than before and she no longer worried about something geographically so far away. At that moment, what made her feel uncomfortable was the discrepancy between her job and her talents. She now realized that she could use her talents in other ways, including helping other Chinese immigrants dealing with their losses and critical adjustment issues, such as finding a job and learning the new language and culture. She became more aware of her stress level as it was related to her loss of sleep and worries. After the first intervention period, even without the social worker's intervention during the second baseline period, Mrs Shen felt very relaxed and was able to sleep more.

Hint 4

Alternative medicine is created and/or envisioned by the client.

Implications 4

API American clients need to be empowered to think more about their strengths than their problems. They continue to look for what they can contribute to the society. Evaluation will focus on before- and after-intervention patterns of behaviors.

STEP 5: ANALYZING DATA

Mrs Shen helped the social worker plot the data on the graph. By means of a single system experimental replication design (called 'ABAB' where A is a baseline measure without intervention and B is the intervention phase), the social worker presented to Mrs Shen, with concrete data, a downward trend of loss of sleep and stress level (see Figure 14.1). Although improvement on her stress level occurred during the first baseline, Mrs Shen talked about what contributed to these outcomes. Mrs Shen liked the intervention because it helped her relax and think. Within this intervention, 'the challenge of thinking patterns' and 'the talking part' of the therapy were significantly addressed, but the client perceived these two components as 'outcomes'.

Hint 5

Visual presentations are powerful tools especially for those who are not expressive.

Implications 5

Some APIs may see the outcomes as 'the intervention', while others see the intervention as the outcomes. Do not overstress or correct the clients' own perceptions. Clients who make the connections from either direction receive the intended benefits.

STEP 6: REPORTING RESULTS AND MAKING RECOMMENDATIONS

Mrs Shen became aware of the importance of talking about her stress, and felt that her stress level was higher during the second intervention stage and her sleeping pattern more irregular and less stable. Mrs Shen could visualize the connection between feelings and behaviors. The social worker suggested that Mrs Shen take five minutes before going to bed to relax. Self-massage methods were instructed. The client was motivated to relax herself and let go of emotions that would create negativity toward life.

Hint 6

Body–mind connections are considered outcomes, not means.

Implications 6

API clients enjoy participating in the therapeutic process. Follow-up data were not always presented to them in the medical environment that they were previously accustomed to. They appreciate knowing their current health and/or mental health conditions but are usually afraid to ask more specific questions about themselves. The interventions package and the outcomes are inseparable

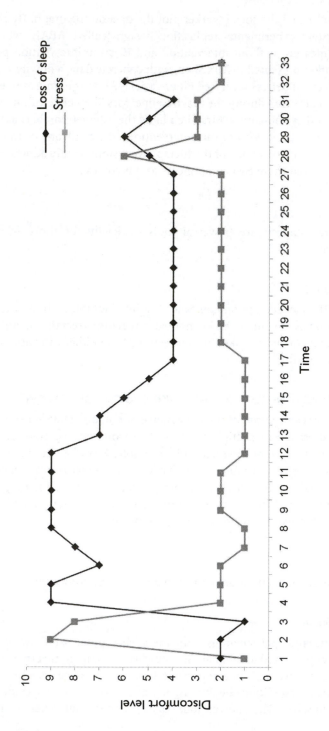

Figure 14.1: Evaluation outcome

and it should not alarm when clients define the intervention as desirable outcomes. Evaluation will focus on graphing the outcomes and analyzing what intervention would be prescribed next.

Working with a family

STEP 1: DEFINING THE SERVICE TARGET

Jan called seeking help because her sister Ming (28) was mentally ill. Her family had tried everything but nothing seemed to work. Jan defined her service target as finding social services that would help Ming to live a happier life. Ming attempted suicide twice but no services were available as a result of the language barrier. After further examination of how the problem had been affecting the family, Jan disclosed her discomfort and believed that her family *should be able* to help, rather than seeking help. She thought that social service agencies would only assist with the mental illness, not the family's distress. Although the family's distress was an important matter to Jan, she thought that it was unnecessary to talk about the family's reactions to outsiders since Ming's first suicide attempt.

Hint 1

Never push clients to define the problem based on the professional's perspective. Clients will eventually find a way to express other issues that they are facing in relation to the presenting problem.

Implications 1

Many API clients define mental health in a narrow sense. New immigrants usually have a stigma attached to mental health that they personally feel uncomfortable with. It is important to recognize this feeling and praise the family's courage in sharing information with professionals. Whether or not solutions to the original problems are discovered, by sharing their personal concerns, they have already solved half of their issues.

STEP 2: SETTING GOALS AND OBJECTIVES

It was important to help Jan set up goals and objectives because she perceived the problem as an individual problem rather than a family issue. Without goals and objectives, she believed that this intervention process was unnecessary. One indication was that she refused to disclose the names of other family members because she felt that everyone had done their share to help and they did not need to be involved. Although she believed that the care for a mentally ill patient was a family problem, the family's involvement was not a concern. According to Jan, the major goal was to find something for Ming to do in order to occupy her time so that she would not feel meaningless in life; her objective was to find an adult day program so Ming could learn new skills to reestablish her confidence. After stating her goal and objective, the professional then helped Jan identify various means to achieve them.

Once Jan perceived the professional's willingness to help, she began opening up herself and understanding the importance of involving family members to help Ming. As a result, she became more relaxed in the interview. She also identified that all family members were stressed and would benefit from some emotional support. In order to be realistic, she agreed to learn new coping skills and bring in her family members once she could handle her own stress.

Hint 2

Family is an integral part of life.

Implications 2

API clients have the potential to realize that they can do something during the intervention process to make the family healthier without involving the family in the initial step. However, it is essential to address the importance of their involvement at a later stage.

STEP 3: IDENTIFYING CONSTRAINTS AND RESOURCES

Jan found that Ming's problems were related to her lack of interpersonal skills. They were refugees and had come to the United States with no expectations. However, they soon found that they could not survive without knowing the language and necessary skills to find a job. Cultural constraints put Ming into a difficult position so she decided to leave home to join a religious group. Strengths included her strong family ties and religious values. Constraints included her language skills and inability to relate to others. In evaluating Jan's ability to help Ming, Jan revealed that she could locate and provide transportation to health care facilities for Ming.

Hint 3

Family members' participation in the planning process is an essential element of intervention with API population.

Implications 3

The anticipated change may not include the means of achieving such change. It is of critical significance to involve the family members in providing informal support including talking with the identified client and locating resources to support the client and the family.

STEP 4: MEASURING THE TARGET AND MONITORING ACTIONS

Jan identified three major steps for change. One was to find Ming a day program to learn interpersonal and language skills. The second step was to involve her family in recording Ming's progress. The third step was to help Ming realize her potential and ability through learning and participating in counseling. These actions were monitored by both Jan and the professional. Ming's perceptions of change were also measured during individual therapeutic sessions. However, Ming's lack of communication skills always made her feel unimportant. As a result, she did not like to verbalize her change in front of her sister. Ming negatively perceived any change observed by the professional through her expressed concerns about her future. The incongruence between the family data and the client's self-observation became an issue in progress assessment.

Based on the family's input that Ming was good at writing, the professional's evaluation plan was modified to include a writing process. Ming would write about her change and the possible reasons for such change. When writing, she did not have to use interactive eye contact, which always made her feel uneasy. In addition, the focus was on the past and present. Ming did not need to address how such change would impact her future, which was one of her fears. Ming was then able to express positive perceptions about herself. Jan was invited to talk about her feedback separately from these sessions.

Hint 4

Individual and family observations are important tools in practice evaluation.

Implications 4

Past- and present-oriented approaches and creative intervention strategies are important avenues to help evaluate the client's progress. During this process of evaluation, the lack of data may be caused by the client's discomfort in participating rather than an inability to make a change.

STEP 5: ANALYZING DATA

Ming reexamined her writing from time to time. Since Ming would not fill out quantitative measures, Jan's participation in this evaluation process was essential. Data were analyzed both quantitatively and qualitatively with Jan and Ming, individually and in family sessions. Family members were informed about the progress.

Hint 5

Data may serve as reinforcers for API clients since they often believe they should record their progress concretely.

Implications 5

Family involvement in this progress recording process helps the professional understand the resistance factors for change. It is not always feasible to obtain quantitative data from the client, but it is helpful to learn about their reactions through creative interactive means, such as writing or drawing out their feelings.

STEP 6: REPORTING RESULTS AND MAKING RECOMMENDATIONS

Ming's family was aware of her progress and continued working with the professional. Ming's parents did not understand the therapeutic goals between Jan and the professional, but they realized the importance of having someone there to provide emotional support for Ming. The unintended consequence of providing emotional support for Jan was not reported. It was culturally appropriate for working with this family to focus on individual-related problems and link family members in the helping process.

Hint 6

Individual issues are family issues; family issues are individual issues too.

Implications 6

Recommendations based on observations from the family are acceptable to the family as well as the individuals involved.

Conclusion: Connecting evaluation to practice

As previously described, the most common approach for evaluating practice with API clients and their families is a client-centered collaborative model. It is a practice-evaluation integrative approach to actively involve the client and the family. This model has three major principles:

1. A culturally competent view: helping professionals must constantly evaluate their cultural competencies.

2. A view of choices: it is important to adopt a customized framework involving the client's own assessment and choice of assessment procedures.

3. An integrative view: it is a strong commitment for helping professionals to engage in an integrative evaluation plan including cultural components familiar to the clients.

A culturally competent view

Respect is the number one ingredient for the achievement of service effectiveness. API individuals often feel that their territory or boundary is invaded because of their cultural differences. They may feel threatened by any intervention even though it is intended to help them. However, many API clients will continue receiving services despite their discomfort since they consider commitment more important than the expected outcome. Therefore, a culturally competent professional must recognize this strong commitment and identify alternatives for clients to consider if the service is evaluated and deemed inappropriate for the client.

A view of choices

Evaluation is governed by the choices given to clients and one aspect is related to *respect.* Since API cultures emphasize respect, people in these cultures always agree with the authority. In mental health services, although clients would have preferences concerning services, they would not disagree with the professional's recommendations. In their vocabularies, respect means agreement. As a result, helping professionals often hear positive answers when they ask a yes/no question. In the process of evaluating the intervention, this 'yes' answer may be indicative of the clients' obligation to say 'yes' and thus alter the actual measurement of success. In reference to this cultural characteristic, helping professionals must remember that although respect means agreement, agreement in turn means *harmony, respect for authority, and an easy expression.* Especially for those who have difficulty expressing themselves in English, it is easier to agree than to disagree and provide an explanation. Therefore, it is important to evaluate the meaning of 'yes' before focusing on the outcome.

Another aspect of choices is related to *the reward system.* Many API families feel that they have to give something back to the professional when they receive services. This feeling is especially strong if they cannot afford payment or if their insurance plans do not cover it. In health care settings, it is common for API patients to send trophies or mirrors engraved with their names and acknowledgments to their physicians. In mental health settings, however, public recognition is not a norm because of the stigma of *craziness.* As a result, their choices become limited. When services are evaluated, they may feel ashamed to share their feelings due to the fact that they have not rewarded the professional. Therefore, it is essential for helping professionals to acknowledge the spiritual aspect of their reward, e.g. job satisfaction, especially when they have to decline the receipt of gifts based on agency policy.

An integrative view

'Starting from where the client is' is a major principle when working with API clients and families. Cultural competencies in knowledge, skills and attitude are integrated toward the acceptance of where the client is, i.e., as an individual and as a member of a family. Learning about the family culture and the individual's definition of culture is a *starting point* for evaluation purposes.

In the evaluation process, first, the professional must help the clients identify their own assessment of the problem. Then the professional must encourage the clients to find out family and cultural information about this assessment. Based on cultural or religious values, clients may identify the problem differently from the professional. It is culturally appropriate to ask the clients about their feelings and then understand how their problem definition has affected themselves and their family. Without this encouragement, clients would most likely agree with the practitioner's definition.

Finally, the evaluation plan has to integrate both the clients' and professionals' input. A family may feel comfortable using multiple services but not disclosing them to the mental health professional. Their intent of multiple service usage is related to maximizing time and efficiency through use of the best possible resources. This practice may be also related to the multiple belief systems operated under the manifestation of their cultural value (such as the worship of multiple gods, the emphasis of multi-generational respect). However, they may not want the mental health professional to know that they are also trying other methods to solve this same problem, such as religious healing, natural remedies, services provided by other professionals and supernatural powers. For example, coining (*Gua Sha*) and cupping (*Ba Guan*) are considered acceptable healing methods (see Hansen 1998) because many Asian immigrants are open to the concept of 'bad wind' treatment where blood circulation will be improved if the 'bad wind' is chased to the surface. The Chinese clients may not want to disclose the use of these traditional health care methods for their body ailments because of their perceived integration into the western culture. Therefore, API clients feel peace of mind when they sense the professional's willingness to accept their concept of 'multi-utilization,' acknowledging the function of these multiple interventions, and empowering the clients to discuss their available resources.

Helping professionals may also work with the traditional healer to understand the supernatural power of certain rituals for practice evaluation. They may encourage clients to evaluate treatment from an integrative perspective to include cultural treatment methods, such as meditation, herbal medicine treatment, coining, or religious rituals, along with the professional's intervention.

It is imperative for helping professionals to learn about various cultural definitions of social services and take the client's perspective into consideration when assessing and evaluating practice. When working with API American clients, helping professionals must overcome their own biases toward unfamiliar and unknown methods of treatment. Confucius once said, 'People who follow different courses cannot possibly take counsel together,' to stress the importance of mutual understanding. One common course between the professional and the API client is the attitude of shared responsibility and mutual respect. The client's definitions of problem assessment and outcome evaluation are key concepts in any practice evaluation design. Self-enhancement is considered an enrichment process and the outcome-based alternative seeking behavior is considered a norm.

References

Bloom, M., Fischer, J. and Orme, J.G. (2006) *Evaluating Practice*. 5th edn, Boston: Allyn and Bacon.

Cheung, K.M. (1995) 'Minority Issues: A Social Work Perspective.' In A. Romaine-Davis, J. Boondas and A. Lenihan (eds) *Encyclopedia of Home Care for the Elderly*. Westport, CT: Greenwood Press.

Corcoran, K.J. (1993) 'Practice Evaluation: Problems and Promises of Single-system Designs in Clinical Practice.' *Journal of Social Service Research 18*, 1–2, 147–159.

Dinh, K.T., Sarason, B.R. and Sarason, I.G. (1994) 'Parent–child Relationships in Vietnamese Immigrant Families.' *Journal of Family Psychology 8*, 4, 471–488.

Fang, S.W. and Wark, L. (1998) 'Developing Cross-cultural Competence with Traditional Chinese Americans in Family Therapy: Background Information and the Initial Therapeutic Contact.' *Contemporary Family Therapy: An International Journal 20*, 1, 59–77.

Feldman, L.A. (1993) 'Distinguishing Depression and Anxiety in Self-report: Evidence from Confirmatory Factor Analysis on Nonclinical and Clinical Samples.' *Journal of Consulting and Clinical Psychology 61*, 4, 631–638.

Fong, R. (1994) 'Family Preservation: Making it Work for Asians.' *Child Welfare 73*, 4, 331–341.

Hansen, K.K. (1998) 'Folk Remedies and Child Abuse: A Review with Emphasis on Caida de Mollera and its Relationship to Shaken Baby Syndrome.' *Child Abuse and Neglect 22*, 2, 117–127.

Kim, H. (1997) *Policy Information Report: Diversity among Asian American High School Students*. Princeton, NJ: Policy Information Center, Educational Testing Service.

Kline, M.V. and Huff, R.M. (1999) 'Tips for Working with Asian American populations.' In R.M. Huff and M.V. Kline (eds) *Promoting Health in Multicultural Populations: A Handbook for Practitioners*. Thousand Oaks, CA: Sage.

Rubin, K.H. (1998) 'Social and Emotional Development from a Cultural Perspective.' *Developmental Psychology 34*, 4, 611–615.

Wallerstein, N. and Bernstein, E. (1988) 'Empowerment Education: Freire's Ideas Adapted to Health Education.' *Health Education Quarterly 15*, 4, 379–394.

Watson, D.L. and Tharp, R.G. (1997) *Self-directed behavior: Self-modification for Personal Adjustment*. Pacific Grove, CA: Brooks/Cole.

Welzler, S. (ed) (1989) *Measuring Mental Illness: Psychometric Assessment for Clinicians*. Washington, DC: American Psychiatric Press.

Wong, S.S., Heiby, E.M., Kameoka, V.A. and Dubanoski, J.P. (1999) 'Perceived Control, Self-reinforcement, and Depression among Asian American and Caucasian American Elders.' *Journal of Applied Gerontology 18*, 1, 46–62.

Yu, M.M. (1999) 'Multimodel Assessment of Asian Families.' In K.S. Ng (ed) *Counseling Asian Families from a Systems Perspective*. Alexandria, VA: American Counseling Association.

Part 3

Advancing Evaluation

Chapter 15

Developing an Outcome Evaluation Framework for Use by Family Support Programs

Charles Bruner

Introduction: The challenge of evaluating family support

Family support programs defy neat categorization. Their defining characteristic is that they adhere to family support principles in working with families – taking an ecological focus, building on strengths, and partnering with families in defining and reaching goals. Family Support America has described these core principles of family support practice (Best Practices Project 1996), but they are also part of reform efforts across many social service systems (Kinney *et al.* 1994). There is a great deal of research literature indicating that families thrive when they have strong social connections with their communities, their talents are recognized and used to benefit themselves and others, and they have control over their futures – e.g. that they live in a family support environment. This research is the basis of the resiliency literature of Bonnie Benard and Nan Henderson (Henderson, Benard and Sharp-Light 1999), the asset literature of Peter Benson and the SEARCH Institute (Benson 1997), and the risk and protective factor literature of Richard Catalano and David Hawkins (Catalano and Hawkins 1996), as well as the foundation of sociology and social psychology.

In the United States, family support programs have generally been established as voluntary institutions that often form a bridge between professional services and voluntary supports, either:

- located in neighborhoods where there is a sparsity of other voluntary institutions to provide support, or

- focusing upon families who otherwise have been marginalized from mainstream services and supports and experience social isolation.

While all families need support, the focus of most family support programs is to help families create environments where their members can thrive. They may do so through specific programs and curricula, but they create the environment through relationships. Different family support programs may work with poor families with young children, immigrant families, families seeking to leave welfare for work, grandparents raising their grandchildren, or families with an incarcerated parent. Often, they draw strength from the fact that participating families share some common history and can support one another in addressing the consequences of that history (Bruner 2004; Kagan and Weissbourd 1994).

While it is recognized that family support is essential to families thriving, it is not as clear whether and how family support programs can build or strengthen that support for the families and within the communities they serve. On the one hand, there are case studies of exemplary family support programs that clearly have helped families thrive, even in very tough circumstances. Lisbeth Schorr has not only described a variety of successful programs embodying family support principles in her work, she has also enumerated the common attributes they share, which starts with dedicated and caring staff (Schorr 1988).

On the other hand, however, a good share of the evaluation literature regarding family support offers little to support the premise that family support programs produce dramatic or certain results. A meta-analysis of family support program research conducted by Abt Associates for the United States Department of Health and Human Services found generally minor gains from family support programs, with many showing little or no change in terms either of family functioning or child development (Layzer *et al.* 2001).

One of the leaders in the resiliency research field, Marc Freedman, suggests that one reason for the lack of much definitive research is that the focus of much evaluation is wrong. 'They've [the substance abuse prevention field] spent lots of money on program evaluations – and they never look at relationships, only program content.' (Benard 2000, p.12) Freedman goes on to emphasize that it is less how the program is conducted (its focus, curriculum and content) that matters, and more the environment through which genuine relationships are developed that help sustain and support people in their continued growth and development. Carl Dunst and Carol Trivette (Dunst and Trivette 2001a, 2001b) represent two of a small group of researchers who are actually examining the relationship side of family support, with their pioneering work suggesting that family support programs which adhere to family support principles do build supportive relationships that nurture growth and development, but those that do not show limited effects.

It is essential for the field of family support to build a better evaluation framework, for two reasons. First, policy makers and funders are increasingly demanding results from the programs and services they fund. They want to know that what they are funding is making a difference. They need credible evidence that programs and services work. Second, the family support field needs better guideposts by which to measure itself. Family support programs need to know whether what they are doing is making a difference (and with which families and under what conditions). They need to know whether their practices and programs adhere to family support principles and build the types of relationships needed to foster family and community growth.

In short, the field of family support evaluation needs to be built – and it needs to be built upon achieving results for children, families, and communities. If it is to be true to family support principles, it also needs to be built with, and not imposed upon, family support practitioners and the families who participate.

The need to reformulate an outcomes framework for family support

This also means that family support program evaluations recognize the current political context for outcome evaluation. Policy makers and funders have recognized the need for new evaluation frameworks, ones which focus not on measuring 'inputs and processes' but rather on measuring 'impacts and results.' Moreover, policy makers and funders recognize that achieving some of the outcomes they want for children and families extends beyond one categorical system's responsibility or capacity. Students bring more than educational needs into the classroom; pregnant women bring more than medical needs into the obstetrician's office; families bring more than employment needs into the welfare or job training program. Further, unless these other needs are met, students are at risk of educational failure no matter what the teacher does in the classroom; women face the prospect of poor birth outcomes no matter how well the medical issues around pregnancy are diagnosed and addressed; families have difficulty sustaining employment no matter how well their skill levels fit the jobs they seek. In addition, students are more likely to get into trouble with the law or pregnant as teens; mothers are more likely to have health problems of their own and difficulties providing a stable environment where their infants achieve appropriate developmental milestones; families are more likely to experience stress and even family violence that is damaging to child growth and development.

Therefore, policy makers and funders have been seeking to restructure the way they look at budgeting to focus upon outcomes. The failure of categorical programs to fully achieve their own outcome objectives leaves new and more holistic, family support approaches as a potential option.

Mark Friedman's outcomes framework (Friedman 2000) has been particularly popular with state and community policy makers and funders and is in use by many state and community collaboratives. His framework emphasizes the need to first identify broad community outcomes and then work backward toward programs and strategies. By doing so, his outcome framework seeks to 'loosen' categorical thinking by focusing on the outcomes rather than the systems and their individual charges and responsibilities.

While different community or state collaboratives may frame the outcomes they wish to achieve in different language, they generally include:

- stable and supportive families

- healthy infants, children, youth, and adults

- school readiness and success

- economic self-sufficiency

- individual, family and community safety

- positive socialization and contribution to community (Bruner 1997, pp.42–45).

When communities establish specific indicators for these outcomes, they often select indicators that represent minimum rather than optimal expectations for children and families – recognizing a point at which government and community have a responsibility to intervene. Thus, on the continuum of educational success, they do not select the proportion of youth who will go to college or graduate school, but rather focus on youth graduating from high school. It is not yet the expectation in society that all children should obtain post-secondary education, but it is the expectation that they graduate from high school.

Thus communities often select indicators and goals that are defined in terms of falling below a minimum acceptable level, e.g. deficits:

- reducing teen pregnancy

- reducing child abuse and neglect

- reducing school dropout

- reducing low birth weight/infant mortality

- reducing juvenile delinquency and drug use.

In effect, each relates to points on a continuum relating to:

- responsible sexuality

- responsible parenting

- learning and education

- health and well-being

- responsible social behavior.

Family support programs also have these goals for the children and families and communities they serve. Children and families who participate in programs also want these things for themselves and their communities.

It therefore might seem logical to start with this set of outcomes and indicators in seeking to define the outcomes and indicators on which family support programs should be measured (and held accountable). Unfortunately, however, although the framework for starting with community-wide outcomes 'loosens' categorical thinking when applied at the collaborative level, imposing this framework at the family support program level can simply re-categorize that thinking, looking at discrete elements of a family support program directed toward a specific objective rather than the totality of the program and its environment supporting growth at multiple levels.

Measuring relationships and personal and community growth in family support

There is, however, a different initial approach to evaluating family support. It does two things. First, it starts with what we recognize really vibrant and effective family support programs are able to achieve, one not bounded by a set of pre-established outcomes. These exemplary family support programs can show both the potential and the limitations of family support. Next, it describes how these achievements/impacts fit within the community outcomes framework, clearly describing the logic model or theory of change (Connell *et al.* 1995) that links those impacts to the community outcomes. This also can help identify what else needs to be in place for family support program impacts to endure and be built upon.

This approach stems from the recognition, stated earlier, that family support is not just about the specific curricula or activities that may be established within a family support program. It is about the relationship development that occurs through the presence of the program and its staff that enables children, families, and communities to grow and develop. Family support is more about relationships than it is about programs. Much of the real value of family support is in creating opportunities for families to build relationships, which often occurs through activities, gatherings, and open-ended events rather than formal programs. It also recognizes that one of the values of family support programs is their open-ended nature. Specific activities within family support programs often are defined or developed by participants as much as by staff. Some of these also are directed to improving community conditions or resources, which often benefit program participants but also benefit the community as a whole.

Traditional evaluations, particularly as they focus upon discrete elements of family support programs, such as parenting programs or case management activities, often miss these gains. Specific classes or curricula themselves tend to be defined and delimited to specific subject areas and discrete objectives. Activities and opportunities tend to be open-ended and subject to multiple possibilities. While classes and curricula are an element of most family support programs, they are only an element and must be conducted in a manner that builds relationships and creates opportunities for 'teachable moments.' They are likely to be truly effective only insofar as they create more open-ended relationships and opportunities for children and families. The resiliency literature is very clear on this point, as is the research on such effective programs as Big Brothers and Big Sisters (Tierney, Grossman and Reisch 1995). One of the best representations of what makes youth programs work is found in *Urban Sanctuaries* (McLaughlin, Irby and Langman 1994) and it is all about relationships and the qualities of the staff who build them.

In short, many of the impacts that family support programs produce are ones that must be described in terms of relationships and personal growth that will vary widely from one family to another (one reason for using a results mapping (Kibel 1999) or goal attainment scaling framework as a methodological tool). In visiting centers, I have found two approaches particularly useful in assessing a family support program's impact.

First, I find it useful to ask staff (and participants) for some examples of their greatest successes – where they really feel they have made a difference (e.g. results mapping). From staff, I often get the story of a family that was isolated and disconnected from any systems of support and felt dragged down by and even hostile to public 'helping' systems and services. That family usually was unwilling to make contact with staff in the first several attempts. Through persistence and faith in the family, however, staff eventually made that connection and now the parent or parents are leaders at the center and in the community in helping others. Their children are thriving in school. I have heard this story and met the parents and children too many times to consider this an isolated occurrence, although it is clear that this level of transformation usually occurs with only a small portion of program participants and often through serendipity. I also have been able, through hearing the rich detail of these stories, to identify specific measurable points in the families' success stories that show evidence of growth – the impacts that family support programs helped produce. Participants who relate these experiences almost inevitably state that they opened up to the staff because staff went the extra mile. Further, they often state that the staff member who built the first relationship was the first person from a 'helping' system who really cared about them and understood them and would be there for them.

Second, I find it useful to get staff and families to describe successes at three different levels – specifically in terms of adult growth and development, child growth and development, and community growth and development. The latter is particularly important, as individual family stories often only hint at the community-wide impacts family support programs can produce.

Based upon visiting vibrant family support programs and talking with both staff and participants on their accomplishments, I have constructed a list of commonly identified signs of success or steps in the growth process. These are set out in Tables 15.1, 15.2 and 15.3 and include impacts at the parent, child, and community levels.

Table 15.1: Parent growth and development witnessed through participation at family support programs

Parents stabilize living situations:

- obtain stable and decent housing
- insure resources last to end of month
- address crises that impede other forward action.

Parents establish realistic goals with measurable steps:

- plan for the future
- take steps to accomplish plan.

Parents effectively navigate systems to meet basic needs:

- secure income supports (welfare and housing benefits, food stamps, child care subsidies, etc.)
- get children into Head Start or other preschool programs, or developmentally appropriate child care
- establish regular sources of health (medical, dental, optometric) care, primary and preventive services and a medical home.

Parents broaden positive social ties:

- establish new relationships
- take and give help
- strengthen personal support systems
- invite others to join and participate.

- Parents think positively:
- gain confidence in self (improve personal grooming)
- reduce depression
- heighten spirituality.

Parents share their talents:

- contribute time and effort (volunteer) to help others
- take responsibility for activities (programs, meals)
- voice views and act on them
- help other participants and staff.

Parents strengthen their parenting:

- establish realistic expectations regarding child development
- play with and nurture their (and others') children
- identify and respond to child health needs
- advocate for their child at school
- broaden their children's experiences
- insure children always are in safe environment (choose friends, care providers, etc.) set boundaries.

Parents manage personal relationships:

- set boundaries
- avoid co-dependency, abusive relationships.

Parents manage adult responsibilities:

- manage work and parenting
- negotiate systems
- fulfill obligations, legal and otherwise.

Parents advocate for themselves and others in community:

- organize to produce change in a system that affects them (school, welfare agency, etc.)
- help another parent navigate a system to get what they need.

Table 15.2 Child growth and development witnessed in family centers

Children socialize:

- enjoy and seek participation
- connect with adults in caregiving roles
- relate in positive ways to other children
- join groups, engage in extra-curricular activities, take leadership roles.

Children learn:

- begin to enjoy school and take pride in school work
- go to school regularly
- engage in developmentally appropriate activities
- take pride in accomplishments
- reach out to new challenges.

Children connect with their own family:

- value their parents
- help and support siblings
- take on household responsibilities.

Table 15.3 Family support program impacts on community

Programs serve as community anchors:

- mediate community issues
- build cultural understanding and recognition
- insure community voice in decisions affecting people's lives.

Programs contribute to community economic well-being:

- provide employment and bridge jobs to careers
- serve as reference for job seekers
- partner in community development activities.

Programs unleash human capital:

- increase volunteer and community self-help activities
- sponsor community policing, park clean-ups, and cultural days.

Programs broaden size of supportive community:

- reconnect those disconnected from community
- improve inclusion, work to see there are no 'out' groups.

Programs model family support practices for other systems.

- help schools be more responsive and open to parents
- provide new diversion opportunities from juvenile court
- help frontline staff in child welfare look at families in different light.

Each family is unique and the growth experienced will be rich and varied across families. Each program operates in a particular community setting and can be expected to impact that setting in its own way. This list is only a preliminary one of family support impacts, but should be sufficient to show the variety of impacts family support programs can achieve and help family support program practitioners be clear about the outcomes areas they are seeking to impact.

From an evaluation perspective, each of the elements on the list is capable of measurement, although there may need to be greater reliance upon family reports and triangulating perceptions than upon pre-post tests and psychometric scales. Randomized controlled trials as a means for establishing a counterfactual may be inappropriate at several levels, not the least of which is violating the principle of family support as being open and inclusive to everyone. At the same time, it may well be possible to identify alternative counterfactuals to a comparison group to determine program impact (Bruner *et al.* 2002).

In drawing the links between these family support program outcomes and community outcomes, some of the elements on the list will have direct connections as intermediate measures (direct evidence of progress) of the outcomes, but others will not. Although this list is long, it should be noted that it does not include such community outcomes as teen pregnancy reduction, reductions in delinquency or violence, reductions in low birth weight, or increases in high school completion. This is where the construction of a logic model or theory of change is important. All these do relate to building resiliency and constructing more supportive communities, which themselves are known to affect these community outcomes. They represent necessary, but not entirely sufficient, conditions for achieving those outcomes.

These elements represent fair measures for the types of impacts we should expect family support programs to produce. Lisbeth Schorr has quoted Sister Mary Paul from Sunset Park as saying, 'A good program never says to a participant, I know that is what you need, but that is not what we provide' (Schorr 1988, p.176). Paraphrasing that statement, a good evaluator should never say to a family support program, 'I know that is what you do, but that is not what we measure.' The logic model or theory of change will help to show what else might need to be in place to achieve those community outcomes and build upon the impacts family support programs are able to achieve. These additional necessary ingredients to achieve full impacts of family support may include good schools, culturally competent services, and economic opportunity.

Advice to family support program practitioners on their own program's evaluation

Evaluation can seem a daunting task. Outcome-based evaluation, particularly when funding streams are on the line, raises the stakes even higher. Yet people are continually evaluating their actions and the impacts of those actions –

considering what to do next and why, what would constitute hoped-for results and what actually occurred, and what generalizations might be drawn about what did happen to inform the next round of actions.

Rather than shying away from calls for evaluations (or, when evaluation is required for funding, setting evaluation off as a separate activity to be conducted by a possibly sympathetic external evaluation specialist), family support program practitioners can seek to take a more hands-on role in shaping evaluations. This is important both so the outcomes that are established and the ways they are measured fairly reflect what the program seeks to achieve and so the program itself can learn from its experiences. At their best, evaluators can help family support programs be more systematic and rigorous in examining their practices, making practitioners' own evaluations of what they observe less subject to subjective bias or selective memory.

As practitioners look to evaluation, they will need to determine what they are trying to achieve and give some specificity to those achievements. The lists in the previous section represent a basis for this work. These can be developed both for the overall family support program and for any of its individual activities. In short, they need to determine what they would consider 'success.' Ideally, this should be created and presented in such a manner that it becomes deeply ingrained in the program, by frontline staff and by program participants. The more staff and participants are involved in creating the outcomes by which programs seek to be measured, the more effective the program will be in achieving them. Practitioners must work to integrate any tracking of family progress into their own way of working with families, in family case records they keep and decisions they make with families on what to do next.

Practitioners also will need to determine how they hope to achieve these successes with families, and how they would know that they were actually practicing in this manner. Are their staff truly adhering to the principles of family support practice, and, when they do, are they getting different or better results? Evaluating family support programs requires attention to how the program operates and how well it adheres to family support principles, with a number of promising self-evaluation tools developed in this respect (Ahsan and Cramer 1998).

Practitioners also need to establish some realistic expectations for their efforts and what degree of change is needed to justify their work. Families are messy units of analysis and do not fit into regression equations easily. Family change and growth is not linear. What works with one family will not work with another. Some families will show no visible signs of change, and others may experience crises that set them back, or simply not engage and leave. Therefore, it is essential to set expectations that do not overstate what family support programs can achieve. At the same time, it is important to enumerate the overall gains that family support programs can demonstrate and to describe them in the context of the family support program budget (Bruner 1996).

Generally, if evaluation is left to an outside evaluator, however skilled that evaluator may be, there will be limited benefit to the program from that evaluation beyond the potential use of the results to justify funding. Moreover, there is a good likelihood that the evaluation will be inconclusive in its findings and will require additional staff time to complete forms that are not used for any other purpose. Practitioners who take a hands-on approach to evaluation, however, are more likely to get what they want from the evaluation, and to use it to improve practice and performance. In addition, practitioners who come forward as supporting outcome measurement as opposed to resisting it will be better politically positioned to receive policy maker and funder support.

Conclusion: thoughts on the sufficiency of the outcomes evaluation framework

This chapter has worked to align two important purposes for an outcomes evaluation framework for family support:

1. To help family support programs establish guideposts for their work that will enable them to assess themselves and improve their own effectiveness.

2. To respond to policy makers and funders seeking assurance that they are funding programs that help produce the outcomes they have determined to be important.

On the first point, this framework not only can and should be useful to family support programs, but it is the only framework that does not introduce biases that might lead programs and centers away from their strengths and goals. Moving to another set of outcomes may get programs and centers to 'teach to the test' rather than to adhere to the principles of building upon strengths and partnering with families in setting goals. From a self-evaluation perspective alone, this framework should also help programs better determine whether they really are adhering to family support principles in their practice and relationship-building.

On the second point, this is likely to be an iterative process. If there were a set of indicators that policy makers and funders recognize as important that family support programs could credibly assert they could achieve, regardless of outside factors or conditions, there would not be a problem. By and large, however, this is not the case. Particularly when working with families with young children, impacts upon long-term school success and high school graduation or avoidance of adolescent parenting or juvenile delinquency are in the distant future and will be filtered through other experiences and systems. While prevention and early intervention family support programs working with families with young children may be among the most needed programs to address these social concerns, these measures cannot be used for determining program impact or guidance program development. Certainly there will never be a 'one size fits all' set of indicators for family support programs, applicable to the diverse array of family support centers and the people they serve.

At the same time, however, policy makers do recognize that building resiliency is a key building block to achieving these community outcomes. Policy makers lack confidence, however, that programs of any type can predictably build that resiliency. It will take a growing body of research that publicly funded family support programs can achieve the types of impacts outlined in this paper to build this confidence. This must be coupled with education of policy makers and funders on the critical importance of achieving these impacts in order to achieve the other, more distant community outcomes (Bruner *et al.* 2002).

This is not a simple task, but it is a doable one, particularly as it makes common sense. Further, on an individual program and family base, results can be shown in very visible and compelling ways, which often have as much salience to policy makers as statistical evaluations. To achieve this, however, requires building a research and evaluation field that also recognizes the value of measuring family support program impacts in these ways and can translate, in credible ways, the results of such an evaluation approach. Family support practitioners can be leaders in this process, not shying away from outcome or evaluation but requesting it, provided it fairly reflects what family support programs are designed to accomplish.

References

Ahsan, N. and Cramer, L. (1998) *How Are We Doing? A Program Self-Assessment Toolkit for the Family Support Field.* Chicago, IL: Family Support America.

Benard, B. (2000) 'Mentoring as the Most Promising Prevention: An Interview with Marc Freedman.' In N. Henderson, B. Benard and N. Sharp-Light (eds) *Mentoring for Resiliency: Setting Up Programs for Moving Youth from 'Stressed to Success'.* San Diego, CA: Resiliency in Action.

Benson, P. (2000) *All Kids Are Our Kids: What Communities Must Do to Raise Caring and Responsible Children and Adolescents.* San Francisco, CA: Jossey-Bass Inc.

Best Practices Project (1996) *Guidelines for Family Support Practice.* Chicago IL: Family Support America.

Bruner, C. (1996) *Thoughts on Statistical and Substantive Significance – Are We Selling Programmatic Efforts Short?* Des Moines, IA: National Center for Service Integration and Child and Family Policy Center Occasional Paper #20.

Bruner, C. (1997) *Defining the Prize: From Agreed-Upon Outcomes to Results-Based Accountability.* Des Moines, IA: National Center for Service Integration.

Bruner, C. (2004) 'Rethinking the Evaluation of Family Strengthening Strategies: Beyond Traditional Program Evaluation Models.' *The Evaluation Exchange 10*, 2, 24–27.

Bruner, C., Greenberg, M., Guy, C., Little, M., Schorr, L. and Weiss, H. (2002) *Funding What Works: Exploring the Role of Research on Effective Programs and Practices in Government Decision-Making.* Des Moines, IA: National Center for Service Integration and Center for Schools and Communities.

Catalano, R. and Hawkins J. (1996). 'The Social Development Model: A Theory of Antisocial Behavior.' In J. Hawkins (ed) *Delinquency and Crime: Current Theories.* New York, NY: Cambridge University Press.

Connell, J., Kubisch, A., Schorr, L. and Weiss, C. (eds) (1995) *New Approaches to Evaluating Community Initiatives: Concepts, Methods, and Contexts.* Washington, DC: Aspen Institute.

Dunst, C. and Trivette, C. (2001a) *Parenting Supports and Resources, Helpgiving Practices, and Parenting Confidence.* Asheville, NC: Winterberry Press.

Dunst, C. and Trivette, C. (2001b) *Benefits Associated with Family Resource Center Practices.* Asheville, NC: Winterberry Press, 2001.

Freedman, M. (1993) *The Kindness of Strangers: Reflections on the Mentoring Movement.* San Francisco, CA: Jossey-Bass, Inc.

Friedman, M. (2000). *Reforming Financing for Family and Children's Services.* Sacramento, CA: Foundation Consortium.

Henderson, N., Benard, B. and Sharp-Light, N. (1999) (eds) *Resiliency in Action: Practical Ideas for Overcoming Risks and Building Strengths in Youth, Families, and Communities.* San Diego, CA: Resiliency in Action.

Kagan, S. and Weissbourd, B. (eds) (1994) *Putting Families First: America's Family Support Movement and the Challenge of Change.* San Francisco, CA: Jossey-Bass.

Kibel, B. (1999) *Success Stories as Hard Data: An Introduction to Results Mapping.* New York, NY: Kluwer Academic/Plenum Publishers.

Kinney, J., Strand, K., Hagerup, M. and Bruner, C. (1994) *Beyond the Buzzwords: Key Principles of Effective Frontline Practice.* Des Moines, IA: National Center for Service Integration.

Layzer, J., Goodson, B., Bernstein, B. and Price, C. (2001) *National Evaluation of Family Support Programs: Final Report, Volume A: The Meta-Analysis.* Cambridge, MA: Abt Associates, Inc.

McLaughlin, M., Irby, M. and Langman, J. (1994) *Urban Sanctuaries: Neighborhood Organizations in the Lives and Futures of Inner-City Youth.* San Francisco, CA: Jossey-Bass Inc.

Tierney, J., Grossman, J. and Reisch, N. (1995) *Making a Difference: An Impact Study of Big Brothers/Big Sisters.* Philadelphia, PA: Public/Private Venture.

Schorr, L. (1988) *Within Our Reach: Breaking the Cycle of Disadvantage.* New York, NY: Anchor Press Doubleday.

Chapter 16

School- and Family-level Income Effects in a Randomized Controlled Prevention Trial: A Multilevel Analysis

W. Todd Abraham, Daniel W. Russell, Max Guyll, Linda Trudeau, Catherine Goldberg-Lillehoj and Richard Spoth

Introduction

Recent adolescent alcohol use estimates suggest that children encounter alcohol at relatively early ages, and that use increases across adolescence. Approximately half of all 8th grade students report having used alcohol; by the 12th grade, reports of lifetime use exceed 80 per cent (Rountree and Clayton 1999). Concerning current alcohol use, approximately 20 to 25 per cent of 8th grade students report frequent use, whereas by the 12th grade the number of students reporting frequent use approaches 50 per cent (Fitzgerald and Arndt 2002; Rountree and Clayton 1999). Perhaps more startling are reports of alcohol use among children as early as the 6th grade. For example, in a sample of 6th grade students from the Midwestern United States, 5 per cent report current use of alcohol and 3 per cent report heavy use, defined as five or more drinks within a few hours on any single day within the last month (Fitzgerald and Arndt 2002).[1] Such reports of early and frequent alcohol use that increases across adolescence have resulted in numerous efforts to develop programs that effectively curb adolescent alcohol involvement.

---

1 Age ranges for 6th, 8th and 12th grades are 11–12, 13–14, and 17–18.

Our goal in this chapter is to address a number of issues relevant to the development and efficacy of such programs. We do so in the context of tough choices faced by policy makers on the allocation of scarce resources and the corresponding increase in demand for evidence about effectiveness and comparative benefits of programmes (Weiss 2002). Our strong view is that those designing and implementing family support programmes must engage the possibilities offered by rigorous quantitative research and particularly randomised control trial approaches. Not only do such approaches allow us to answer the basic question 'Does it work?', they also afford the opportunity for deeper understanding of the key individual level and contextual factors that affect program effectiveness.

Currently of particular interest among intervention researchers is the impact of socioeconomic status (SES) on substance use. Although poverty tends to be associated with greater adolescent substance use, a review of the literature yields inconsistent relationships between adolescent substance use and SES once family resources are above the poverty threshold (Hawkins, Catalano and Miller 1992). That is, research has demonstrated relationships between substance use and SES that are positive, negative, or nonexistent (Smart, Adlaf and Walsh 1994). These mixed findings have led to an examination of neighborhood socioeconomic factors and their impact on delinquent or problem behaviors. Such research suggests that neighborhood poverty influences criminal behavior (Lynam *et al.* 2000), drug use (Smart *et al.* 1994), dropping out of high school, teen pregnancy (Harding 2003), and alcohol use (Jones-Webb *et al.* 1997; Smart *et al.* 1994). In fact, studies have shown that neighborhood poverty influences rates of alcohol use net of other neighborhood factors, such as the number of outlets that sell alcohol (Duncan, Duncan and Strycker 2002).

The findings reviewed above suggest an intriguing possibility; namely, that school-level income may more strongly predict an adolescent's alcohol use than does the income level of that adolescent's own family. This runs counter to the typical finding that family-level variables are more strongly associated with youth outcomes than are community-level variables (Leventhal and Brooks-Gunn 2000).

The purpose of the current analysis is to investigate the relationship between school-level income and adolescent substance use, and to explore the importance of school-level income relative to family-level income. The chapter will also test whether school- and family-level incomes serve to moderate the effectiveness of two established intervention programs designed to reduce adolescent alcohol use.

Study description

Participants

The study involved the families of all 6th grade students enrolled in 33 rural Iowa schools. Schools were targeted for inclusion based on eligibility for subsidized school lunch programs and size (i.e. community population ≤ 8,500). Participating schools were divided into comparable groups of three based on the proportion of students that resided in lower-income households and school size. Schools within these triads were then randomly assigned to one of three experimental conditions, which included two intervention conditions and a minimal contact control condition. Therefore, treatment condition represented a characteristic of schools and not of participating families. Randomly assigning schools to condition effectively limits contact between participants in different study conditions, providing a method of controlling for potential contamination of experimental treatments due to participants in different conditions having contact with one another (termed resentful demoralization; see Cook and Campbell 1979).

Of the 1,309 families contacted within the 33 schools, 667 families (approximately 51%) agreed to participate in the study. The gender of the children from participating families was approximately equal (51.7% girls, 49.3% boys), with an average age of 11.34 years ($SD = 0.50$ years) at the beginning of the study. Most participating children lived with two parents (86%); and within dual-parent families, the majority of participating children (64%) lived with both biological parents. Nearly all of the study participants identified themselves as Caucasian (98.6%).

Treatment conditions

Schools and participating families were randomly assigned to one of two family-based intervention programs or a minimal contact control condition. Preparing for the Drug-Free Years (PDFY; see Catalano *et al.* 1999; Spoth, Redmond and Shin 1998; Spoth *et al.* 2004) requires families to attend five sessions that are administered over a five-week period, with each session lasting for two hours. Parents receive instruction on risk factors associated with adolescent substance abuse, the development of clear behavioral guidelines regarding adolescent substance-related behavior, how to enhance parent–child bonding, discipline, and how to manage anger and conflict. Participating children are required to attend one of the five sessions, during which they receive instruction on peer resistance. Of the 221 families assigned to the PDFY condition, 124 (56%) participated in the intervention. Ninety-four percent of these latter families attended three or more sessions and 61 per cent attended all five sessions.

The Iowa Strengthening Families Program (ISFP; Molgaard and Spoth 2001; Spoth *et al.* 1998, 2004) requires that parents and children attend seven weekly sessions, including six two-hour sessions and a single one-hour session. The two-hour sessions commence with separate and simultaneous one-hour sessions for parents and children, followed by a one-hour family session. The seventh session consists of only the one-hour family session. During ISFP sessions, parents are taught to clarify their expectations, use appropriate disciplinary practices, manage strong emotions, and communicate effectively with their children. Content of the ISFP sessions for children generally mirrors that for the parents, with the addition of instructions on how to cope with peer pressure. The ISFP family sessions also provided time for families to practice what they have learned during the preceding parent and child sessions. Of the 238 pretested families assigned to the ISFP condition, 117 (49%) participated in the intervention. Ninety-four percent of these families attended five or more sessions and 62 per cent attended all seven sessions.

The remaining 208 families were assigned to a minimal contact control condition. Control families received four leaflets via mail concurrent with the PDFY and ISFP interventions. The leaflets contained information regarding developmental changes that occur during the adolescent years.

Measures

Adolescent alcohol use was assessed using child answers to four questions, including whether they had ever used alcohol (e.g. beer, wine or other liquor), ever used alcohol without parental permission, and ever been drunk, as well as how many times they had used alcohol during the previous month. Responses of 'Yes' and 'No' to the first three items were scored as 1 and 0, respectively, whereas responses to the fourth item indicating any use during the past month were scored as 1 and responses indicating no past month use were scored as 0. Child scores to these four items were summed to yield an Alcohol Use Composite Index (AUCI). Children completed the AUCI items as part of a larger assessment survey on four separate occasions, including a pre-test assessment before condition assignment and intervention implementation, a post-test assessment after intervention implementation approximately six months after pre-testing, as well as during two follow-up assessments that occurred 18 and 30 months after the pre-test. AUCI scores were generally reliable across the four waves of assessment (KR-20 coefficient was 0.67, 0.75, 0.78, and 0.83 across waves 1–4, respectively).

Family-level income was assessed during in-home interviews conducted as part of the Rural Family and Community Drug Abuse Prevention Project. Specifically, mothers and fathers reported total income over the previous week or month, and these reports were then appropriately adjusted to calculate total annual household income. Information concerning school-level income was obtained from a previous survey of nearly all households in the Rural Family Project schools of families who would subsequently be recruited for participation in the Rural Family Project. Family incomes within each school were averaged to yield the school-level income measure.

Results

Assessment of clustering

Because condition assignment and interventions occurred at the school level and not independently for each family, the study design introduces the potential for non-independence or clustering within the data. Clustering occurs when units at one level of analysis (e.g. individuals) share characteristics with similar units at a higher level of analysis (e.g. schools). When clustering occurs, units at the lower level of analysis appear more homogeneous because of the shared higher-level characteristics. From a statistical standpoint, clustered (or nested) units violate the assumption of independence necessary for statistical techniques that test for group differences. When dependencies within the data exist (i.e. clustering), common statistical tests for differences between treatment groups become positively biased because the within-group variability is artificially reduced. As a result, common statistical methods for testing treatment effects (such as analysis of variance) yield inflated estimates. From a practical standpoint, failure to account for dependencies within the data can lead to erroneous conclusions concerning intervention efficacy (i.e. Type 1 errors, or concluding that a treatment is effective when, in fact, it is not).

One method of assessing the degree of dependency within data involves examination of the intraclass correlation coefficient (ICC). Dependence (i.e. clustering) exists within the data to the degree that the ICC differs from zero. The ICC can be obtained from the results of a one-way analysis of variance (ANOVA) in which the higher-level unit serves as the grouping or class variable (see Snijders and Bosker 1999, p.22). When using such an approach, evidence of clustering exists if the F-ratio associated with the ANOVA indicates there is a statistically significant difference on the dependent variable as a function of the grouping or class variable. Table 16.1 presents the results obtained from a one-way ANOVA with school as the grouping variable. These results indicate that dependence exists within the AUCI variable data, and that the dependence increases across the four waves of assessment. Although the ICC may often be rather small in magnitude, values as low as 0.01 can result in seriously biased statistical tests (see discussion by Murray and Short 1996; Raudenbush and Bryk 2002; Snijders and Bosker 1999).

Table 16.1: Evidence of school clustering across the four waves of alcohol involvement assessment

Assessment	F ratio	p	ICC	% of variance due to school
Time 1[a]	1.07	0.366	0.006	5.1
Time 2[b]	1.28	0.140	0.025	7.4
Time 3[c]	1.72	0.010	0.061	11.1
Time 4[d]	2.21	<0.001	0.099	14.8

ICC = intraclass correlation coefficient
[a] df = 32, 632
[b] df = 32,517
[c] df = 32,438
[d] df = 32,405

Increase in alcohol use over time

Before proceeding to examine the efficacy of the PDFY and ISFP interventions in curbing adolescent alcohol use, we first examined whether there was any observable change in alcohol use over the four waves of assessment. Figure 16.1 presents a plot of average AUCI scores across the four waves of assessment for all children collapsing across condition assignment. As one might expect, alcohol use increased as participants moved from the 6th through the 8th grade (i.e. middle school). Consistent with Figure 16.1, statistical analyses indicated that alcohol use increased both linearly and curvilinearly across time. That is, alcohol use increased across the duration of the study (linear change), and the slope of the increase in alcohol use became steeper with time (curvilinear change).

Growth curve analysis

Currently, the most commonly used method for analyzing clustered data involves the use of multilevel regression methods (e.g. Duncan *et al.* 2002; Rountree and Clayton 1999). Although the details of this analytic strategy are beyond the scope of this work (for excellent sources, see Raudenbush and Bryk 2002; Singer and Willet 2003; Snijders and Bosker 1999), a simplified overview will aid understanding of the analyses that follow. In a multilevel regression model, individual or lower level outcomes are predicted by individual or lower level factors as in a standard linear regression. The Level 1 regression yields average estimates of the intercept and slope components as well as associated estimates of variability in the intercept and slope across levels of

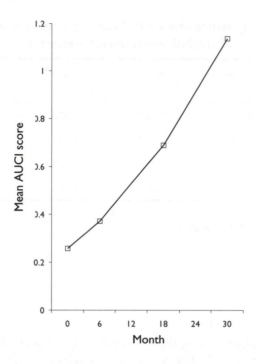

Figure 16.1: Alcohol use over time averaged across all children.

higher order factors. One can then include second-level factors in the model to directly predict the Level 1 outcomes, as well as to account for variability in the first-level intercept and slope components. These models take into account the clustered nature of the data and allow for the investigation of cross-level inter-actions. When applied to longitudinal data, as in the present case, the Level 1 equation specifies the prediction of change in some outcomes as a function of individual-level factors (e.g. time), given that the repeated assessments are nested within individuals (see Singer and Willet 2003 for applications with longitudinal data). One can then specify second-level equations that include higher-order factors (e.g. school-level characteristics, such as treatment condi-tion or average family income in each school) as predictors of both the Level 1 outcome and the variability associated with the Level 1 (individual level) intercept and slope components.

Dealing with dropouts

As with any longitudinal design, the current study experienced attrition over the four waves of data collection. Of the 667 families who participated in the study, only 62.5 per cent of the families (*N* = 417) completed all four assessments. Participant dropout presents a problem for the analysis of treatment effects because differential attrition across the three intervention conditions may introduce bias that potentially distorts treatment conclusions. One potential solution is to analyze data for only those families that completed all four assessments. However, it is possible that the reason for dropping out of the study directly relates to the outcome of the treatment. For example, families for whom the intervention is not working may be more likely to leave the study. Ignoring this possibility by analyzing data only from families who provide complete data often leads to biased and inaccurate conclusions regarding the effectiveness of a given intervention program. A more appropriate solution to handling dropouts involves testing for systematic differences over time between those who drop out and those who remain in the study.

Investigation of differences due to attrition is easily incorporated into multilevel modeling analyses (see Hedeker and Gibbons 1997). One need only create a series of predictor variables reflecting the amount of data provided by each family (i.e. how many assessments each participating family completed). These variables are then included in a model to examine both direct influences on the outcome and moderation of the effects of other predictor variables on the outcome measure. For example, if a variable representing complete versus incomplete data directly predicts alcohol use, one would conclude that rates of alcohol use are higher or lower among participants who subsequently dropped out of the study. Similarly, if the same variable moderates a treatment by time interaction, one might conclude that the effectiveness of the intervention was different for families who remained in the study compared to those who discontinued participation. By incorporating attrition into a multilevel analysis, this approach maximizes the information available from the data, in that parameters are estimated based on all available data regardless of whether or not a given participating family provided complete data across all waves of the study.

In the present study, we investigated the potential influence of dropping out by including predictor variables reflecting whether participants completed Wave 1 only, Waves 1 and 2 only, Waves 1 through 3 only, or all four waves of assessment. Results from these analyses indicated that there were no significant direct effects on level of alcohol involvement related to dropout status. Figure 16.2 presents the average level of alcohol use over time for participants who did and did not complete all four assessments. The figure clearly shows that initial rates of alcohol use did not differ for those who dropped out of the study before the six-month follow-up. In addition, rates of increase in alcohol use did not differ significantly for dropouts versus participants who remained in the study. Finally, none of the relationships among the variables discussed below were affected by dropout status.

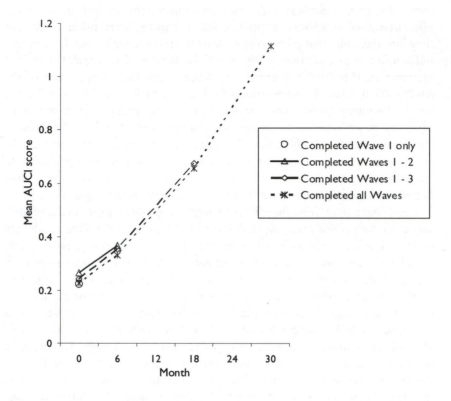

Figure 16.2: Alcohol use over time by dropout status

Treatment effects

Recall that assignment to condition is a school-level characteristic due to the design of the current study. As a result, investigation of intervention effects requires specification of the Level 1 model such that change in alcohol use is a function of time, whereas variables representing intervention exposure are specified as Level 2 factors that influence change in alcohol use across assessments. Evidence for effects due to a specific intervention relative to the control condition exists if a cross-level interaction between an intervention variable and time (e.g. ISFP*Time, ISFP*Time2) is statistically significant. In comparison to the control condition, results indicated that alcohol use increased at a slower rate in the ISFP condition, as revealed by a significant ISFP*Time interaction term. In addition, the non-significant ISFP*Time2 interaction suggests that the slower rate of change among those who experienced the ISFP intervention does not exhibit a dramatic change in increase (i.e. remains linear) over time. With respect to PDFY, the non-significant PDFY*Time interaction suggests that the linear increase in alcohol use does not differ between those in the PDFY and control conditions. However, the significant PDFY*Time2 interaction indicated that the curvilinear component of increased alcohol use increased more slowly in the PDFY condition than in the control condition. Examination of the results presented in Figure 16.3 indicates that those adolescents exposed to the ISFP intervention experienced a slower increase in alcohol use over time than did adolescents in the control condition. In addition, the amount of upward curvature in the alcohol trajectory across the study was lessened among those in the PDFY condition relative to control condition children.

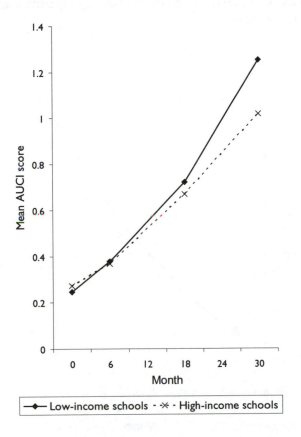

Figure 16.3: Alcohol use by treatment condition

School-level income

As noted in the introduction, research suggests that peer influences and school context are important factors to consider when examining adolescent drinking and drug abuse. To investigate possible contextual effects in this study, we expanded the treatment effects model discussed above to examine the influence of contextual characteristics of the school on adolescent alcohol involvement. To do so, we entered average family income for each school as a Level 2 predictor of alcohol use. Results indicated a statistically significant interaction between school-level income and time, indicating that rates of adolescent alcohol use differed across schools as a function of the financial composition of each school. Figure 16.4 shows that alcohol use increased more quickly among adolescents attending lower income schools than among participants attending higher income schools.

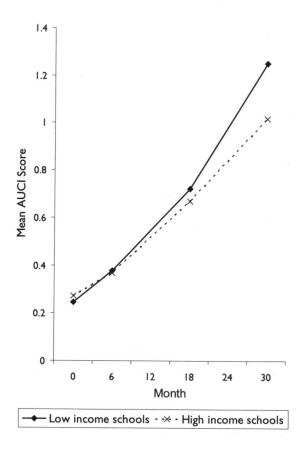

Figure 16.4: Alcohol use by school-level income

In addition to the interaction presented in Figure 16.4, the three-way interactions between school income, ISFP treatment exposure, and both the linear and quadratic components of time (i.e. Time and Time2) were statistically significant. However, it is important to recall the ISFP treatment variable reflects the effect of ISFP treatment relative to the control condition, which makes it challenging to interpret such complex interactions. Therefore, to better understand these interactions, simple effects analyses were conducted in which the effect of school-level income was tested separately for the ISFP, PDFY and control conditions. Compared to their counterparts in higher-income schools, these analyses revealed that adolescents in lower-income schools experienced both greater rates of alcohol use, and more quickly increasing rates of alcohol use, but only in the control condition. That is, both the income by time interaction, t (2078) = 4.17, p <0.001, and the income by Time2 interaction, t (2078) = -3.34, p <0.001, were statistically significant for participants in the control condition. By contrast, school-level income was not significantly associated with differences in alcohol use trajectories among adolescents in the ISFP or PDFY condition schools.

Figure 16.5 presents a plot of alcohol use over time as a function of experimental condition and school-level income. Consistent with the findings described above, lower-income schools in the control condition appear to exhibit not only steeper slopes, but also slopes that become steeper over time, as compared to high-income control condition schools. For schools in the two treatment conditions, the alcohol use trajectories for higher- and lower-income schools are more similar.

At first glance, these findings might suggest that school-level income moderated the effectiveness of the ISFP intervention. However, subsequent simple effects analyses revealed no differences between the income groups in the ISFP condition, suggesting a different interpretation. Alcohol use rates in the control condition increased more quickly for adolescents from lower-income schools than for adolescents from higher-income schools. Thus, the three-way interaction of ISFP, time, and school-level income appears to have emerged because ISFP treatment reduced alcohol use in both lower- and higher-income schools to similar levels, with the amount of reduction relative to the control condition being greater for lower income schools. Although one might conceptualize this as greater effectiveness of ISFP for lower-income schools, it could with equal justification be conceptualized as reflecting a greater vulnerability for adolescents in lower-income schools in the absence of intervention, and that ISFP treatment both removes this additional vulnerability for adolescents in these schools and provides a similar general benefit to all participants.

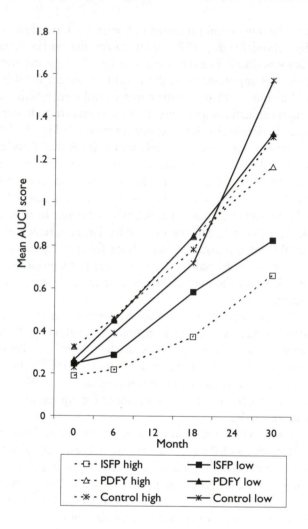

Figure 16.5: Alcohol use by treatment condition by school income

Family-level income

The observed influence of school-level income on alcohol use in the control condition raises an important issue. Specifically, do these results suggest that family-level income affects alcohol use? To investigate this possibility, we expanded the model discussed above to include the reported income of each family. If the earlier results regarding school-level income occurred because of individual family income, then family-level income should predict alcohol involvement and moderate the effects of the intervention exposure variables on alcohol use. However, results indicated that family-level income did not directly predict alcohol use, nor did it moderate the effects of either intervention variable. Furthermore, the effects associated with school-level income remained statistically significant when the model accounted for the influence of family-level income. These findings suggest that the effects associated with school-level income on alcohol involvement reflect a characteristic of the schools and not the individual families.

Conclusions

These results suggest that school-level factors in general, and school-level income in particular, are associated with adolescent alcohol use. Although it is not immediately clear *how* school-level income influences adolescent alcohol use independently of family-level income, several existing theoretical frameworks suggest possible mechanisms. Leventhal and Brooks-Gunn (2000) review a number of income-relevant neighborhood factors important to adolescent outcomes, including resources associated with institutions (police availability, affordance of healthy environments for learning and socializing) and residents (monitoring by community adults, preponderance of positive role models). In addition to the possibility that factors at higher levels, such as neighborhood or school characteristics, may exert direct influences on adolescent alcohol use, it is also likely to be the case that such relationships are complex and can be influenced by individual level variables as well. For example, Parcel and Dufur (2001) demonstrated that parental resources such as monitoring could compensate for school deficiencies, including an environment that accepts adolescent drinking. Similarly, Fitzgerald and Arndt (2002) found that peer influences on drinking prevalence are moderated by the existence of reference groups within the school, home, or neighborhood that disapprove of alcohol use. Clarity concerning the relationships among neighborhood, school, family, and individual factors is further obscured by mixed findings from studies that focus on only one part of the puzzle. That is, neighborhood factors may impact drinking in the absence of school or individual-level factors, yet appear unimportant when school or family factors are included. Such a pattern of results would be expected if neighborhood influences are not direct but rather operate through school or family characteristics (Ennett *et al.* 1997).

The present results do provide evidence against the conclusion that school-level contextual effects are always mere proxies for effects that stem from individual or family-level variables. For example, alcohol use in the current data was greater among those attending lower-income schools, but alcohol use was not greater among adolescents of lower-income families, indicating that family financial status per se is not the influential factor. Clearly, the mechanisms through which school-level income influences alcohol involvement deserve further attention by those who design, implement, and assess intervention efforts.

A clear conclusion from the present investigation is that focusing on multiple levels of analysis is vital when assessing the efficacy of an intervention program. Without attention at the school level, one may miss the fact that in the absence of the intervention, adolescent alcohol involvement rates differ across economically diverse schools. In addition, without attention to associations both within and across levels of analysis and treatment conditions, one may prematurely and perhaps erroneously conclude that intervention efficacy is dependent upon the setting.

The purpose of this investigation was to draw the attention of program developers and evaluators to such key issues. Such careful analysis will inform decisions regarding whether it is better to pursue a strategy of implementing universal interventions designed for general population families, or of developing specialized interventions designed to benefit distinct at-risk groups that might otherwise not benefit (e.g. low income schools). Continued assessment and evaluation of interventions through randomized controlled trials allows researchers to determine whether or not program efficacy differs by contextual or individual-level variables, and whether or not modifications should be considered to maximize intervention effectiveness in specific settings. For the reflective Family Support practitioner, manager and policy maker, the benefits of randomized controlled trials should be apparent.

References

Catalano, R., Kosterman, R., Haggerty, K., Hawkins, D. and Spoth, R. (1999) 'A Universal Intervention for the Prevention of Substance Abuse: Preparing for the Drug Free Years.' In R. Ashery, E. Robertson and K. Kumpfer (eds) *NIDA Research Monograph on Drug Abuse Prevention Through Family Interventions.* Rockville, MD: National Institute on Drug Abuse.

Cook, T.D. and Campbell, D.T. (1979) *Quasi-Experimentation: Design & Analysis Issues for Field Settings.* Chicago, IL: Rand McNally College Publishing Company.

Duncan, S.C., Duncan, T.E. and Strycker, L.A. (2002) 'A Multilevel Analysis of Neighborhood Context and Youth Alcohol and Drug Problems.' *Prevention Science 3,* 125–133.

Ennett, S.T., Flewelling, R.L., Lindrooth, R.C. and Norton, E.C. (1997) 'School and Neighborhood Characteristics Associated with School Rates of Alcohol, Cigarette, and Marijuana Use.' *Journal of Health and Social Behavior 38,* 55–71.

Fitzgerald, J.L. and Arndt, S. (2002) 'Reference Group Influence on Adolescent Alcohol Use.' *Journal of Alcohol & Drug Education 47,* 42–56.

Harding, D.J. (2003) 'Counterfactual Models of Neighborhood Effects: The Effect of Neighborhood Poverty on Dropping Out and Teenage Pregnancy.' *American Journal of Sociology 109,* 676–719.

Hawkins, J.D., Catalano, R.F. and Miller, J.Y. (1992) 'Risk and Protective Factors for Alcohol and Other Drug Problems in Adolescence and Early Adulthood: Implications for Substance Abuse Prevention.' *Psychological Bulletin 112,* 64–105.

Hedeker, D. and Gibbons, R.D. (1997) 'Application of Random-effects Pattern-mixture Models for Missing Data in Longitudinal Studies.' *Psychological Methods 2,* 64–78.

Jones-Webb, R., Snowden, L., Herd, D., Short, B. and Hannan, P. (1997) 'Alcohol-related Problems among Black, Hispanic and White Men: The Contribution of Neighborhood Poverty.' *Journal of Studies on Alcohol 58,* 539–545.

Leventhal, T. and Brooks-Gunn, J. (2000) 'The Neighborhoods They Live In: The Effects of Neighborhood Residence on Child and Adolescent Outcomes.' *Psychological Bulletin 126*, 309–337.

Lynam, D.R., Caspi, A., Moffitt, T.E., Wikström, P.H., Loeber, R. and Novak, S. (2000) 'The Interaction between Impulsivity and Neighborhood Context on Offending: The Effects of Impulsivity are Stronger in Poorer Neighborhoods.' *Journal of Abnormal Psychology 109*, 563–574.

Molgaard, V. and Spoth, R. (2001) 'Strengthening Families Program for Young Adolescents: Overview and Outcomes.' In S.I. Pfeiffer and L.A. Reddy (eds) *Innovative Mental Health Programs for Children: Programs That Work*. Binghamton, NY: Haworth Press.

Murray, D.M. and Short, B. (1996) 'Intraclass Correlation among Measures Related to Alcohol Use by School Aged Adolescents: Estimates, Correlates and Applications in Intervention Studies.' *Journal of Drug Education 26*, 207–230.

Parcel, T.L. and Dufur, M.J. (2001) 'Capital at Home and at School: Effects on Child Social Adjustment.' *Journal of Marriage and Family 63*, 32–47.

Raudenbush, S.W. and Bryk, A.S. (2002) *Hierarchical Linear Models: Applications and Data Analysis Methods*, 2nd edn, Thousand Oaks, CA: Sage Publications, Inc.

Rountree, P.W. and Clayton, R.R. (1999) 'A Contextual Model of Adolescent Alcohol Use across the Rural-urban Continuum.' *Substance Use & Misuse 34*, 495–519.

Singer, J.D. and Willett, J.B. (2003) *Applied Longitudinal Data Analysis: Modeling Change and Event Occurrence*. New York: Oxford University Press.

Smart, R.G., Adlaf, E.M. and Walsh, G.W. (1994) 'Neighbourhood Socio-economic Factors in Relation to Student Drug Use and Programs.' *Journal of Child & Adolescent Substance Abuse 3*, 37–46.

Snijders, T. and Bosker, R. (1999) *Multilevel Analysis: An Introduction to Basic and Advanced Multilevel Modeling*. Thousand Oaks, CA: Sage Publications Inc.

Spoth, R., Redmond, C. and Shin, C. (1998) 'Direct and Indirect Latent-variable Parenting Outcomes of Two Universal Family-focused Preventive Interventions: Extending a Public Health-oriented Research Base.' *Journal of Consulting and Clinical Psychology 66*, 385–399.

Spoth, R., Redmond, C., Shin, C. and Azevedo, K. (2004) 'Brief Family Intervention Effects on Adolescent Substance Initiation: School-level Growth Curve Analyses 6 Years Following Baseline.' *Journal of Consulting and Clinical Psychology 72*, 535–542.

Chapter 17

Towards an Inclusive Approach to Family Support Evaluation

Jackie Sanders and Robyn Munford

Introduction

This chapter will explore how inclusive approaches can inform the evaluation and development of family support services. We will begin with a brief exploration of family support and identify the contribution evaluation can make to the enhancement of practice. A major focus of the chapter is on how to include family support workers and clients in all aspects of research and evaluation. We will use our research and evaluation practice to illustrate a number of key themes implicit in an inclusive approach to evaluation. These themes include:

- the value of involving all agency members in evaluation processes
- inclusiveness as a strategy for building effective evaluations
- the connections between good social service practice and good evaluation practice
- the synergies that occur when evaluation works effectively with family support practice so that evaluation outcomes are used in everyday practice.

While the experience of family support referred to in this chapter is located in Aotearoa/New Zealand the examples provided have relevance for the international context.

A key focus of the chapter is on building evaluation into the daily practices of organisations and to demonstrate how evaluation is connected to the development of a critically reflective practice in family support services. We will demonstrate how approaches that adopt a strengths philosophy are connected to inclusive evaluation approaches. We hope that the chapter will encourage practitioners, policy makers and managers of family support services to explore the link between evaluation and the achievement of positive outcomes for families. The challenge is to see evaluation embedded in organisational policies and practices and to view evaluation as a key strategy in ensuring that family support interventions remain relevant to clients and that positive outcomes can be achieved in the short and long term.

Family support – some key elements

When we talk of family support, we are referring to a particular type of intervention that is primarily home and community-based. In such services practitioners typically visit families, rather than families attending agency rooms for support. Home-based support has been found internationally to contribute to enhanced outcomes, where changes in the style or nature of family life are considered to be important (Katz and Pinkerton 2003a). Bringing practitioners into home and community environments increases their sensitivity and understanding of the practical and emotional constraints faced by families in their daily lives and support work is more relevant and targeted as a result. In addition to the value of workers being familiar with the daily reality families face, our work with home-based family support services (Munford and Sanders 1999, p.164) has noted three other benefits of home-based work:

1. Clients interpret the willingness of practitioners to come into their home territory as evidence of their commitment to work with them through all the issues they face.

2. Barriers to access, such as the cost of transport or the challenges of finding safe adequate child-care are reduced.

3. Home-based support reduces the degree of intimidation that families can feel when asking for help and which often creates a sense of loss of personal power and control. Home-based support, by definition, locates the discussion of challenges, issues or problems in the place in which they commonly occur. This reduces the likelihood that planning and practising for change will feel remote from daily life.

Family support work also often combines practical and emotional components and the capacity of family support services to work on both of these levels is often identified by families as a critical dimension in their success (Munford and Sanders 1999, pp.165–172). Support to meet concrete daily needs is an important component of relationship building and provides many opportunities to establish trust and credibility (Scott and O'Neil 1996, p.6). Practical support often constitutes a significant part of the beginning of the intervention, where it can be used to secure an early sense of achievement and a focus while the worker and family build an effective relationship (Munford *et al.* 1998, p.67).

Family life is usually something that people have strong feelings about. When family life becomes difficult, family members will typically experience distress, worry, anxiety, anger, grief and a range of other intense emotions. Working with emotional responses to challenging situations and experiences is therefore a particularly critical dimension of family support work. Our research has shown that effective emotional support that provides a safe place to talk about very intense feelings and experiences and to develop new ways of problem solving and resolving past hurts is an important component of family support work. When we have tracked families that have used family support services, they have told us of the emotionally debilitating impact of the issues they faced and the significance of finding another adult who could support them to work constructively through these intense emotions to find resolution. As we have noted elsewhere, while practical support and information is important when families seek change, these types of assistance alone will not increase the capacity of parents to nurture children effectively (Munford and Sanders 1999, p.172). In fact, developing the capacity of parents to nurture is often required, and this can only happen when they are able to accept caring themselves. Dore (1993) has also noted that developing the capacity to accept care is a critical first step in the creation of parents who are able to nurture effectively. Emotional support work, then, is a fundamental aspect of family support, focusing as it does upon capacity to provide care for children, but also for oneself and for other adult family members.

Family support works best when it is delivered in a variety of modalities. Providing opportunities for group and individual work, linking families into other services outside of the agency (such as early childhood care and education, clinical and therapeutic services, such as counselling for specific issues) and encouraging families to identify different ways in which their needs may be met, are all important aspects of the work provided by family support agencies. Because one size does not fit all, these different modalities ensure that many opportunities are found to meet needs. They also create opportunities for families to meet a range of people, both providers and members of their communities, and this is important in terms of developing the capacity of families to continue to meet their own needs with the help of naturally occurring networks once they no longer need to be involved with the family support agency (Munford and Sanders 1999).

In Aotearoa/New Zealand this point is particularly pertinent for Maori families (Maori are the indigenous population of Aotearoa/New Zealand) where successful solutions to the daily challenges of family life and to more complex issues are often sought outside the immediate family living within a household. Here, successful family support interventions can harness the naturally occurring networks of the extended family to support family members and are central in seeking and achieving change (Munford and Sanders et al. 2001).

As can be seen from the preceding discussion, the creation of an effective working relationship is a critical ingredient in effective family support (Sanders and Munford 2003, p.184). The relationship is the vehicle through which work takes place and where changes can be attempted. The helping alliance that is forged by family support workers with clients is critical in the change process. It underpins the processes and strategies discussed above. In fact, the process of effectively supporting families to embark on complex processes of change is premised upon the establishment of an effective, unconditional relationship. Strong relationships provide a safe place within which families can be open and honest. For many families, the relationship they have with their family support worker may be their first experience of a respectful, honest relationship with another adult (Munford and Sanders 1999, p.171). Modelling positive, respectful relations is also an important form of teaching that support workers can engage in. By their own actions in building the support relationship they are able to demonstrate new ways of working through contentious, stressful, challenging and possibly hurtful situations to find constructive solutions. Clients who have been part of our research frequently refer to the ways in which they learned new ways of relating to children, partners and state agencies (such as schools, police, state social workers and so on) as a result of watching how their family support worker interacted with them and with others.

As we have seen, it can be argued that there are many positive aspects to family support work, but how do we know that what we are doing with clients is working and can be sustained over time? In order to develop best practice and be accountable in our practice we do need to participate in reflective practice. From time to time, this will also need to extend to more formal evaluation procedures in order to critically explore all aspects and processes of the helping relationship including identifying what constitutes positive outcomes for those using family support services and what sorts of support do not help families to move forwards (Canavan, Dolan and Pinkerton 2000; Katz and Pinkerton 2003a; Maluccio, Canali and Vecchiato 2002).

Evaluation – some key elements

There are many definitions of evaluation, some of which take an external view of its purpose and emphasise the specification by others of the value gained from a practice or programme (Saville-Smith 2003, p.77): the process by which we examine, assess and make judgements about the relative or absolute value of an action, a process a practice or an investment while others (see, for example, Lishman 1998, p.10) take into account the potential contribution evaluative activity can make to a range of stakeholders:

evaluation examines our effectiveness and can help us to improve it, can increase our accountability to users and clients, develops our knowledge and identifies gaps in knowledge, and helps us develop new models of practice and service delivery.

Shaw (1996, p.184) takes this approach still further and argues for the role of evaluation in empowerment and social change:

> Evaluating in practice is not limited to determining whether social work is effective, but must be a means of empowerment and social change... Evaluating in practice challenges social work to new understandings and new methodology... More importantly, it holds the promise of keeping social work honest.

When talking about evaluation in the context of family support services, we are attracted to the sorts of definitions offered by Shaw (1996, 1999) and Lishman (1998) because of the emphasis they place on evaluation's role in development and change within services, as well as with the quantum of impact such services are able to have in clients/families' lives. In working with agencies over the past decade we have learned of evaluative experiences that were less than optimal – evaluations that seemed to take information from family support agencies and give nothing back. These experiences, often as a result of national-level government requirements that funded programmes are externally evaluated, have created an environment of distrust and anxiety about evaluation. They also seem to us to represent wasted opportunities because the flow of information has been predominantly one way – from the agency to the funder. There is a number of models of evaluation practice that encourage a more open, responsive approach to evaluation, even when purchase agreements require external validation of effectiveness and value. Action- and empowerment-based approaches (Duigan 2003, pp.77–78) are but two of an increasing array of evaluation methodologies that enable providers and users to participate in design, development and implementation of evaluation activity. Like good family support work, successful evaluation relies heavily upon the relationships that evaluators are able to construct with all stakeholders and with the extent to which they are able to sustain open and honest approaches to their work.

As others have noted (Duigan 2003; Saville-Smith 2003; Shaw 1996) power and politics play a critical, if often unnamed role in evaluative activity. The process of setting out to ascribe some sort of value to a programme (as implied in the root of the term evaluation) places evaluators in the position of being able to make claims about effectiveness. It also raises insider and outsider issues (Munford and Sanders 2003b, p.268) where evaluators as outsiders become privy to insider knowledge. Furthermore, particularly in external evaluations, evaluators are able to choose, often with little oversight from others, which information they utilise in evaluating the programme, and which they will not. All of these are intensely political issues, raising as they do matters to do with the control of information. For these reasons, we favour action-oriented evaluative activity, where relationships and power issues are made an explicit part of the overall process, and where clear processes are agreed upon at the outset for dealing with the information generated. These sorts of processes aim for inclusion of participants in all aspects of the evaluation.

Key principles in inclusive evaluation approaches

Involvement of all key stakeholders

We define stakeholders as all of those people who have an interest in the process and outcomes of the evaluation, including those who have commissioned the research and those whose practices are being evaluated. Maluccio *et al.* (2002, p.2) suggest that as evaluations, especially outcome evaluations, increasingly become an accepted part of the work of agencies, thought needs to be given to how those closest to service delivery can be included in these processes. This includes administrators, practitioners and consumers. In attempting to achieve an inclusive approach to evaluation one needs to identify the key stakeholders and their roles in the evaluation. This involves being realistic about the purposes of the evaluation and achieving clarity about who has the authority over design, methods and use of data (McKie 2002; Shaw 1999). As McKie (2002) and Shaw (1999) point out, participation in evaluation requires careful consideration in that many of the stakeholders involved, for example, the workers, are having their work evaluated and from this decisions about future services are likely to be made.

Despite the challenges, there are possibilities for stakeholders to become involved and at the very least to be fully informed about evaluation procedures. The following points have emerged from our experience and represent a commitment to achieving inclusive evaluation approaches:

- It takes time to adequately prepare for the evaluation and time must be put aside throughout the evaluation to confront issues as they arise. Careful planning is always required. This includes taking the time to build key relationships so that all participants can take time to understand the processes being used and the interpretations being made (Chaskin 2002, p.32). Time is also required to reflect on how to achieve the purpose of the evaluation by using methods that take account of the 'lived realities of policy and practice' (Pinkerton and Katz 2003, p.16).

- Care must be taken to identify how the key questions are to be addressed and how the range of methods to be used can facilitate participation. Evaluators must understand that those whose work is being evaluated are experts in their field and have much to offer the evaluation process. Evaluators, merely because they have been assigned the role of evaluating a project, are not the only experts involved in the evaluation. Where possible participants can be involved in providing comment on the data collection methods and can also be involved in collecting and analysing data (Canavan and Dolan 2003, p.260) With adequate preparation this can generate data that can lead to more comprehensive analysis and interpretation.

- Evaluations can be more responsive by incorporating the practices of the agency in the processes used to collect data (Walsh Tapiata 2003). For example, in Aotearoa/New Zealand there is an expectation that when evaluators collect data from Maori participants cultural norms will be respected and incorporated into the process, including using kaumata (respected tribal elders) who can introduce the evaluators and facilitate meetings with participants. In this setting time is also taken to get to know the whakapapa (family connections) of a family and this needs to be done before a relationship can proceed. The local and cultural contexts of agencies need to be understood before embarking on the evaluation. Significant information can be missed simply because an evaluator has misunderstood the importance of certain agency norms and ways of operating.

- Evaluators need to find ways of keeping all participants informed throughout the process and if issues arise they need to be prepared to address these and take responsibility for any role they may have had in causing these. This open approach is strongly linked to success in the dissemination stage of evaluation and in the uptake of findings. Practitioners are more likely to utilise findings if they are confident that data collection and analysis is robust and subject to rigorous scrutiny and that it takes cognisance of the realities of working in their specific practice situation.

- At all times one must remember that a central goal of evaluation is focused on ways to develop more effective policy and practice in social service agencies. If stakeholders have felt involved in the evaluation and are aware of its potential to contribute positively to practice, they may be more willing to be part of the implementation of new policies and programmes.

Learning for all participants

A key theme that has guided our research and evaluation work and that is strongly connected to the involvement of key stakeholders is to acknowledge that the evaluation can result in learning for all participants. Much learning can take place when all aspects of family services (intake, provision, outcomes) are openly analysed and evaluated (Berry, Bussey and Cash 2001). All evaluations (those from externally commissioned projects to those that have been instigated by the agency) can provide opportunities for learning both in terms of what emerges in the findings, but also from what is learned throughout the course of the evaluation. A process of knowledge generation where all participants are seen as being able to learn from the process and findings of the evaluation offers new possibilities that are likely to result in constructive outcomes for all participants (Munford et al. 2003).

A commitment to dialogical inquiry where all participants can engage in reciprocal learning (Freire 1998) has greater possibilities for achieving positive change. While one must be realistic about the politics of evaluation (Canavan, Dolan and Pinkerton 2003; Katz and Pinkerton 2003b) where it may be difficult for practitioners always to engage positively with findings, we argue that where possible, processes for achieving dialogical inquiry should be established at the beginning of all evaluations. This is in line with a strengths approach that would see evaluation being embedded within a commitment by the agency to work from a perspective that respects the diversity of knowledge and where a search for solutions guides practice. If we believe that our work as practitioners is about sharing knowledge and about enabling our clients to develop their own opportunities for creating knowledge that can assist them to find solutions, the evaluation process has the potential to enable clients and workers to develop new skills and knowledge. Seeing practitioners learn alongside clients and reflect on practice together can have a positive and lasting effect on service development (O'Neil 2003). This can form the basis of a learning-organisation approach to evaluation which has an ongoing commitment to forming partnerships between those who are implementing family support programmes and those who are 'traditionally thought of as evaluators' (Wright and Paget 2002, p.130).

A commitment to critical reflection on all aspects of the evaluation

We have argued elsewhere (Munford and Sanders 2003a) that critical reflection is a vital part of research and evaluation. Doing research and evaluating practice, including the evaluation of the processes of service delivery and the measurement of practice outcomes, locates us within ongoing, busy relationships and our presence may be disruptive for the daily practice of the agency. This requires careful management. We have found that a commitment to ongoing critical reflection on our evaluation procedures assists us to be aware of the issues that may arise and how these can be overcome. It is not sufficient to provide participants with the contact details of evaluators and an encouragement to be in touch if things become difficult. Reflection is an active process and requires a commitment on the part of the evaluators to ensure that moments for reflection are built into the evaluation process and are taken seriously in terms of what may emerge from these discussions. Importantly, this requires that evaluators be willing and able to receive both positive and negative feedback on their own practice and to respond to criticism of this practice constructively, even when it may not have been offered in the most constructive manner.

A critical reflection process mirrors best practice in service delivery and can be achieved in all types of evaluations, even those commissioned by an external agency. We have been involved in advisory roles in commissioned evaluations and have found that the quality of the data is strongly influenced by the ways in which the evaluation team has been able to establish clear feedback mechanisms for participants. When effective feedback and reflection mechanisms are in place, data is likely to be of a high quality with fewer instances of missing data. There are also minimal disruptions to access to participants when they have been fully informed of their rights and how they can provide comment on processes and evaluation activities. While these processes are strongly linked to consent to participate, a signed consent form at the beginning of the evaluation is not sufficient to guarantee that participants continue to feel that they are willing participants in the process. This has to be constantly reviewed and negotiated when issues arise.

Many evaluators, given time pressures, find it difficult to commit fully to the process of critical reflection, However, from experience we have learned that the following factors will help maintain the momentum of the evaluation and achieve more streamlined and effective evaluations, in terms both of processes and outcomes:

- ensuring that there is time to reflect on the ongoing impact of the evaluation

- being clear that social service interventions are not interrupted

- respecting the knowledge of social service workers and their clients

- involving practitioners in identifying what data (information) can be collected and the most effective ways of achieving this.

Implications for practitioners

The challenge for practitioners is to think about how they can become actively involved in evaluation (see Haviland 2004). While externally directed evaluations of their work will be required in order to measure the effectiveness of their programmes and to measure the outcomes of interventions and social service programmes, there will be many opportunities for practitioners to identify what sorts of evaluations would contribute to the enhancement of practice. There are many factors to consider here and we have identified two areas that are likely to be of central concern for practitioners.

Asking the critical questions about evaluation and the contribution that evaluation can make to enhancing best practice

We encourage practitioners to critically engage with evaluations and to ask the following sorts of questions:

- What is the purpose of the evaluation and has this been clearly articulated to all stakeholders? Who has control of the evaluation and how can practitioners ensure that they can become involved in evaluation procedures? Do they have a role in determining the questions to be asked, the data to be collected and the procedures for data analysis and interpretation?

- Are concepts clearly defined, for example, how is family support defined? Do the evaluators have a clear understanding of the nature of the services being provided and the key elements of family support services? Are the local and cultural frameworks used within the agency acknowledged and taken into account by the evaluators?

- How are consumers and clients involved in the evaluation? Have mechanisms been put in place to ensure that their interests are protected?

- Are feedback mechanisms in place to ensure that accountability to key stakeholders is maintained throughout the evaluation?

- How and in what form, will findings be disseminated? What contribution will these make to the enhancement of best practice and to ensuring that effective services can be sustained over the long term and in a range of service interventions and locations? For example, does an evaluation of a new family support service programme or intervention in a particular area have the potential to influence the development of services in other areas?

- What sorts of resources and support are available to assist with the implementation of findings?

The greater the level of involvement of agency staff the greater the likelihood that findings will be used to develop and enhance practice. We suggest that the answers to these questions are written down as an agreement between the evaluators and the agency. They can then be used as a reference point for discussion and reflection as the evaluation unfolds.

The evaluation process is complex, but with systematic planning it can meet the requirement of the evaluators to achieve rigorous processes and of social service organisations that want to improve practice and to maintain those interventions and strategies that are making a positive difference for clients. A central goal of evaluation should be a commitment to achieving best practice. Much has been said about the potential of evaluation to make a difference to practice. However, many practitioners are unsure about how to implement evaluation strategies and how to incorporate monitoring and evaluation into their daily practice. We suggest that one of the key strategies is to identify how monitoring and evaluation can be built into the ongoing activities of the agency and to extend and transform these into systematic investigation of the delivery of family support services.

Building evaluation into everyday practice

Family support workers often engage in regular supervision where they meet with a senior practitioner to reflect on their practice and where they may also meet with peers and others in their team to share knowledge and develop new skills. Taking the time to critique one's work with clients, so that all aspects of this work can be explored and where strategies for improving practice can be identified, is critical to the ongoing development and maintenance of good practice. When social service agencies have a commitment to reflective practice they are more likely to remain responsive to families, to test out what really works and to have a commitment to ensuring that organisational practices parallel the relationships that are being established with clients (Munford and Sanders 1999).

A commitment to reflective practice can provide a foundation for developing more formal evaluations of practice. Evaluation can emerge out of the practices of reflection. Having opportunities to meet in teams can involve a focus on the monitoring and evaluation of practice. This can begin slowly and in a way that does not impact on the daily work of the organisation (Sanders and Munford 2003). Staff can take on a commitment to evaluate one aspect of practice. For example, the engagement of clients in the agency and relationship building as part of the assessment and intervention process, can be a key focus of evaluation. Understanding how clients come to the agency, the nature of the relationship between the social worker and the client and how services match the diverse needs of clients are matters that deserve close scrutiny as fundamental elements of family support services. This kind of reflection and evaluation focuses on inputs (funding, worker contributions, programme methodologies); processes (types of interventions) and outputs (client and programme outcomes) as well as the dynamic interplay of all these factors (Fein 2002).

Reflective practice and evaluation can be empowering for workers as it enables them to take charge of their work and to critically engage with their daily practice. Research and evaluation may provide an opportunity to analyse their practice so that good practice can be sustained over time. The ongoing development of our understanding of effective support processes is essential in order to procure adequate resources for social service work. In partnership with clients, it may also be an opportunity to understand what it is that really does make a difference in the lives of clients (Munford and Sanders 1999, p.200). Self-reflective practice can give a 'voice to the voiceless', for clients and for workers, and will assist in defining effective service delivery strategies by re-analysing situations to generate new knowledge and frameworks for practice (Allan 2003). Gaps in services can also be identified and the contribution family support can make to addressing entrenched issues faced by those living in impoverished circumstances and experiencing social exclusion can also be revealed (May-Chahal, Katz and Cooper 2003).

Family support workers can be encouraged to keep information that can be used in evaluation processes. Team meetings can include some evaluative activities that are based on the interpretation of certain aspects of family support interventions. The challenge is to maintain a commitment to the establishment of a learning organisation where the approach to evaluation is focused on family support agencies becoming involved in evaluation that produces meaningful results and that can have immediate and lasting benefits for agencies (Wright and Paget 2002).

Conclusion

Successful evaluations are able to address complex issues and are driven by the desire to strengthen family support policies and enhance the effectiveness of social service interventions. We argue that the greater the involvement of practitioners in all aspects of the evaluation, the greater the likelihood that the processes of the evaluation will be successful and that results will be incorporated into agency practices. Family support workers have much to offer these processes as those who engage in critical reflection on their practice demonstrate a commitment to ensuring that their practice does indeed make a positive difference for families.

References

Allan, J. (2003) 'Practising Critical Social Work.' In J. Allan, B. Pease and L. Briskman (eds) *Critical Social Work: An Introduction to Theories and Practice.* Sydney: Allen and Unwin.

Berry, M., Bussey, M. and Cash, S.J. (2001) 'Evaluation in a Dynamic Environment: Assessing Change when Nothing is Constant.' In E. Walton, P. Sandau-Beckler and M. Mannes (eds) *Balancing Family-Centered Services and Child Well-Being: Exploring Issues in Policy, Practice, Theory and Research.* New York: Columbia University Press.

Canavan, J. and Dolan, P. (2003) 'Policy Roots and Practice Growth: Evaluating Family Support on the West Coast of Ireland.' In I. Katz and J. Pinkerton (eds) *Evaluating Family Support: Thinking Internationally, Thinking Critically*. Chichester: Wiley.

Canavan, J., Dolan, P. and Pinkerton, J. (2000) *Family Support: Direction from Diversity*. London: Jessica Kingsley Publishers.

Canavan, J., Dolan, P. and Pinkerton, J. (2003) 'Optimising the Relationships between Research, Policy and Practice: A Systemic Model.' In R. Munford and J. Sanders (eds) *Making a Difference in Families: Research that Creates Change*. Sydney: Allen and Unwin.

Chaskin, R. (2002) 'The Evaluation of 'Community Building': Measuring the Social Effects of Community-Based Practice.' In A.N. Maluccio, C. Canali and T. Vecchiato (eds) *Assessing Outcomes in Child and Family Services: Comparative Design and Policy Issues*. New York: Aldine de Gruyter.

Dore, M. (1993) 'Family Preservation and Poor Families: When Homebuilding is not Enough.' *Families and Society 74*, 9, 545–556.

Duigan, P. (2003) 'Approaches and Terminology in Programme and Policy Evaluation.' In N. Lunt, C. Davidson and K. McKegg (eds) *Evaluating Policy and Practice: A New Zealand Reader*. Auckland: Pearson Education.

Fein, E. (2002) 'The Black Box: Accounting for Program Inputs when Assessing Outcomes.' In A.N. Maluccio, C. Canali and T. Vecchiato (eds) *Assessing Outcomes in Child and Family Services: Comparative Design and Policy Issues*. New York: Aldine de Gruyter.

Freire, P. (1998) *Pedagogy of Freedom*. Oxford: Rowman and Littlefielt Publishers.

Haviland, M. (2004) 'Gathering Information to Inform Action.' *Bulletin (Australian Institute of Family Studies)* 5, 3–5.

Katz, I. and Pinkerton, J. (2003a) *Evaluating Family Support: Thinking Internationally, Thinking Critically*. Chichester: Wiley.

Katz, I. and Pinkerton, J. (2003b) 'International Convergence and Divergence: Towards an Open System Model in the Evaluation of Family Support.' In I. Katz and J. Pinkerton (eds) *Evaluating Family Support: Thinking Internationally, Thinking Critically*. Chichester: Wiley.

Lishman, J. (1998) 'Personal and Professional Development.' In R. Adams, L. Dominelli and M. Payne (eds) *Social Work: Themes, Issues and Critical Debates*. London: Macmillan.

Maluccio, A.N., Canali, C. and Vecchiato, T. (2002) *Assessing Outcomes in Child and Family Services: Comparative Design and Policy Issues*. New York: Aldine de Gruyter.

May-Chahal, C., Katz, I. and Cooper, L. (2003) 'Social Exclusion, Family Support and Evaluation.' In I. Katz and J. Pinkerton (eds) *Evaluating Family Support: Thinking Internationally, Thinking Critically*. Chichester: Wiley.

McKie, L. (2002) *Engagement and Evaluation in Qualitative Inquiry*. London: Sage.

Munford, R. and Sanders, J. (1999) *Supporting Families*. Palmerston North, NZ: Dunmore Press.

Munford, R. and Sanders, J. (2003a) 'Introduction: Making a Difference.' In R. Munford and J. Sanders (eds) *Making a Difference in Families: Research that Creates Change*. Sydney: Allen and Unwin.

Munford, R. and Sanders, J. (2003b) 'Action Research.' In C. Davidson and M. Tolich (eds) *Social Science Research in New Zealand: Many Paths to Understanding*. Auckland: Pearson.

Munford, R., Sanders, J., Tisdall, M., Henare, A., Livingston, K. and Spoonley, P. (1998) *Working Successfully with Families, Stage Two*. Wellington, NZ: Barnardos.

Munford, R., Sanders, J. with Andrew, A., Butler, P., Kaipuke, R. and Ruwhiu, L. (2001) 'Aotearoa/New Zealand – Working Differently with Communities and Families.' In C. Warren-Adamson (ed) *Family Centres and their International Role in Social Action*. Aldershot: Ashgate.

Munford, R. and Sanders, J. with Andrew, A., Butler, P. and Ruwhiu, L. (2003) 'Action Research with Families/Whanau and Communities.' In R. Munford and J. Sanders (eds) *Making a Difference in Families: Research that Creates Change*. Sydney: Allen and Unwin.

O'Neil, D. (2003) 'Clients as Researchers: The Benefits of Strengths-Based Research.' In R. Munford and J. Sanders (eds) *Making a Difference in Families: Research that Creates Change*. Sydney: Allen and Unwin.

Pinkerton, J. and Katz, I. (2003) 'Perspective through International Comparison in the Evaluation of Family Support.' In I. Katz and J. Pinkerton (eds) *Evaluating Family Support: Thinking Internationally, Thinking Critically*. Chichester: Wiley.

Sanders, J. and Munford, R. (2003) 'Lessons from the Evaluation of Family Support in New Zealand.' In I. Katz and J. Pinkerton (eds) *Evaluating Family Support: Thinking Internationally, Thinking Critically.* Chichester: Wiley.

Saville-Smith, K. (2003) 'Power and Politics: The Shaping of Evaluation Research in New Zealand.' In N. Lunt, C. Davidson and K. McKegg (eds) *Evaluating Policy and Practice: A New Zealand Reader.* Auckland: Pearson Education.

Scott, D. and O'Neil, D. (1996) *Beyond Child Rescue: Developing Family-centred Practice at St Lukes.* Sydney: Allen and Unwin.

Shaw, I. (1996) *Evaluating in Practice.* Aldershot: Ashgate.

Shaw, I. (1999) *Qualitative Evaluation.* London: Sage.

Walsh Tapiata, W. (2003) 'A Model for Maori Research: Te Whakaeke i te Ao Rangahau o te Maori.' In R. Munford and J. Sanders (eds) *Making a Difference in Families: Research that Creates Change.* Sydney: Allen and Unwin.

Wright, L. and Paget, K. (2002) 'A Learning-Organization Approach to Evaluation.' In A.N. Maluccio, C. Canali and T. Vecchiato (eds) *Assessing Outcomes in Child and Family Services: Comparative Design and Policy Issues.* New York: Aldine de Gruyter.

Chapter 18

Reflecting for Action: The Future of Family Support

John Canavan

The motives for putting together this collection are firmly rooted in a belief that while family support has grown in importance as a strategic direction in services for children and families globally, as yet it lacks a foundational base in terms of its theory, policy, operational management, practice and evaluation. Such a base is necessary to guide its development in a coherent and optimally valuable way. It is also necessary to assess the quality and effectiveness of family support in meeting the needs of children and families. This book is a contribution to addressing this foundational deficit. In Chapter 1 the book suggests a cupped model of family support in which the needs of children and young people are seen as being met through the support of their families, which in turn are part of an series of supportive relationships through extended family and friends, school and community, organisational networks and national policy and legislation. Reflecting that model a provisional definition for family support is suggested and backed by ten practice principles. What then follows is a set of 16 content-rich chapters on various dimensions of family support policy, organisation, practice and evaluation.

For some readers, engagement with the book will have been selective, focusing only on specific areas of interest. For others, their engagement will have been more comprehensive and analytical, in which case the book chapters can be seen as individual case studies for testing out the meaning and relevance of the definition and principles of family support provided at the outset. Running through the book has been a key orientation towards reflective practice. This can be seen as a mode of operation in social, educational and other service provision very much in sympathy with family support. It fits well with the emphasis within the field on the role of the practitioner and the significance of their style of work. Importantly, a reflective practice mode also allows the organic creation of knowledge that the relatively new field of family support requires. Continuing in reflective mode, this final chapter considers the opening definition in light of the subsequent chapters, offers some suggestions as to future directions for family support and proposes reflective practice as a key strategy in consolidating its knowledge base.

Reflecting on the definition

How then does the definition (see Box 18.1) stand up as the basis for developing family support into the future? My argument is that assessing it against the contents of this book is a good starting point for answering the question. Thus, if this diverse set of chapters, which were not assembled on the basis of having a tight fit with the definitional material, still reflect its various elements, then the definition must have a core validity. So, does the definition hold up? In answer to that question, based on a detailed reading of the chapters, it appears that the material gathered together is highly representative of the definition, with some dimensions featuring more strongly than others.

For example, one of the first aspects of the definition for family support is the recognition that it is a broad enterprise representing a wide range of activities and types of service. The range of experience all taking place under the banner of family support reflected in the foregoing chapters serves to confirm this as a significant characteristic. Less well reflected in the book is the extent to which family support should be seen to involve integrated programmes, although Ilan Katz in Chapter 2 highlights the possibility of schools operating as a key partner in such arrangements. Going back a step, an essential element in the development of the definition and practice principles has been the recognition that these depend on explicit policy choices. Both Michelle Millar and Alex Wright confirm the significance of this argument – Millar in Chapter 6 by identifying and illustrating the value of comparative policy analysis for reflecting on family support and Wright in Chapter 5 by setting out a specific framework for analysing policy implementation as a key part of the policy making process.

Perhaps the dimension of the definition most strongly reflected throughout the book relates to social support and the role of informal social networks. Chapters 13 by Pat Dolan, 10 by Pat Dolan and Brian McGrath, 8 by Jeff Fleischer and Judy Warner, 9 by Rosemary Kilpatrick, 11 by Fatima Husain and 14 by Monit Cheung and Patrick Leung all illustrate the significance of these concepts to the practice of family support. The definition's emphasis on the role of the community and school is exemplified by Ilan Katz and by Robert J. Chaskin respectively. Katz offers much food for thought on the issues involved in school-based provision. Chaskin's chapter provides clear frameworks for thinking about and making the connection between community and family support. Katz' chapter also reflects the importance of accessibility and flexibility of services. This is something represented strongly in the contribution by Fleischer and Warner on the YAP programme.

Box 18.1: Family support definition and practice principles

Definition:

- a style of work
- a set of activities
- reinforces positive informal social networks
- delivers through integrated programmes combining statutory, voluntary community and private services
- primarily focused on early intervention across all levels of needs and services
- promotes and protects the health, well-being and rights of all children, young people and their families
- in their own homes and communities
- pays particular attention to those who are vulnerable or at risk.

Practice principles:

- working in partnership with children, families, professionals and communities
- needs led and striving for the minimum intervention required
- clear focus on the wishes, feelings, safety and well-being of children
- reflects a strengths-based/resilience perspective
- strengthens informal support networks
- accessible and flexible incorporating both child protection and out-of-home care
- facilitates self-referral and multi-access referral paths
- involves service users and front-line providers in the planning, delivery and evaluation
- promotes social inclusion, addressing issues of ethnicity, disability and rural/urban communities
- outcomes-based evaluation supports quality services based on best practice.

The importance of family support provision being needs led also features strongly throughout the book. The intervention outlined by Kilpatrick, the case studies from Cheung and Leung's chapter and the tool for developing interventions based on identified needs provided by Dolan all reflect this practice principle strongly. The more specific point about service user involvement in planning, delivery and evaluation is also well reflected, for example in the chapters by Chaskin, Jackie Sanders and Robyn Munford and Alex Wright.

Chapters 12 by John Pinkerton and 7 by Ruth Gardner highlight the fact that family support is not just about preventive work. In the former, Pinkerton locates preparation for leaving care within an overarching policy goal of family support, while for Gardner, family support reframes child protection work to be 'positive and inclusive wherever possible, rather than defensive and risk-averse'. Both chapters are also significant in illustrating the point that a key imperative of family support is its focus on vulnerable, hard-to-reach and at-risk children. In turn, this aspect of the definition connects to the wider service principle of social inclusion. The chapters by Kilpatrick, Husain and Cheung and Leung illustrate the role of family support for children and families excluded from full participation in society because of disability- and ethnicity-related barriers.

Dolan's chapter provides the most explicit representation of family support as a style of work. He outlines its significance and suggests a self-appraisal tool for addressing it in a structured way. Peter Steen Jensen and Rene Junker in Chapter 4 also consider style of work in underscoring a positive approach to children and families. They contrast this with a culture of diagnosis and trouble-shooting. Both of these chapters link the notion of style of work to underpinning principles and protocols for practice. In both, the particular style of work illustrated reflects a strengths-based, resilience approach, which is one of the family support practice principles set out above. This principle is most explicitly represented in the YAP programme described by Fleischer and Warner, where it is a core guiding principle of the model.

It is not surprising that the chapters focusing on evaluation most emphasise the family support service principle of building measures of success into practice. Charles Bruner in Chapter 15 underlines the importance of practitioners taking a lead in family support evaluation. He provides a useful framework of indicators that could be directly adopted or easily adapted by interested projects. Sanders and Munford suggest that the challenge for evaluation in family support is to embed it in organisational policies and practices. Their view of evaluation as a key strategy in ensuring that family support interventions remain relevant to clients and ensuring positive short- and long-term outcomes is directly in line with the tenth practice principle. In illustrating what RCT approaches look like in practice, W. Todd Abraham and his colleagues in Chapter 16 remind us that family support evaluation should strive for the highest standards of evidence and the most sophisticated statistical analysis. Among the other chapters, while more focused on the issue of cultural appropriateness in working with families, Cheung and Leung's contribution also offers a very concrete way of linking practice to measurement in family support.

Running throughout the book is an emphasis on the well-being and health of children. Less apparent is an emphasis on the rights of children. As noted earlier, chapters for this book were not selected to illustrate the definition and principles and so it is important not to over-interpret this point or engage in an extended analysis of what it might mean. On the other hand, in arguing in favour of the definition, based on the fact that the invited contributions reflect key elements of it, I must also question this aspect of the definition, given that the chapters don't reflect it. Looking at this point from a discourse perspective, it could be argued that a family support discourse runs the risk of 'back-grounding' children in terms of the focus of intervention and shifting the balance of resource-use away from children to adults. Although only hinted here, it is certainly an issue requiring research and debate as family support develops further. The only other area where the book doesn't reflect elements of the definition and the service principles in an explicit and robust way is in relation to the significance of family support as early intervention across a range of levels and needs. As with the issue of rights, the relationship between prevention, early intervention and family support policy models could be a focus for a valuable debate.

Developing future directions

Moving forward, the challenge now is to consolidate and build on the knowledge base in family support. This something that will require further elaboration, adaptation and refinement of its concepts, processes and practices. My reflections on the definition and the rich diversity of the chapters' contents suggest a wide range of areas needing developmental, research and evaluation work. For example, starting with the linchpin concept of social support, much more needs to be done to develop the links between existing knowledge in this field and family support. Formulating and testing more comprehensive and detailed materials for practitioners in the form of practice guides, protocols and resource packs for working with different target groups, at different levels of need, is also a key task. Exploring issues of children's rights and resource allocation as these are played out in family support service delivery is among a number of politics and policy-related questions. Also important here is the question of the discursive meaning of family support, its adoption by different groups for different political ends and what the implications are for the development of the field. At an organisational level, more needs to be done to establish how to reorientate services toward a family support stance. There is a critical need to develop and implement rigorous research and evaluation programmes that seek to establish whether family support really makes a difference to children and families and in what ways. There are also more far-reaching questions about whether family support as a policy and practice orientation has something to offer adult services, for example in the fields of mental health and aging.

Traditional strategies for consolidating the family support knowledge base are available in the form of scholarly and applied research and evaluation activities. Notwithstanding the requirement of commissioners for specific answers to specific questions of policy and intervention, often within limited timeframes, scope exists for 'family support interested' applied researchers and evaluators to build wider questions into their designs. In doing so, they should be able to both add value to their work on behalf of the commissioner and extend the body of knowledge for the field in general. For academics, less constrained by the demands of commissioners, there is possibly greater scope to engage in more foundational work on the theoretical issues in family support. In order to be most useful, this work needs to be translated into easily accessible working papers, journal articles, books and chapters.

In addition to these traditional modes, one way for managers at organisation and intervention levels and front-line practitioners to move the family support agenda forward is to return to the practice principles suggested in Box 18.1. This set of principles offers an opportunity for reflection on family support using four questions. These questions can each be asked of the ten principles in relation to any specific example of family support:

- What are the indicators of the achievement of the principle?

- What level of performance is being achieved by the intervention/service/organisation?

- What actions need to be taken to achieve the principle in practice?

- What has been learnt from trying to implement the principle?

So, for example, it might be that partnership is indicated at the level of a community-based project with adolescents to the extent to which planning explicitly includes sections on young person's and parents' views on the issues and how they can be resolved. An early-years intervention team might use a simple subjective rating scale to score themselves on the accessibility and flexibility of their service. A service manager with responsibility across all care and welfare services might develop an action plan to ensure that all services are inclusive and non-discriminatory, based on a prior process of self-assessment in relation to the social inclusion principle. Finally, a parent-training-course provider might document her own learning and that of the group from emphasising informal networks in their work together.

The four questions can either be posed as part of a continuing process of reflection within day-to-day practice or serve as the basis for regular six-monthly or annual reviews, for example. As well as impacting in an iterative fashion on activities at organisation, service and intervention level, if properly documented, data and analysis generated from such reflection could feed into wider efforts at practitioner-led research. In this way the questions will help ensure that the development of family support is informed by experiences from the front line.

The role of reflective practice

This book aimed to work to an explicit reflective practice agenda. Thus, as well as making sets of ideas available for practitioners, it aimed to equip the reader with the means to translate these into meaningful practice that meets the needs of children and families. To a large degree, the reflective practice agenda was apparent throughout the book and the formal and informal models drawn on enriched the substantive material in the chapters. For the future, reflective practice has the potential to be the key strategy for consolidating and developing the family support knowledge base. One risk of this is that reflective practice may be seen to be just for care and welfare practitioners, and not for those involved in policy, planning, management and research. However, reflective practice should have resonance for 'practitioners' at all levels.

Yet reflective practice is hard to do. For all of us involved in the day-to-day of our work, it is most difficult to build structured time into our work processes for 'reflection on action', and even more so for developing skills for 'reflection in action'. There is always the service user to be seen, meetings to attend, reports to be finished; these all take priority in increasingly demanding work settings. Such increased demands require changes in the balance of our work, not that we try to fit in ever more into our schedules. One way of addressing this is to move outside narrow models and engage in a more thoroughgoing approach to reflective practice.

Thompson, who has written extensively on practice in social work, suggests a means of doing so. His starting point is that concepts and frameworks are 'made to measure' by the skilful work of the reflective practitioner, thus bridging the gap between theory and practice (2000, p.89). Yet he identifies significant barriers to bridging this gap, including for example: elitism of academic processes and practices on one side and anti-intellectualism (of weak and strong varieties) of practitioners on the other; organisational issues linked to time and work pressures; and eclecticism in practice (resulting in a diminution of the value of individual theories). In spite of these, he is optimistic about the value of reflective practice and outlines 15 strategies to stimulate its development. Accepting that Thompson regards this set of strategies as neither comprehensive nor definitive, they do cluster fairly well into three groupings to do with value positions, reflection techniques and organisational imperatives. These are listed in Box 18.2.

Even if it is not possible to pursue all of these strategic imperatives, following Thompson's framework offers a supportive structure within which to frame reflective practice for the development of family support.

Connecting the strands

This book is a self-conscious attempt to address the 'foundations-building' agenda facing family support. It is based on setting out an explicit, albeit provisional, position on definition and practice principles and inviting sharing of knowledge and experience which can be used to explore, modify or develop the stated position. In line with that approach, developing family support further and ensuring its place within the global operation of child welfare (and other human services) will require sustained intellectual work. For example a significant challenge will be to bring together, in a coherent fashion, the mass of knowledge that currently exists and that will emerge in the future, from the collective actions of front-line workers, operational managers, policy makers and researchers. The concluding points below suggest a way of undertaking that task, and are primarily, but not exclusively, aimed at researchers. They are as follows:

- Start with the definition provided in this book, using it as a basis for description, analysis, critique and conceptual reformulation.

- Accumulate existing family support knowledge around four clusters:
  - policy and politics
  - organisation, management and planning
  - direct work with children and families
  - research and evaluation.

All four clusters need to have empirical and theoretical dimensions to them.

- Develop strong family support policy, practice, research and training networks backed by a literature (including 'grey literature', websites and research databases) that will capture and disseminate knowledge from policy and intervention and from the efforts of reflective practitioners.

Box 18.2: Thompson's strategies for bridging the practice–theory gap (2000, pp.94–107)

Value positions

1.	Going beyond practice wisdom	Recognising the danger of taking practice as 'art' too far
2.	Going beyond theoryless practice	Recognising that all practice has a theoretical base, acknowledged or not
3.	Going beyond common sense	Recognising that 'common sense' involves unquestioned assumptions
4.	Going beyond elitism and anti-intellectualism	Recognising the need to make theory accessible and applicable and to avoid anti-intellectual approaches that don't engage in theory

Reflection techniques

5.	Using cycles of learning	An active, cyclical approach linking concrete experience to previous learning and experience, before re-engaging in new practice
6.	Developing research-minded practice	Developing creative, participatory approaches to practice that follow the logic of research
7.	Using the critical incident technique	Focusing on particular incidents that make an impression on staff
8.	Developing a group approach	Setting up groups to promote learning / understanding of particular issues
9.	Problematising	Opening up opportunities for learning by looking behind everyday routines and standard practices
10.	Using enquiry and action learning (EAL)	Using case-study approaches to work from practice to relevant theory.

Organisational imperatives

11. Promoting continuous professional development	Ensuring ongoing opportunities for learning for staff involving in-service training, supervision, appraisal
12. Developing interprofessional learning	Offering reflective practitioners in different disciplines the opportunity to learn with and from each other
13. Balance of challenge and support	Taking steps to find out what makes an appropriately balanced, challenging and supportive work environment, a key factor in creating a context for reflective practice
14. Developing staff care	Recognising and tackling stress and other work pressures that act as barriers to reflective practice
15. Using mentoring	Providing opportunities for all staff at all stages of their careers to be mentored; outside of line-supervision arrangements if necessary

Reference

Thompson, N. (2000) *Theory and Practice in Human Services.* Buckingham: Open University Press.

List of Contributors

W. Todd Abraham is a doctoral candidate in social psychology at Iowa State University and a graduate research assistant at the Institute for Social and Behavioral Research. His current research interests focus on applications of quantitative methods including structural equation and multilevel regression modelling, methods for dealing with missing data, and approaches to testing mediation.

Charles Bruner holds a PhD in political science from Stanford University and served twelve years in the Iowa General Assembly as a state legislator. He directs the Child and Family Policy Center and has written extensively on linking policy and research on issues vital to children and families, with a particular emphasis upon family support.

John Canavan, MA is joint manager of the HSE/NUI, Galway, Child and Family Research and Policy Unit and teaches part-time at NUI, Galway, on the Diploma/MA in Family Support Studies. He has over ten years' experience as an evaluator, having worked at policy and project level, and is currently completing doctoral research on the evaluation of social interventions with young people.

John Pinkerton is involved in teaching, researching and writing in the areas of family support and care leaving. He is External Examiner to the MA in Social Work course at Trinity College Dublin, a member of the editorial board of the British Journal of Social Work, a member of the advisory board of the Children's Institute, University of Cape Town, and consultant to the Northern Ireland Government on the development of a Northern Ireland Children's Strategy.

Ilan Katz is Professor and Acting Director of the Social Policy Research Centre at the University of New South Wales in Sydney, Australia. He trained as a social worker in South Africa and worked in the UK in a number of local authorities and NGOs. He was Head of Practice Development and Research at the NSPCC and has subsequently worked for the DfES and the Policy Research Bureau in London. He was an investigator on the National Evaluation of Sure Start and is now Chief Investigator of the evaluations of both the Australian Government's Stronger Families and Communities Strategy and the NSW Government's Early Intervention Program. He is a member of the Consortium Advisory Group of the Longitudinal Study of Australian Children, and the NSW Department of Community Services Research Advisory Group. He has written extensively on child protection, family support, parenting, race and ethnicity, comparative child welfare regimes and early intervention.

Robert J. Chaskin is an Associate Professor at the School of Social Service Administration and a Research Fellow at the Chapin Hall Center for Children at the University of Chicago, US. His research interests include community organising and development, community social organisation, comprehensive community initiatives, youth development, associations and nonprofits, philanthropy and social change, knowledge utilisation and evaluation, and cross-national research. He has published widely on the subjects of community building and community capacity. Professor Chaskin received his AM in Anthropology and PhD in Sociology from the University of Chicago.

Dr Monit Cheung, MA, MSW, PhD, LCSW, is Professor and Chair of Children and Families Concentration, and is Principal Investigator of the Child Welfare Education Project, a state partnership program funded federally by Title IV-E for training child welfare social workers. She is a Licensed Clinical Social Worker specialising in family counselling, child/adolescent counselling, and incest survivor treatment. She is also a volunteer clinician providing counselling and case consultation at the Asian American Family Counseling Center, and a consultant trainer for the Hong Kong Social Welfare Department and the Hong Kong Police Force.

Dr Pat Dolan is joint manager of Western Health Board/NUI, Galway, Child and Family Research and Policy Unit and is the director of the forthcoming MA in Family Support Studies at the National University of Ireland. He is directly involved in research on family support and is a recognised international expert in the field.

Jeff Fleischer is the Chief Executive Officer of the Youth Advocate Program Inc. He has developed strength-based programs for young people and families at high risk of institutionalisation for the past 30 years throughout the US and Europe. Jeff has provided training and has participated in efforts to change youth service systems so that they rely less on out-of-home placements and institutions. He is a member of the Committee for International Human Rights Inquiry and has developed a partnership with the Street Childrens' Movement in Guatemala. He received a Masters Degree in Social Work from Rutgers University and is a Licensed Clinical Social Worker in the State of New Jersey.

Ruth Gardner has combined practice, research and writing throughout her career. As a researcher she has delivered national studies for the Department of Health on consulting and involving children in the looked after system and on preventive social work. Recently completed research for the NSPCC concerns the content and process of effective family support in deprived areas, including children's perceptions. These three studies have each produced a single authored book, the most recent of which was endorsed by Lord Laming. The NSPCC has now commissioned research into the integration of children's services to achieve Every Child Matters Outcomes.

Catherine Goldberg-Lillehoj is a Research Scientist at the Institute for Social and Behavioral Research at Iowa State University. Her principal research interest is the prevention of adolescent substance use with school-based intervention programs, specifically with rural populations.

Max Guyll is a Research Scientist at the Partnerships in Prevention Science Institute at Iowa State University. His research interests include issues related to the prevention of substance use, problem behaviors, and obesity in children and adolescents.

Fatima Husain is a Senior Research Fellow at the National Family and Parenting Institute, London. Her main area of specialisation is ethnic minority families and children.

Peter Steen Jensen is a General Manager of the Department of Children and Young People in Local Government in Odense, Denmark. In recent years, he has been at the forefront of community planning in Odense having previously worked both as school teacher and school inspector for many years in the Department of Education, Copenhagen, Denmark.

René Junker is Head of Social Services in Odense, Denmark. Having initially studied at the University of Aalborg Denmark, he has many years experience at both development and management levels of family support services.

Dr Rosemary Kilpatrick is acting director of the Institute of Child Care Research in Queen's University, Belfast. Prior to this she was senior lecturer in the Graduate School of Education in the same university with special responsibility in the field of learning disability. She is a chartered forensic psychologist and has much professional experience in the juvenile justice and care systems in Northern Ireland as well as in the voluntary sector. Her particular area of interest is children and young people who are at risk of being socially excluded and much of her research has been on this topic, with findings having been used to inform policy and practice within both the education and child care sector.

Dr Patrick Leung, Associate Professor and former Doctoral Program Director at the University of Houston Graduate School of Social Work (UH-GSSW), TX, teaches program evaluation, research methodology, survey design and doctoral level multivariate statistics. Currently, he is the chair of the Texas Title IV-E (Child Welfare Training) Roundtable Evaluation Committee and Board of Director of the US Council on Social Work Education. His research areas include child welfare training and evaluation, substance abuse treatment, Asian cultural sensitivity training, immigrant mental health issues, domestic violence and gerontology.

Michael B. Marks is a former administrator and now Internal Senior Consultant for Youth Advocate Programs, Inc. (YAP). He has over 25 years' experience in government and the charity sector. He previously served as Deputy Executive Director for the Society for Seamen's Children, the largest child welfare and family services organisation on Staten Island, New York City. Mr. Marks is in the process of completing a PhD in Social Welfare from the University of Albany (NY, USA). He is participating as an action researcher, overseeing and studying the methods, processes and impacts of new pilot programming within YAP, that involves juvenile offenders and dependent children partnering with staff in serving as resources, contributors and change-agents to further YAP's mission as well as improve their neighborhood/community.

Carla J. McCulty has worked with Youth Advocate Programs, Inc. since 1998 in both domestic and international juvenile justice, child welfare, and mental health programs. She most recently worked as Consultant to New York City's Administration for Children's Services through an Annie E. Casey grant. Ms McCulty helped in the creation of the YAP National Training Curriculum, provides training and program development support, chairs the YAP Leadership Engagement And Development (LEAD) Program, and sits on a number of YAP-wide committees. She received her BA in Psychology from Pennsylvania State University, her MA in Social Work from Marywood University, and is working on completing her MA in International Administration from the University of Miami.

Dr. Michelle Millar, BA, MA, PhD (Limerick) is College Lecturer teaching Public and Social Policy at the Department of Political Science and Sociology, NUI, Galway. Her research interests focus on social policy change and evaluation and the involvement of service users in health care planning and delivery.

Robyn Munford is the Professor of Social Work and Head of the School of Sociology, Social Policy and Social Work, Massey University, New Zealand. She teaches social and community work practice focusing on community development and disability studies while her current research focuses on families and communities.

Dr Brian McGrath is Course Director of the MA in Community Development at the National University of Ireland, Galway. His research interests are in the areas of youth, education, social exclusion, rural sociology, and community development. He has published on these themes in international and national journals. He has previously worked as a principal researcher on international collaborative research for the European Commission and has undertaken research on behalf of various development agencies.

Daniel W. Russell is currently conducting research in several different areas related to loneliness and social support. He also continues an active program of work focused on methodological issues including multiple imputation procedures as an approach to missing data and issues related to multilevel regression analysis and testing structural equation models with multilevel data.

Dr Jackie Sanders is a Senior Researcher within the School of Sociology, Social Policy and Social Work, Massey University, New Zealand. She manages two research programmes, and supervises post graduate student research in the areas of social and community work practice, projects utilising qualitative methodologies and action methods frameworks.

Richard Spoth, PhD, is the F. Wendell Miller Senior Prevention Scientist and Director of the Partnerships in Prevention Science Institute at Iowa State University. Dr Spoth is a NIH-NIDA MERIT Award recipient; he serves on federally-sponsored expert and technical review panels addressing issues in prevention research and research-practice integration.

Linda Trudeau is currently a research scientist interested in evaluating the effectiveness of programs designed to prevent adolescent problem behaviors and in exploring mechanisms whereby programs achieve their effects. In addition, she is interested in exploring etiological factors related to problem behaviors, including individual characteristics, such as personality and temperament, and socialising factors, such as family and peer relations.

Judy Warner is a professional writer who has worked in the human services field for over 15 years. She holds a Bachelor's degree in Marketing and earned a Master's degree in Journalism from Temple University at Harrisburg, PA. Ms Warner has been associated with Youth Advocate Programs, Inc. since 1991, most recently serving as Chief of Communications and Development at the agency Support Center in Harrisburg. She is the former president of Warner-Snyder Inc., a grant writing and consulting firm. She is currently employed as the Communications and Financial Developer for Rejoice, Inc. Foster Care and Adoption Agency in Harrisburg.

Dr Alexandra Wright is Assistant Professor in the Faculty of Social Work at the University of Manitoba. Her research and teaching interests include social service organisational theory, administration and practice, family centered services, children with special needs and children who have experienced maltreatment.

Subject Index

Abacus 137
Abt Associates 238
advice support 14
Africa 165
Alaska [Wraparound] Youth Initiative 120
alcohol use
  increase over time averaged across all children 255
  increase over time by dropout status 258
  by school-level income 260
  by treatment condition 259
Alcohol Use Composite Index (AUCI) 253
American Youth Policy Forum 131
Annie E. Casey Foundation 131
anti-discrimination legislation 166
Aotearoa, New Zealand 22, 266, 268, 272
Asian and Pacific Islander (API) clients, working with 34, 111, 214–33
  case examples 221–30
    working with family 227–30
    working with individual within family system 222–7
  connecting evaluation to practice 230–3
    culturally competent view 231
    integrative view 232–3
    view of choices 231–2
  steps and procedures 215–21
    analysing data 219–20, 225, 229–30
    defining service target 21617, 222–3, 227
    identifying constraints and resources 218, 223–4, 228–9
    measuring target and monitoring actions 218–19, 224, 229
    reporting results and making recommendations 220, 225–7, 230
    setting goals and objectives 217–18, 223, 227–8
  uniqueness of evaluating services with 214–15
assessment
  of clustering 254–5
  strength-based 126–7
  tools 196–200
Australia 89, 94–5

Bangladeshis 34
Barriers and Promising Approaches to Workforce and Youth Development for Young Offenders, Program Profiles 131

Canada 89
capacity-building agenda and community 51–3

care, cultural competence as system of 172–7
Caribbean 165
child and youth policy of Municipality of Odense 63
Child Care Act 1991 90
child growth and development 244
Childhood Fund 137
children
  and adolescent mental health services 38
  at risk, implementing common language for defining 70–1
Children Act 1989 92, 103, 135
Children Order (NI) 1995 135
Children's Commissioner 93
Children's Fund 29
Children's Service Plans 145
Children's Strategy (Making it R Wrld 2) 135
choices 231–2
Christchurch Health and Development study 105
Climbié, Victoria 93
closeness 14
clustering, assessment of 254–5
Commission on the Family Report (1998) 91
common language for defining children at risk, implementing 70–1
Commonwealth 94
communication competence, intercultural 173–4
'Communicative Family Support Model' 168
community
  and capacity-building agenda 51–3
  as target of intervention 49
  as unit of identity and action 49
community advocacy 121–2
community-based practice
  family support as 42–57
  from remediation to support 44–6
  why community? 46–9
community capacity 51–3
  implications for family support practice and policy 54–7
community connections 57
community environment 55
community growth in family support, measuring 241–5
community linkages/interests 126
Community Mothers Programme 151
community social organizations 56–7
comparisons, making 89–90
competence
  intercultural communication 173–4
  linguistic 174–5
concepts, using 21, 101–233
concrete support 14
Connexions 29
cultural awareness 170–1

cultural competence
  in care 168–72
  evaluating 176–7
  in Family Support 168
  and sensitivity 165–78
  as system of care 172–7
cultural knowledge 170
cultural reflexivity 171
cultural sensitivity 171–2
  evaluating 176–7
Culturally Competent Family Support Model 168
cupped model of family support 15–17

Danish National Institute of Social Research 65
Danish University of Education 67
data collection and analysis 219–20, 225, 2219–30
decision-making, social worker's basis for 68
definition of family support 15–17
Denmark 20, 61–73
Department of Child, Youth and Family (NZ) 96
Department of Child, Youth and Family Services
    (Denmark) 64
Department for Education and Science (UK) 28
Department for Education and Skills (UK) 31
Department for Health and Social Security (DHSS)
    138
Department of Health and Children (Ireland) 155
Department of Health and Human Services (US)
    238
desirability 15
disabled children, supporting families with 134–47
dropouts, dealing with 256–7

Early Years Development Fund 137
Eastern Regional Health Authority 130
Education Welfare Officers 27
educational opportunities 111
emotional support 14
empowering practitioners 75–86
England 89, 92–3, 135
environment, community 55
esteem support 14
Ethnic-Sensitive Inventory (ESI) 177
European Union 166
evaluation
  advancing 22
  advice to family support program practitioners
      on 245–7
  asking critical questions about 273–4
  building into everyday practice 276
  commitment to critical reflection on all aspects
      of 273–4
  connecting to practice 230–3
  contribution to best practice 273–4
  of family support, challenge of 237–9
  framework for family support programs 237–48

key elements 269–71
  outcome 226
Every Child Matters 29, 30, 31, 93, 135
extended activities, developing 32
extended schools 31–3
  developing 32
Extended Schools Pathfinder Initiative 31, 32

families, approaching 'difficult' 120
Families Commission (NZ) 97
Families Commission Act 2003 (NZ) 97
Families First 94
family
  and school-level income effects in randomised
      prevention trial 250–64
  transformation of 61–2
  whole 40
Family and Community Service Resource Centre
    programme 90
family-focused intervention 128–9
Family Group Conferencing (FGC) 88
family policy and developments in school 28–30
Family Service Centres 96
Family Services Committee 94
Family Start (NZ) 96
family support
  advice 14
  concrete 14
  and cultural competence 214–21
    and sensitivity 165–78
  definition 15–17
    and practice principles 281–4
  emotional 14
  esteem 14
  exploring space for 88–98
  intervention tool 200–3
  key elements 267–9
  levels of 185
  local government and 61–73
  model 15–17
  principles 16–17
  program
    advice to practitioners on evaluation 245–7
    impacts on community 244
  reflective 108–12
  reframing practice as 181–94
  sample practice manual for services 208
  sample practice standards for services 206–7
    challenges in providing 35–9
  self-appraisal tools 203–11
  types and qualities of 14–15
  underpinning with social support theory 13–15
  understanding 13
  and young people in need 149–62
Family Support Agency (FSA) 90
Family Support Agency Act 2001 90, 91

Family Support America 237
Family Support Program (FSP) 94, 119, 119–32
Family Support Services Scheme 94
Family Support Strategy 12
Family Teams 127
feedback, seeking and using as evidence of needs
    Metropolitan Outskirts project 112–16
    Metropolitan Suburbs project 108–12
formal support networks for young people 151
    practical support through 159–60
frameworks, using 21, 101–233
'From Welfare to Well Being' strategy 96

goals and objectives, setting 113, 217–18, 223,
    227–8
group work programme, planning 181–4
growth curve analysis 255–6

Home Office 29
Home Start 30

identity and action, community as unit of 49
implementing family support policy 75–86
inclusive approach to famiy support evaluation
    266–77
    key principles 271–4
        commitment to critical reflection on all
            aspects of evaluation 273–4
        involvement of all key stakeholders 271–2
        learning for all participants 273
income effects in randomised prevention trial
    250–64
Indians 34
Individual Service Plan (ISP) 125
individualized service planning 125–6
informal support networks for young people 150
informed judgement and action 117
'inner child' workshop 114
inner-city London borouh 34
Integrated Power Approach (IPA) 79–80, 86
integrative view 232–3
inter-agency trust 114–15
intercultural communication competence 173–4
intervention, family-focused 128–9
Intervention Matrix Model (IMM) 196, 200–3
    background and context 200–1
    case example 203
    description and administration 201–3
    potential limitations 203
Iowa Strengthening Families Program (ISFP) 253,
    255, 258, 261
Ireland 149, 151–2, 155, 200
Irish Department of Health and Children 12
'Is It Saturday?' project 137
    background 134–6
    establishing project 138–9

outcomes 140–1
    benefits for children 140
    benefits for parents 140
    unforeseen 141
    play and leisure facilities 137–8
    reflections 141–6
Israel 89

'journey to recovery' workshop 113–14

Kilkenny Incest Investigation 90

learning
    for all participants 273
    and reflective practice 104–5
        and family support 107–8
    in risky environment 105–7
Less Cost, More Safety 131
leaving care 181–94
    coping wheel 190
    delivering as family support service 188–91
    preparation for 192
levels of family support 185
    linking care career to 187
life domain bubble chart 126
linguistic competence 174–5
Local Co-ordination (NZ) 96
Local Education Authorities 31
local government, family support through 61–73
local knowledge 114–16
local strategy, developing 32
location in system 182–6

Maori families 89, 268
measuring target and monitoring actions 218–19,
    224
Mental Health and Learning Disability Review (NI)
    136, 146
Metropolitan Outskirts project 112–16
    applying reflective learning 113–15
    clear goal-setting and monitoring effectiveness
        113
    feedback on project 115–16
Metropolitan Suburbs project 108–12
    adapting services on basis of reflective practice
        112
    parents' activities, social and educational
        opportunities 111
    views of project 111–12
Ministry of Social Development (NZ) 96, 97
mobilising support 151–2
model of family support 15–17
monitoring actions 218–19
monitoring effectiveness 113
Mønsterbryderprojektet (Mould-breaker Project) 67

municipal organization, new demands on 68–73
    cooperation with normal service units 71–3
    implementing basis for decision 69–70
    implementing common language for defining
        children at risk 70–1
    from trouble-shooter to resource scout 71
Muslims 175

National Agreements 92
National Anti-Poverty Strategy 92
National Association of Local Authorities in
    Denmark 65
National Children's Strategy 92
National Development Plan 92
National Family and Parenting Institute (NFPI) 33,
    34, 166
National Program 94
National Society for the Prevention of Cruelty to
    Children (NSPCC) 108, 110, 115, 116
    Metropolitan Suburbs project 108–12
National University of Ireland 130
needs-led approach 122–3
neighbourhood
    -based recruitment of staff 128
    concentration of social problems 47
Neighbourhood Youth Project (NYP) study 152–6,
    200
    continuity and change over time 154–5
    forms of support 155–6
    key sources of support 153–4
New Labour 93
New Zealand 22, 89, 95–7, 266, 268, 272
'no reject, no eject' policy 123
normal service units, cooperation with 71–3
Northern Area Health Board, Ireland 130
Northern Ireland 119, 135
Norway 89

Odense, Municipality of (Denmark) 61–73
    child and youth policy 63
Omnibus Reconciliation Act 1993 42
On Track 29
operational policy process 83–6
    recommendations 8'5–6
optimism 129–30
organization
    municipal, new demands on 68–73
    and policy 76–80
        engaging with 20–1, 25–100
organizational capacity 55
organisational structure, social service 77
outcome evaluation framework
    developing for family support programs 237–48
    need to reformulate for family support 239–41
    sufficiency of 247–8

Pakistanis 34
paradigm shift: from remediation to support 44–6
parent growth and development 243
Parent Information Point (PIP) 30, 31, 33–5
Parenting Fund 29
parents
    activities 111
    true partnership with 128
'parents under stress' workshop 113
peer support, activating 157–8
Performance Action Team (PAT) Reports 29
personal and community growth in family support,
    measuring 241–5
play and leisure facilities for disabled children
    137–8
policy
    examples with PIF 81–3
    and organization 76–80
        engaging with 20–1, 25–100
Policy Implementation Framework (PIF) 80–1, 86
    policy examples within 81–3
power
    dimensions to process of exercising 79
    Integrated Power Approach (IPA) 79–80
    policy and organizations 76–80
    worker discretion as alternative source and
        location of 77–8
practical support through formal sources 159–60
practice–theory gap, Thompson's strategies for
    bridging 288–9
Pre-Employment Consultancy Service (PECS) 138
Preparation for Adulthood 21
Preparing for the Drug-Free Years (PDFY) 252,
    255, 259, 261
primary and secondary schools 39
principles of family support 16–17
Privacy Act 1993 (NZ) 96
problem indicators 220
provision, basic description of 184

Race Directive (EU) 166
Race Relations Act 1976 166
Race Relations Amendment Act 166
reciprocity 14–15
record keeping 221
reflecting
    for action 280–9
    on family support definition and practice
        principles 281–4
reflective learning, applying 110, 113–15
    clear structure and ethos 114
    continuity of staffing, local knowledge and
        inter-agency trust 114–15
    'inner child' workshop 114
    'journey to recovery' workshop 113–14
    'parents under stress' workshop 113

reflective practice
  adapting services on basis of 112
  approach to 17–20
  and family support 112–16
  learning and 104–5
  role of 286–7
  Self Appraisal Model (SAM) 203–9
  working with adolescent and their social
    networks 161
reflexivity 171
reframing practice as family support 181–94
relationships in family support, measuring 241–5
remediation to support 44–6
reporting results and making recommendations 220,
    225–7, 230
research and practice 167–8
resource scouting 71
risk factors 66–8
risky environment, learning in 105–7
Rural Family and Community Drug Abuse
    Prevention Project 253
rural/urban issues 38–9

Safeguarding Children Boards 104
school- and family-level income effects in
    randomised prevention trial 250–64
  implications for practitioners 274–7
    asking critical questions about evaluation
      273–4
    building evaluation into everyday practice
      276
    contribution evaluation makes to best
      practice 273–4
  results 254–63
    assessment of clustering 254–5
    dealing with dropouts 256–7
    family-level income 262–3
    growth curve analysis 255–6
    increase in alcohol use over time 255, 256
    school-level income 260–1
    treatment effects 258–9
  study description 252–4
    measures 253–4
    participants 252
    treatment conditions 252–3
school-based family support services 27–40
  barriers to accessing 36–8
  challenges in providing 35–9
    family must mean whole family 40
    one size doesn't fit all 39
    school staff must be engaged 40
  developments in, and family policy 28–30
Scotland 80
SEARCH Institute 237

Self-Appraisal Model (SAM) 196, 203–9
  administration 205–8
  background and context 203–4
  case example 209
  key elements 205
  sample practice manual 208
  sample practice standards 206–7
semi-formal and natural supports, development of
    124
service delivery criteria 189
service developments 31–5
  extended schools 31–3
service planning, individualized 125–6
single system design 215
'Social Coalition' (Australia) 95
Social Exclusion Unit 29
social-intervention cost levels, rise in 64–5
Social Network Questionnaire (SNQ) 152
social opportunities 111
social problems
  characteristics of 63–4
  neighbourhood concentration of 47
Social Provisions Scale (SPS) 152, 196, 197–200
  administration 199
  background and context 197
  case example 199–200
  description 197–8
  potential limitations 199
social service organisational structure 77
Social Services Act (Denmark) 63
social support
  qualities of 14–15
  theory, underpinning family support with
    13–15
social work theories, developments in 166–7
social worker, basis for decision-making 68
Social Workers in Schools (NZ) 96
South Africa 89
South Asia(ns) 165, 175
Springboard Family Support Programme 91,
    154–5, 200
staffing, continuity of 114–15
Strategic Management Initiative 92
Strategy for Children and Young People with High
    and Complex Needs (NZ) 96
'Strengthening Families' strategy 96–7
strength-based assessment 126–7
strength-based planning tool 127
strengths
  focus on 125
  inventory 126
stress, parents under 113
'Stronger Families and Communities Strategy' 95
Supported Work program 124
Sweden 89

target
defining 216–17, 222–3, 227
measuring, and monitoring actions 218–19, 229
Targeted Family Service (NZ) 96
Tarrant County Advocate Program (TCAP) 131
Tarrant County Juvenile Services 131
Teen Parenting Programme 200
Texas Youth Advocate programs 131
Third Way 93, 97, 98
Thompson's strategies for bridging practice–theory gap 288–9
Together from the Start 146
'Together into Play' 113
tools, using 21–2, 101–233
transformation of family 61–2
treatment effects 258–9
trouble-shooting 71
true partnership with parents 125
trust relationships with young people and families 121–2

UK 20, 28, 30, 33, 39, 89, 92, 165-6, 167, 177, 200
unconditional care 129
and commitment to 123
UN Convention on the Rights of the Child (UNCRC) 11, 135
Urban Sanctuaries 242
USA 20, 42, 44, 45, 50, 51, 89, 119, 168, 200, 237, 250
juvenile justice programming in US 131

VanDenBerg, Dr 120

Wales 135
Western Health Board, Ireland 130
worker discretion as alternative source and location of power 77–8
working with individual within family system 222–7
Wraparound 120

YAP/Ireland 119
YAP/UK 119
young people in need 149–62
case studies
Neighbourhood Youth Project (NYP) 152–6
Youthreach 156–60
sources of support 149–52
formal 151
informal 150
mobilising 151–2
youth advocacy 118–32

Youth Advocate Programs, Inc. (YAP) 118–32, 200
evaluations and outcomes of programs 130–1
Family Support Program 119–32
Family Team meeting and development of individual service plan 127–30
family-focused intervention 128–9
neighbourhood-based recruitment of staff 128
optimism 129–30
true partnership with parents 128
unconditional care 129
four pillars of YAP's community-based care 121–4
community advocacy 121–2
development of semi-formal and natural supports 124
needs-led approach 122–3
'no reject, no eject' policy and commitment to unconditional care 123
guiding principles of YAP model 125–6
focus on strengths 125
individualized service planning 125–6
history, context and overview of model 119–20
juvenile justice programming in US 131
Thames Programme, London 130
youth policy of Municipality of Odense 63
Youthreach 156–60
activating peer support 157–8
practical support through formal sources 159–60
relationships with workers 158–9

Author Index

Aber, J.L. 46, 48
Abouchaar, A. 28, 40
Adams, L. 137
Adams, R. 19, 20
Adely, F. 51
Adlaf, E.M. 251
Adshead, M. 88
Ahlbrandt, R.S. 49
Ahmad, B. 167
Ahsan, N. 246
Aldgate, J. 182
Allan, J. 277
Allen, M. 50
Anderson, M. 158, 159
Arndt, S. 250, 263
Audit Commission 136
Austin, M. 84, 85
Aymanns, P.14

Baginsky, M. 40
Baldwin, N. 109, 110
Ball, M. 29
Barker, M. 13, 182
Barkin, C. 151, 200
Beardsworth, A. 136
Becher, H. 167, 168
Becker, G. 51, 57
Becker, H. 66, 74
Behn, J.D. 177
Beishon, S. 167
Bell, N.J. 150
Bell, R.W. 150
Belsky, J. 14, 150, 200
Benard, B. 237, 238
Benson, P. 237
Beresford, B. 137
Berger, L. 62
Bernstein, E. 215
Berry, M. 273
Best Practices Project 237
Bhabra, S. 34
Biegel, D. 15, 152, 154
Bloom, M. 215
Bloomer, M. 157
Blythe, D.A. 46
Boldt, S. 151
Bømler, T. 64, 66
Bosker, R. 254, 255
Boud, D. 18
Bowes, A.M. 168
Box, L. 168

Brady, B. 210, 211
Briggs, X. 50
Brockbank, A. 104, 105
Brody, G.H. 46
Bronfenbrenner, U. 44
Brooks, S. 75
Brooks-Gunn, J. 46, 48, 251, 263
Brown, A. 191
Brown, D. 131
Brown, K. 155
Brown, L. 89
Brugha, T.S. 197
Bruner, C. 22, 238, 240, 245, 246, 248, 283
Bruns, E.J. 120
Bryk, A.S. 254, 255
Burford, B. 168
Burleson, B. 14
Burt, R.S. 56
Bussey, M. 273
Butt, J. 168

Campbell, D.T. 252
Campbell, K.E. 49
Campinha-Bacote, J. 169, 170, 173
Canali, C. 269
Canavan, H. 13
Canavan, J. 9, 11, 13, 22, 45, 150, 151, 153, 197, 200, 209, 210, 269, 272, 273
Carballeira, N. 169, 170
Carruthers, L. 109, 110
Cash, S.J. 273
Catalano, R.F. 237, 251, 252
Center for Mental Health Services (CMHS) 176
Chand, A. 168
Chaskin, R.J. 20, 43, 46, 50, 51, 52, 53, 55, 271, 281, 283
Chen, G.M. 173, 174, 177
Cheung, K.M. 283, 284
Cheung, M. 22, 281
Christensen, E. 68
Clark, J. 173
Clarke, M. 204
Clayton, R.R. 250, 255
Clegg, S.R. 17, 76, 77
Cochran, M. 14
Cohen, B.J. 84, 85
Cole, V. 14, 150, 151, 164
Coleman, J. 51, 56, 150, 151
Coles, B. 182
Commission for Racial Equality 166
Commission on the Family 91
Commonwealth of Australia 95
Compas, B.E. 151, 200
Conliffe, C. 136
Connell, J.P. 241
Cook, T.D. 252

Cooper, I. 277
Cope, B. 171
Corcoran, K.J. 215
Cotterell, J. 14, 150, 151, 152
Coulton, C.J. 48
Cowie, H. 150
Craig, D. 97
Cramer, L. 246
Crane, I. 48
Cross, T. 169, 170
Crouter, A.C. 48
Crow, G. 89
Cummings, C. 31, 33
Cummins, L. 171
Cunliffe, A. 171
Curtin, C. 200
Cutrona, C.E.13, 14, 56, 150, 151, 152, 154, 197, 198

Dahl, R.A. 76
Dana, R.H. 177
Davies, A. 95
Davies, L. 84
Davis, K. 172
Davis, P. 131
Day 172
Day, D. 50
Dempster, M. 89
Dencik, L. 62
Denney, D. 166
DePanfilis, S. 197
Department for Education and Skills 29, 30, 93, 135, 146
Department of Health 183
Desforges, C. 28
Devine, P. 188
Dinh, K.T. 216
Dolan, P. 11, 13, 14, 21, 45, 90, 91, 150, 152, 153, 182, 197, 198, 200, 209, 210, 269, 272, 273, 281, 283
Dolowitz, D.P. 88
Dominelli, L. 19
Domokos, T.M. 168
Donnelly, M. 89
Dore, M. 268
Dryden, J. 151, 200
Dryfoos, J.G. 151, 200, 210
Dufur, M.J. 263
Duigan, P. 270
Duncan, G.J. 46
Duncan, S.C. 204, 212, 251
Duncan, T.E. 251, 255
Dunst, C. 44, 238
Dyson, A. 29, 31, 33

Earls, F. 48, 52

Eckenrode, J. 13, 150
Egelund, T. 64, 65, 66, 68
Elliot, S.S. 150
Elsborg, S. 67
Ely, P. 166
Ennett, S.T. 263
Exton, K. 13, 182

Fagan, G.H. 151
Family Resource Coalition 43, 51
Family Support America 42, 43, 45
Family Support Australia 94
Fang, S.W. 216
Featherstone, B. 89, 92
Fein, E. 276
Feldman, G.R. 150
Feldman, L.A. 219
Fergusson, D.M. 96
Fernandez, E. 94
Fischer, J. 215
Fisher, M. 18
Fitzgerald, J.L. 250, 263
Fleischer, J. 21, 281, 282, 283
Fong, R. 218
Freedman, M. 238
Freire, P. 273
Friedman, M. 239
Frydenburg, E. 150
Fulcher, G. 78
Fuller, R. 109
Furstenberg, F.F. 46, 48, 49

Gambrill, E. 19
Garbarino, J. 13, 43, 46, 48, 50, 51
Gardner, R. 13, 14, 21, 42, 43, 50, 93, 103, 108, 150, 152, 197, 200, 204, 283
Gardner, S. 44
Gavigan, C. 200
Ghate, D. 34, 37, 150, 151, 197
Gibbons, R.D. 257
Gibbs, I. 204
Gibson, J. 51
Giller, H. 13, 197
Gilligan, R. 43, 45, 152, 197, 200
Glanville, B. 151
Golding, J. 168
Gonwa, T. 177
Gonzalez-Mena, J. 176
Goode, T. 174, 177
Gordon, D. 136
Gottlieb, B.H. 197
Gould, N. 17, 18
Granovetter, M. 56
Grant, G. 84
Grant, K.E. 151, 200
Gray, M. 204

Gregg, E.M. 154
Grossman, J. 210, 242
Groves, W.B. 49
Gubrium, J.F. 156
Gudykunst, W. 173
Gummer, B. 75, 77, 78, 80

Hains, A.A. 200
Halpern, R. 45, 46
Hamilton, S. 13, 150
Hammer, M. 173
Hansen, K.K. 232
Hansen, T.J.. 67
Hansen, V.R. 67
Hanson, M.J. 169
Hardiker, P. 13, 182, 183, 186
Harding, D.J. 251
Hardy, C. 76, 77
Hasenfeld, Y. 77
Hawkins, D. 237
Hawkins, J.D. 251
Hazel, N. 37, 150, 151, 197
Hedeker, D. 257
Hegel, A. 13
Hegel, A. 13, 197
Henderson, N. 237
Hendry, L. 151
Herbert, M. 154
Hessle, S. 65
Higgins, K. 89, 188
Hill, M. 182, 197
HM Treasury 30
Ho, M.K. 177
Holstein, J.A. 156
Holt, C. 91
Holt, S. 14, 152, 200, 210
Houston, S. 18
Howard, S. 151, 154, 200
Hudson, F. 159
Huff, R.M. 217
Husain, F. 22, 166, 167, 168, 281, 283

Ineichen, B. 159

Irby, M. 242
Jack, G. 13, 14, 200, 209
Jencks, C. 48
Johnson, B. 151, 200
Jones, D.N. 38, 41
Jones, W. 174
Jones-Webb, R. 251
Jordan, B. 13
Jørgensen, P.S. 62, 65, 67
Jun, J. 171
Junker, R. 283

Kagan, S.L. 44, 238
Kalantzis, M. 171
Katz, I. 20, 42, 45, 50, 267, 269, 271, 273, 277, 281
Kelly, B. 136
Kemp, S.P. 43, 45, 50
Kibel, B. 242
Kilpatrick, R. 21, 139, 281, 283
Kim Young Yun 73, 179
Kim, H. 216, 233
Kingsley, G.T. 51
Kinney, J. 237
Klaur T. 14
Klein, G. 106
Kline, M.V. 217
Knights, S. 18
Knitzer, J. 51
Kolb, B. 142
Kostelny, K. 43, 50, 51
Krogstrup, H. 64
Kubisch, A. 51

Langenkamp, M. 173
Langman, J. 242
Layzer, J.L. 42, 43, 45, 50, 238
Lee, B.A. 49
Leffert, N. 46
Leigh, J.W. 175
Leung, P. 22, 281, 283, 284
Leventhal, T. 251, 263
Levitan, S.A. 44
Lewis, J. 75, 84
Lightburn, A. 43, 45, 50
Lipsky, M. 75, 77, 78
Lishman, J. 269, 270
Little, M. 200, 209
Lodge, A. 151
Loughran, F. 136
Luchmann, T. 62
Lukes, S. 76, 79, 80
Lynam, D.R. 251
Lynch, E.W. 169
Lynch, K. 151

Macfarlane, A. 168
McAuley, C. 200
McClinton, J. 139
McConkey, R. 136, 137, 144
McCrea, R. 191, 192
McGill, I. 104, 105
McGrath, B. 21, 84, 151, 281
McGuinness, C. 90
McKay, H. 49, 95
McKenzie, B. 75, 84, 87
McKeown, K. 154, 200, 204
McKie, L. 271

McLaughlin, M. 242
McNeely, J.B. 51
McPhatter, A.R. 169
Maluccio, A.N. 269, 271
Mangum, G.L. 44
Marsh, D. 88, 89
Marsh, P. 18, 193
Massachusetts Chronic Disease Improvement
    Network 177
Maternal and Child Health Bureau 177
May-Chahal, C. 277
Mayer, S. 48
Meadows, M. 169
Mendel, R. 131
Michels, R. 76
Middleton, S. 136
Miljan, L. 75
Millar, M. 21, 281
Miller, J.Y. 251
Miller, O. 49
Miller, Z. 46
Millward, A. 31
Minsky, S. 177
Mitchell, J.C. 56
Modood, T. 167
Molgaard, V. 253
Monteith, M. 136
Moon, J.A. 141
Morenoff, J.D. 52
Morgan, G. 76
Morrison, T. 104
Mount, K. 200, 209
Muir, H. 166
Mullin, E. 151
Munford, R. 22, 95, 200, 267, 268, 269, 270, 273,
    276, 283
Munro, E. 105, 106, 107
Murphy, M. 90
Murray, D.M. 254

National Association of Social Workers 169
National Centre for Cultural Competence 173
Nelson, K. 50
Neuman, W. 203
Nishida, H. 173
Norton, D. 44

O'Brien, M. 200
O'Connor, P. 151
O'Neale, V. 168
O'Neil, D. 267, 273
O'Shea, C. 156
Office of Minority Health (OMH) (1999) 176, 177
Office of the First Minister and Deputy First
    Minister 135
Orme, J.G. 215

Orosan, P.G. 151, 200

Paget, K. 273, 277
Pandey, S. 48
Pankaj, V. 168
Papadopoulos, R. 168
Parcel, T.L. 263
Parker, R. 136
Parsons, L. 168
Parton, N. 200
Payne, M. 19
Peel, M. 193
Percy, A. 13, 90, 182, 200
Petch, A. 109
Pines, M.W. 44
Pinkerton, J. 11, 13, 21, 42, 45, 50, 75, 89, 90, 91,
    182, 188, 191, 192, 200, 209, 267, 269,
    271, 273, 283
Poertner, J. 75
Prior, J. 131
Procter, J. 168
Proudfoot, R. 151
Putnam, R. 48, 56

Quane, J.M. 46, 48
Quinn, J. 151, 200
Qureshi, T. 168

Raffo, C. 151
Rankin, B.H. 46
Rapp, C. 75
Rappaport, J. 48
Raudenbush, S.W. 48, 254, 255
Rea, R. 131
Reder, P. 204
Redmond, C. 252
Reed, M. 76, 77, 79, 80
Rees, G. 151
Reeves, M. 151
Reisch, N. 242
Resch, N. 210
Review of Mental Health and Learning Disability
    (Northern Ireland) 136
Ricketts, E.R. 46
Riordan, S. 14, 155, 200
Robinson, J. 84
Robinson, L. 175
Robson, E. 29
Room, G. 56
Rosaldo 167
Rose, R. 88
Rountree, P.W. 250, 255
Rubin, K.H. 218
Ruch, G. 17
Russell, D. 152, 198
Rutter, M. 13, 197, 200

Ryan, S. 156
Ryburn, M. 89

Sachdev, D. 167
Saleebey, D. 165, 167, 176
Sampson, R.J. 48, 49, 52, 56
Sanders, J. 22, 95, 267, 268, 269, 270, 273, 276, 283
Sarason, B.R. 216
Sarason, I.G. 216
Saunders, J. 200
Saville-Smith, K. 269, 270
Sawhill, I.V. 46
Schofield, G. 155
Schon, D. 17, 141
Schorr, L. 44, 238, 245
Schotter, J. 171
Scott, D. 267
Sharp-Light, N. 237
Shaw, C. 37, 49
Shaw, I. 270, 271, 279
Shin, C. 252
Shinar, O. 56
Short, B. 254
Sigrun, H. 14
Sinclair, I. 204
Singer, J.D. 255, 256
Skaarup, P. 64
Sloper, P. 136, 137
Smart, R.G. 251
Smith, B. 95
Smith, D.E. 75, 77, 78
Smith, G. 77, 80
Smith, L. 166, 169, 176, 177
Smith, P. 158
Snijders, T. 254, 255
Spoth, R. 252, 253
Starosta, W.J. 173, 174, 177
Steen Jensen, P. 283
Stein, M. 151
Stokes, D. 157
Strycker, L.A. 251
Sundell, K. 89

Taylor, B.J. 89
Taylor, H. 144
Taylor, I. 17
Tehrani, N. 210
Tharp, R.G. 216, 218
Thoburn, J. 168
Thompson, B. 144
Thompson, N. 286, 288
Thompson, R. 150
Tierney, J. 210, 242
Tirado, M. 177
Todd Abraham, W. 22, 283

Todd, L. 31, 33
Toumbourou, J.W. 154
Tracy, E.M. 15, 150, 152, 164, 197, 209
Trewsdale, M. 136
Trivette, C. 238
Tunstill, J. 13, 92

Van Horn, C.E. 76
Van Meeuwen, A167
Van Meter, D.S. 76
Vecchiato, T. 269
Vinnerlijung, B. 89

Wåhlander, E. 65
Wall, O. 88
Wallerstein, N. 215
Walsh Tapiata, W. 272
Walsh, G.W. 251, 265
Ward, D. 191
Wark, I. 216
Warner, J. 21, 281, 282, 283
Warren, C. 45
Watson, D.L. 216, 218
Weber, M. 77
Weinbach, R. 75
Weiss, C. 177
Weiss, H.B. 160, 200, 210
Weiss, R. 198
Weissbourd, B. 42, 43, 44, 45, 46, 50, 238
Wellman, B. 56
Welzler, S. 219
Wharf, B. 75, 84
Wheal, A. 188
Whittaker, J.K. 13, 209
Wilkin, A. 31
Willet, J.B. 255, 256
Williams, J. 156
Wills, A. 56
Wilson, W.J. 18, 46
Wiseman, R. 173, 174
Wong, S.S. 217
Woolgar, S. 171
Wright, A. 80, 281, 283
Wright, L. 273, 277
Wyers, N.L. 78

Yahle, T. 173
Youniss, J. 150

Zimmerman, M.A. 48